16LIVES

JOSEPH PLUNKETT

The 16LIVES Series

HONOR O BROLCHAIN – AUTHOR OF 16LIVES: JOSEPH PLUNKETT

Honor O Brolchain was brought up and educated in Dublin. On inheriting the considerable papers of her grandmother, Geraldine Plunkett Dillon, sister of Joseph Plunkett, Honor became more involved in the family's history and has since, with additional research, created papers and talks on many aspects of the Plunketts from 1082 to 1948, especially their building enterprises in nineteenth-century South Dublin. This biography of Honor's granduncle, Joseph Plunkett, comes from the wealth of documentary material on the youngest Proclamation signatory executed in 1916. She also produced an edition of Geraldine Plunkett Dillon's lively memoir, *All In The Blood*.

LORCAN COLLINS – SERIES EDITOR

Lorcan Collins was born and raised in Dublin. A lifelong interest in Irish history led to the foundation of his hugely popular 1916 Rebellion Walking Tour in 1996. He co-authored *The Easter Rising – A Guide to Dublin in 1916* (O'Brien Press, 2000) with Conor Kostick. His biography of James Connolly was published in the 16 Lives series in 2012, and his most recent book is *1916: The Rising Handbook*. He is a regular contributor to radio, television and historical journals. 16 Lives is Lorcan's concept, and he is co-editor of the series.

DR RUÁN O'DONNELL – SERIES EDITOR

Dr Ruán O'Donnell is a senior lecturer at the University of Limerick. A graduate of UCD and the Australian National University, O'Donnell has published extensively on Irish Republicanism. His titles include *Patrick Pearse* in the 16 Lives series, *Robert Emmet and the Rising of 1803*; *The Impact of the 1916 Rising* (editor); *Special Category: The IRA in English Prisons, 1968–1978* and *1978–1985*; and *The O'Brien Pocket History of the Irish Famine*. He is a director of the Irish Manuscripts Commission and a frequent contributor to the national and international media on the subject of Irish revolutionary history.

16LIVES

JOSEPH PLUNKETT

Waterford City and County
Libraries

Honor O Brolchain

THE O'BRIEN PRESS
DUBLIN

First published 2012 by
The O'Brien Press Ltd,
12 Terenure Road East, Rathgar,
Dublin 6, D06 HD27, Ireland.
Tel: +353 1 4923333; Fax: +353 1 4922777
E-mail: books@obrien.ie.
Website: www.obrien.ie
Reprinted 2016

ISBN: 978-1-84717-269-3

PICTURE CREDITS
The author and publisher thank the following for permission to use photographs and
illustrative material: front cover, back cover & inside front cover images: courtesy of the
Honor O Brolchain Collection.
Picture section 1, p 7, top left; courtesy of Maeve O'Leary; p 8: courtesy of the Mc-
Donagh family. All other images courtesy of the Honor O Brolchain Collection.
Picture section 2, p 3; courtesy of Henry Fairbrother; p 4, top: courtesy of the National
Museum of Ireland. All other images courtesy of the Honor O Brolchain Collection.
*If any involuntary infringment of copyright has ocurred, sincere apologies are offered and the owners
of such copyright are requested to contact the publisher..*

Printed and bound by CPI Group (UK) Ltd, Croydon, CR0 4YY
The paper used in this book is produced using pulp from managed forests.

DUBLIN
UNESCO
City of Literature

DEDICATION

For my son and daughter, Mahon and Isolde Carmody.

ACKNOWLEDGEMENTS

Assembling historical information is like making a jigsaw out of jelly; each piece disappears into the whole which, in turn, grows bigger and wider. Often it is the very small pieces which make the difference and often they are handed on with great generosity by people who have a real awareness of their value. I have experienced this generosity over and over again and would like to thank all those who offered ideas, facts, anecdotes and documents for this book. This includes those who donate information to the World Wide Web, often without knowing whether it is being used or appreciated.

The following people contributed substantially to the process:

Dr William J. McCormack, the late Donal O'Donovan, James Connolly Heron, Paul Turnell, Art O Laoghaire, Major General (Rtd.) David Nial Creagh, The O'Morchoe, Charles Lysaght, Maeve O'Leary, Jenny and Andrew Robinson, Dr John O'Donnell and Michael O'Donnell, David Lillis, Mary Plunkett, Dr Carla Keating, Dr Anne Matthews, Henry Fairbrother, David Kilmartin, Anna Farmar, Lucille Redmond, Muriel McAuley, Seosamh O Ceallaigh, Grainne Nic Giolla Chearr and Alice Nic Giolla Chearr, Patrick Cooney, Terry Baker, the O'Brien Press team, especially Helen Carr, Lorcan Collins and Ruán O'Donnell.

The following institutions and their curators were, as always, crucial, helpful and civilised: the National Library of Ireland, especially the Reprographic Services who were exceptionally helpful, University College Dublin Archive, and very special thanks to the Internet Archive, the Digital Library of Free Books; the Defence Forces, Ireland, Bureau of Military History; Stonyhurst College Archive, Archivist: David Knight; Catholic University Schools Archive, Archivist: Kevin Jennings; Belvedere College Archive, Archivist: Tom Doyle.

I must also mention two organisations which are personal enablers in my professional life, the National Council for the Blind of Ireland and Irish Guide Dogs for the Blind.

As often happens there is one person who must take the lion's share of thanks: my husband, Brendan Ellis, has, from the beginning, been a major part of all the processes from dictating about one thousand documents to me to store for use on the computer, taping documents, reading, researching and, in the final stages, reading and proofing the manuscript and offering positive and negative criticism. Inestimable, unquantifiable and always kindly done!

16LIVES Timeline

1845–51. The Great Hunger in Ireland. One million people die and over the next decades millions more emigrate.

1858, March 17. The Irish Republican Brotherhood, or Fenians, are formed with the express intention of overthrowing British rule in Ireland by whatever means necessary.

1867, February and March. Fenian Uprising.

1870, May. Home Rule movement, founded by Isaac Butt, who had previously campaigned for amnesty for Fenian prisoners.

1879–81. The Land War. Violent agrarian agitation against English landlords.

1884, November 1. The Gaelic Athletic Association founded – immediately infiltrated by the Irish Republican Brotherhood (IRB).

1893, July 31. Gaelic League founded by Douglas Hyde and Eoin MacNeill. The Gaelic Revival, a period of Irish Nationalism, pride in the language, history, culture and sport.

1900, September. Cumann na nGaedheal (Irish Council) founded by Arthur Griffith.

1905–07. Cumann na nGaedheal, the Dungannon Clubs and the National Council are amalgamated to form Sinn Féin (We Ourselves).

1909, August. Countess Markievicz and Bulmer Hobson organise nationalist youths into Na Fianna Éireann (Warriors of Ireland) a kind of boy scout brigade.

1912, April. Prime Minister Asquith introduces the Third Home Rule Bill to the British Parliament. Passed by the Commons and rejected by the Lords, the Bill would have to become law due to the Parliament Act. Home Rule expected to be introduced for Ireland by autumn 1914.

1913, January. Sir Edward Carson and James Craig set up Ulster Volunteer Force (UVF) with the intention of defending Ulster against Home Rule.

1913. Jim Larkin, founder of the Irish Transport and General Workers' Union (ITGWU), calls for a workers' strike for better pay and conditions.

1913, August 31. Jim Larkin speaks at a banned rally on Sackville Street; Bloody Sunday.

1913, November 23. James Connolly, Jack White and Jim Larkin establish the Irish Citizen Army (ICA) in order to protect strikers.

1913, November 25. The Irish Volunteers founded in Dublin to 'secure the rights and liberties common to all the people of Ireland'.

1914, March 20. Resignations of British officers force British government not to use British army to enforce Home Rule, an event known as the 'Curragh Mutiny'.

1914, April 2. In Dublin, Agnes O'Farrelly, Mary MacSwiney, Countess Markievicz and others establish Cumann na mBan as a women's volunteer force dedicated to establishing Irish freedom and assisting the Irish Volunteers.

1914, April 24. A shipment of 35,000 rifles and five million rounds of ammunition is landed at Larne for the UVF.

1914, July 26. Irish Volunteers unload a shipment of 900 rifles and 45,000 rounds of ammunition shipped from Germany aboard Erskine Childers' yacht, the *Asgard*. British troops fire on crowd on Bachelors' Walk, Dublin. Three citizens are killed.

1914, August 4. Britain declares war on Germany. Home Rule for Ireland shelved for the duration of the First World War.

1914, September 9. Meeting held at Gaelic League headquarters between IRB and other extreme republicans. Initial decision made to stage an uprising while Britain is at war.

1914, September. 170,000 leave the Volunteers and form the National Volunteers or Redmondites. Only 11,000 remain as the Irish Volunteers under Eoin MacNeill.

1915, May–September. Military Council of the IRB is formed.

1915, August 1. Pearse gives fiery oration at the funeral of Jeremiah O'Donovan Rossa.

1916, January 19–22. James Connolly joins the IRB Military Council, thus ensuring that the ICA shall be involved in the Rising. Rising date confirmed for Easter.

1916, April 20, 4.15pm. The *Aud* arrives at Tralee Bay, laden with 20,000 German rifles for the Rising. Captain Karl Spindler waits in vain for a signal from shore.

1916, April 21, 2.15am. Roger Casement and his two companions go ashore from U-19 and land on Banna Strand. Casement is arrested at McKenna's Fort.

6.30pm. The *Aud* is captured by the British navy and forced to sail towards Cork harbour.

22 April, 9.30am. The *Aud* is scuttled by her captain off Daunt's Rock.

10pm. Eoin MacNeill as Chief-of-Staff of the Irish Volunteers issues the countermanding order in Dublin to try to stop the Rising.

1916, April 23, 9am. Easter Sunday. The Military Council meets to discuss the situation, considering MacNeill has placed an advertisement in a Sunday newspaper halting all Volunteer operations. The Rising is put on hold for twenty-four hours. Hundreds of copies of The Proclamation of the Republic are printed in Liberty Hall.

1916, April 24, 12 noon. Easter Monday. The Rising begins in Dublin.

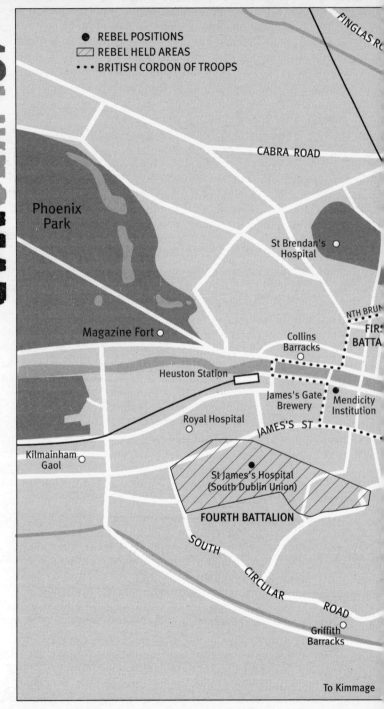

16LIVESMAP

- ● REBEL POSITIONS
- ▨ REBEL HELD AREAS
- • • • BRITISH CORDON OF TROOPS

FINGLAS RO

CABRA ROAD

Phoenix
Park

St Brendan's
Hospital ○

NTH BRUN

Magazine Fort ○

Collins
Barracks ○

FIRS
BATTA

Heuston Station

James's Gate
Brewery

● Mendicity
Institution

Royal Hospital ○

JAMES'S ST

Kilmainham ○
Gaol

St James's Hospital
(South Dublin Union)

FOURTH BATTALION

SOUTH

CIRCULAR

ROAD

Griffith ○
Barracks

To Kimmage

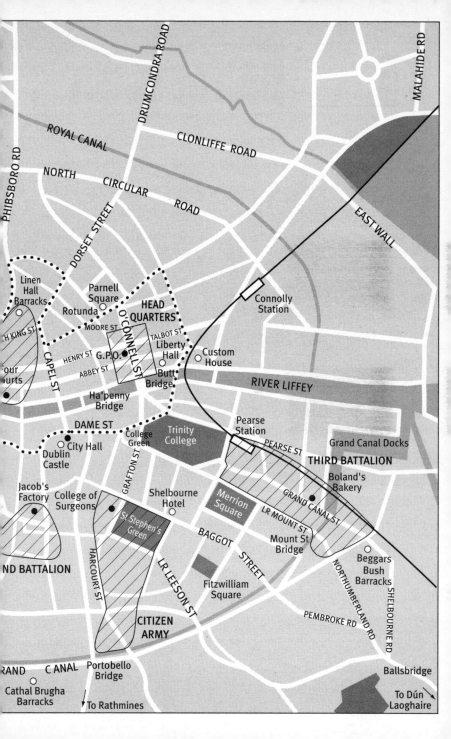

16LIVES – Series Introduction

This book is part of a series called *16 LIVES* conceived with the objective of recording for posterity the lives of the sixteen men who were executed after the 1916 Easter Rising. Who were these people and what drove them to commit themselves to violent revolution?

The rank and file as well as the leadership were all from diverse backgrounds. Some were privileged and some had no material wealth. Some were highly educated writers, poets or teachers and others had little formal schooling. Their common desire, to set Ireland on the road to national freedom, united them under the one banner of the army of the Irish Republic. They occupied key buildings in Dublin and around Ireland for one week before they were forced to surrender. The leaders were singled out for harsh treatment and all sixteen men were executed for their role in the Rising.

Meticulously researched yet written in an accessible fashion, the *16 LIVES* biographies can be read as individual volumes but together they make a highly collectible series.

Lorcan Collins & Dr Ruán O'Donnell,
16 LIVES *Series Editors*

CONTENTS

Introduction

JOSEPH PLUNKETT – eldest son of a Papal Count, afflicted with tuberculosis from early childhood, poet with religious elements whose middle name was Mary – could not have been expected to press his name into history as one of the seven leaders of a revolution and the youngest signatory to its philosophy, but he was and he did. In searching for the real person for this book it was mostly his own writing that rescued his reputation. It revealed the lively mind, the talents and the humour of the very young man in his diffidence and arrogance and in the more mature man, the same characteristics, but more serious, philosophical and humane.

Writer, traveller, reader, experimenter, roller-skater, thinker, crackshot, dancer, lover of women, theatre company director, motorcyclist, actor, editor, philosopher, military tactician, linguist, negotiator and, with all these, talkative, kind, critical and affectionate. This was the Joseph Plunkett who emerged, the man who cheated impending death from tuberculosis, dying instead by firing squad at the age of twenty-eight.

From his late teens he took the writing of poetry seriously and worked very hard at it. Fortunately, he put a date on anything he hoped to have published and when inserted into the story of his life they sit well there, sometimes giving us an insight into his life and sometimes having no apparent relevance at all.

His diaries leave a sense of having met someone and begun to know them and this is part of the great reward of working with him. His variety of passions, his insistence on thinking ideas through and his thread of humour through everything make him a fascinating and surprising discovery and one who deserves a completely new public image.

Honor O Brolchain

CHAPTER ONE

· · · · · ·

1886-1902
The Young Plunketts

WITLESS
When I was but a child
Too innocent and small
To know of aught but Love
I knew not Love at all.

But when I put away
The things I had outgrown
I learnt at last of Love
And found that Love had flown.

Now I can never find
A feather from his wings
Though every day I search
Among my childish things.
Joseph Plunkett

When George Noble, Count Plunkett and his wife returned from their two-year American honeymoon in 1886 Josephine Mary (Countess Plunkett) was already pregnant with their first child. The Plunketts were the beneficiaries of wealth created by their hardworking parents. Their fathers, Patrick Plunkett and Patrick Cranny, had moved from the leather and shoe trade in nineteenth-century Dublin to building on the south side of the city, largely thanks to money provided by their wives, one of whom, Bess Noble Plunkett, had a shop of her own and the other, Maria Keane Cranny, had family money, a dowry. The property built and accrued by Plunkett and Cranny would have come to a considerable amount. It was mostly not intended for sale, but for rental to professionals and civil servants. Count and Countess Plunkett's marriage settlement included eight houses on Belgrave Road, Rathmines and seven houses on Marlborough Road in Donnybrook, three farms in County Clare and a house on Upper Fitzwilliam Street, No. 26, 'an address suitable for a gentleman', and this house was where they lived.

It was comparatively narrow and consisted, essentially, of two rooms on each floor. The basement was mostly used and occupied by the servants, but there was also a lavatory there for Count Plunkett's exclusive use. On the hall floor Count Plunkett had his study in the front beside the hall door to which he retreated for most of the time when he was at home to continue his work on European Renaissance art, Irish history and politics and his many other areas of scholarship and expertise. Behind his study was the dining room with the painting he thought might be a Rubens over the mantelpiece and behind that room a conservatory. From the hall the elegant staircase led past a beautiful window to a landing and two drawingrooms in an L-shape, all designed and proportioned by the Georgian builder for stylish entertaining. The stairs continued past a bedroom on the return to the two bedrooms on the next floor, one for the Count and one for the Countess. From this floor upwards the style and elegance disappeared and a very ordinary and very steep attic-type stairs led to the nurses' and children's quarters, which had a bathroom used by most of the household as well as one room the width of the front of the house and one, half that, at the back. The area behind the house, a garden and yard, was very small in modern terms, not a leisure garden, but an area for the burying and disposal of waste. Behind this was Lad Lane where the Plunketts' carriage was housed and their horses stabled in the livery stables. Count Plunkett filled the house all the way to the nursery at the top with paintings. He also oversaw the decoration of the drawingrooms and cast the house as a place beautiful enough for children to grow up in, but in the forty years they occupied it the Plunketts did no more to improve or decorate it.

The nursery area at the top of the house was home not

only to that first baby, Philomena Mary Josephine (Mimi) and her nurse from Mimi's birth in 1886, but to all seven children as they arrived, their three nurses and one or two nursemaids until they were all young adults. This does not in the least compare with the four or five entire families in one room which occurred in the terrible and extensive poverty of areas of Dublin at the time, but it must have made some of the individuals in those two rooms ache for peace and privacy at times. It was alleviated by visits to the rest of the house to see their parents once a day or less and a walk every day:

> One or two of the nursemaids used to bring all of us children for a walk every day but before we could leave there were seventy little buttons to be done up on my clothes. The walk was always the same, from Fitzwilliam Street along Leeson Street and Morehampton Road to Donnybrook Church and a little way on to the Stillorgan Road, with Jack in the pram and the two small ones, George and Fiona, in a mailcar which was a back-to-back go-car made mostly of bamboo. I had to walk with Joe and Mimi and Moya.
> Geraldine Plunkett Dillon

All seven children were born in the house: Philomena Mary Josephine in 1886, Joseph Mary in 1887, Mary Josephine Patricia in 1889, Geraldine Mary Germaine in 1891, George Oliver Michael in 1894, Josephine Mary in 1896 and John Patrick in 1897, their mother being attended each time by Nurse Keating, her maternity nurse. Countess

Plunkett's name, Josephine Mary, is repeated with incongru-
ous frequency in the children's names but, in fact, they were
usually known as Mimi, Joe, Moya, Gerry, George, Fiona
and Jack. Thirteen months after Mimi, on 21 November
1887, Joe (Joseph Mary) arrived.

The year after the birth of the next child, Moya, in 1889
the Countess organised the first of her famous holidays.
These were as much to get away from her children as to
get away herself. This one was to Tuam in County Galway
where she rented an unfurnished house and had all of the
luggage and furniture sent there from Dublin by canal boat
to Ballinasloe and from there, in thirty carts, to Tuam. She
travelled there with Mimi, Joe and Moya, all under five years
old, but she herself spent most of the time back in Dublin
leaving the children in the care of their nursemaids and the
owner of the house. Joe's sister, Gerry, was born four years
after Joe, in November 1891, and it is to her that we are most
indebted for the detailed personal accounts of the lives of all
her family, especially Joe, whom she greatly loved.

One of her very early memories was a 'howling row', a
battle between Mimi and Joe and the 'horrible' head nurse.
Mimi and Joe told her years later that they were just trying
to draw attention to what was going on. They were at the
mercy of this nurse and her threats. Joe told her that one
of the nurses used to heat the poker until it was glowing
red and threaten to shove it down his throat when he cried.

Another trick was to push the go-car (precursor of the buggy) out over the edge of the canal and threaten to let go; this was supposed to be for 'fun'. Gerry's nurse (each child had a nurse brought in for them) Biddy Lynch was different. She stayed with them for nine years bringing order, affection and pleasure into their lives. In Gerry's description:

> She was kind, sensible, just, clever, intelligent, patriotic (a Parnellite), absolutely reliable, religious, scrupulously exact and honest. She taught us to read and to write and to sing Irish songs, she taught us our religion, she washed us and dressed us, she made our clothes and hats and, in her spare time, knitted stockings for her mother at home in County Westmeath.

Some of the maids lived in, but those who didn't used to finish work at about seven o'clock in the evening and meet up with their friends, often standing and chatting outside the house. On one of these evenings Joe and George decided to drop light bulbs from the fourth floor nursery window onto the basement area and the maids thought the resulting explosions were revolvers. They complained that they knew they had been noisy, but they didn't think they should be shot at!

Joe already had what was known as 'bovine' tuberculosis by that time, probably contracted when he was about two years old from milk. It is a virulent form of tuberculosis, which attacks the glands as well as the lungs and causes weight loss and night sweats. As a disease it was cloaked in ignorance and myth and even the experts underestimated it as a fatal disease. 'Bovine' tuberculosis, transmitted from humans to cows and back to humans is now dealt with by pasteurisation of milk. Joe Plunkett's temperament was active, interested, humorous and lively but he had to suffer the restriction and frustration of being frequently confined to bed with this illness all through his life. In 1895 another long family holiday, this time to Brittany for three months, was undertaken with the Count and Countess, her mother, Maria Cranny, five children, Mimi, Joe, Moya, Gerry and one-year-old George, and Gerry's nurse, Biddy Lynch.

By the time he was seven Joe was being taught by a governess along with his sisters, Mimi and Moya. The Countess often sat in on these sessions and not only interfered, but even competed with the children. In the time-honoured manner, governesses came and went at frequent intervals, but it is to her nurse, Biddy, that Gerry gives the credit for teaching her to read and write. It is likely that this also applied to Joe, although it was usual to take boys' education more seriously and he would have been the focus of attention from both the Countess and whichever governess was there at the time. The Count left the employment of staff and organising children's lessons to his wife, but he talked to his children as he would to any adult and about the same things – art, history, French, Italian, books, Irish history – and with the same enthusiasm and affection, so they were simultaneously acquiring another type of education.

In the winter of 1896 Mimi was sent as a boarder to Mount Anville School, and Moya and Gerry to the Sacred Heart Convent, Leeson Street while living with their grandmother, Maria, in 17 Marlborough Road in Donnybrook. After her husband's death she had moved there from Muckross Park, which her husband built for her. The Countess often sent her children off to other houses and schools and this time she had good reason as she had a small baby, Fiona, at home and was pregnant again.

There was a children's fancy dress party that year given by the Lord Mayor of Dublin, Richard McCoy, and the Countess decided to send her four eldest children, Mimi, Joe, Moya and Gerry. On the day of the party they were taken to a costume hire firm and dressed up, Mimi in an 'Irish' costume, Moya in a Kate Greenaway dress and bonnet, Joe as a Gallowglas and Gerry (who really hated the whole proceedings) as the Duchess of Savoy. Gerry found it stilted and not at all about the children, but there is no record of how the others felt. However the ordeal was not over because they were 'stuffed' into the costumes again the next day and taken to the Lafayette studios on Westmoreland Street to be photographed both as a group and individually. The result is beautiful and dramatic, but taking photographs at that time was a slow process requiring the subject not to move for a long time, always difficult for children, so they used to put their head and neck in a brace to keep them still. In the end the expense was enormous and the pleasure only for the adults.

In 1897 the family rented a house called Charleville in Templeogue on the outskirts of Dublin and the children were sent there with Biddy Lynch. What was supposed to be a few months turned into a year with visits from their father and, occasionally, their mother. This meant that Mimi, Joe, Moya and Gerry were now missing school, but they did have a governess, Mademoiselle Ditter, whom Gerry describes as:

> … small and dark, a wild creature and a terrible tyrant, and she
> always abandoned us if possible. She was supposedly French
> but in fact she came from Alsace and had a strong hatred of
> the French. She used to teach us how to curse the French
> with appropriate gestures and to sing anti-French songs. She
> did also teach us to recite real French poetry and sing more
> conventional songs and to sew and make paper flowers.

Countess Plunkett liked only French to be spoken at the dinner table and the children did learn enough of the language to read French books of all kinds for pleasure. Food was supposed to be sent to Charleville from town on a regular basis, but their mother frequently forgot. Six children, a couple of servants and a wild governess in a country house with no access to money or shops needed to be resourceful. When they ran out of food there were hens but the henhouse was kept locked and the Countess kept the key with her in town so Moya was delegated to break in to it and take the eggs, which she did by squeezing through the hens' door. It was in Charleville also that they got Black Bess, a well-trained, good-mannered four-year-old pony. The older children could ride her and drive her in the trap, enabling them to explore the countryside with great freedom.

Jack Plunkett, the youngest of the seven children, was born that October and shortly afterwards the rest of them were brought back to Fitzwilliam Street.

Count Plunkett's title was bestowed on him by the Pope in recognition of his gift to an order of nuns, The Little Company of Mary (known as The Blue Nuns), of a villa in Rome so that the order could have a house there. He was a nationalist in the Parnellite tradition, having been a friend of both Isaac Butt and Charles Stewart Parnell himself. He stood for election as a Parnellite in constituencies where he was unlikely to win because he could afford to lose his deposit, but could test support and divide the opposition vote. He also undertook, at his own expense, to reform and update the St Stephen's Green electoral register, which covered a large area of Dublin. Count Plunkett bought a typewriter (only invented twenty years before) for his work on the register and when it was finished brought it home where, to their great delight, the children had the use of it. When Parnell was leaving Dublin in 1891 for what turned out to be the last time he called unexpectedly to see the Count in

Fitzwilliam Street and waited a couple of hours for him but, sadly, the Count didn't get back in time; Parnell died only a few months later in Brighton. In 1898 Count Plunkett, who stood for election again that year in the Stephen's Green area and nearly got in, was going round the house singing *Who fears to speak of '98* to celebrate the centenary of the 1798 Rebellion:

Then here's their memory, let it be
To us a guiding light
To cheer our fight for liberty
And teach us to unite!
John Kells Ingram (1823-1907)

Biddy Lynch, who had a great collection of songs, was joining in and adding appropriate songs of her own. As there was hardly any teaching of Irish history in schools or out of them, songs were an important source of information for the many in the populace who were hungry for it. Count Plunkett was rejected as a candidate for the Irish Parliamentary Party by John Redmond in 1900 for being too radical in his nationalism. In 1895 he had said 'Do we vote for the country that crushes us, or for the beginning of our liberty?' – too radical for Redmond.

There were also visible and audible contradictions between the way the Plunketts lived and what they saw around them. The majority of those living on Fitzwilliam Square and Street would have been strongly unionist, that is to say, wishing for the uninterrupted continuation of the union between Britain and Ireland, particularly as it would be the best way to continue their wealth, business and professions, but behind the Square and the Street were lanes full of great poverty and squalor, families living in and over stables with no facilities, regular chaos and violence, which could all be heard from the houses in front. All this had a considerable effect on ten-year-old Joe who from December, 1898, was in school in CUS (Catholic University Schools) Leeson Street, while the girls were back in the Sacred Heart Convent school just across the road. The Countess usually failed or forgot to arrange for her children to have such things as uniforms, copybooks or pens. At this time she was away on a trip so they stayed in various places including their grandmother's in Donnybrook, but most days they went to see their father in Fitzwilliam Street where he was preparing his book on the painter, Botticelli. On Saturdays he gave them pocket money: Mimi and Joe got twopence, Moya and Gerry got a penny.

Joe's time in CUS was very short; four months later in March 1899 he contracted pneumonia and pleurisy. Pneumonia was well documented and the causes known by then but, without proper treatments it was greatly feared and with good reason. It frequently proved fatal for the young, the old and those who, like Joe, had chronic bad health. Its usual symptoms of cough, chest pain, fever and difficulty in breathing were often exacerbated by those of pleurisy, an inflammation of the cavity surrounding the lung which causes stabbing pain in the chest and pain and swelling in the joints; a miserable condition for an eleven-year-old boy. Joe's mother had no training in nursing but she was good at it and had an interest in it which enabled her, with several staff to help her, to nurse invalids, including her father, through long illnesses. On this occasion Joe was not expected to live and his mother nursed him for months until he started to recover; Joe was always grateful to her for this.

Early in 1900 their grandmother, Maria Cranny, died. Joe was still ill so his brothers and sisters were sent to live in her Donnybrook house with their nurse and nursemaid. They, in their turn, contracted whooping cough and measles and were very ill, Mimi nearly died, and they were sent to a house, Parknasillogue, in Enniskerry, to recover. Joe was also convalescing by then but he was not sent to the country, his mother decided to take him to Rome for the winter to recover as he was still very weak after his long illness. When they got to Paris, she changed her mind and instead put Joe in the Marist school in the Parisian suburb, Passy, as a boarder and she stayed in Paris. Joe acquired good French in the school and became expert in local children's games but it could not be called convalescing and Passy, with its northern French climate, tended to be cold and wet and bad for his health. By the time they headed home at the end of the year he had developed an enlarged gland in his neck, the first of many.

CHAPTER 2

• • • • •

1902-1906
Country Life

Count Plunkett's book, *Botticelli and his School*, was published in August of 1900 and with the £300 he was paid
by the publishers, George Bell and Sons, he bought the last
seven years of a lease on a house, Kilternan Abbey, in Kilternan,
County Dublin, eight miles from the centre of Dublin and
very much in the countryside. The Count wanted to give
his children country air, finalising the deal while Joe and his
mother were still away. For the seven children it was, initially,
paradise. Kilternan Abbey was a big house at the top of the
Glenamuck Road on one hundred and twenty acres of land,
all but five let to local farmers, and with a pillared entrance,
there still, on the Enniskerry Road beside the Golden Ball
pub. Being sited in the foothills of the Dublin Mountains
there were wonderful views of Dublin Bay and far beyond
but its design was more suburban than rural. The hall floor

included two sitting rooms, one with a billiards table, much used by Joe and Gerry, a conservatory and a dining-room. The Countess and Joe each had a bedroom on the first floor and the top floor had two front rooms, Mimi's and one shared by Gerry and Moya with the nursery at the back for George, Fiona and Jack and their nurses, Biddy Lynch and Lizzie. There were cellars, yards, outhouses, stables and a bungalow where Count Plunkett lived when he was there. There was also plenty of land for the children to explore, a pond, cows, horses, shrubberies, hillsides, streams, huge glasshouses, and mountains of fruit – figs, plums, greengages, Morello cherries, passion fruit, Muscat vines and thousands of peaches – and they still had their pony, Black Bess.

Gerry writes:

> Joe and I went wild whenever we could, roaming all over the hills behind. We would get up at fantastic hours of the morning, usually somewhere around five o'clock, to have the whole world to ourselves. We would find something to eat in the kitchen, and since the doors were always locked and the keys on Ma's table, we got out a window onto the shed roof or down the fig tree by the kitchen wall. We made a house in one of the evergreen trees in front of the house and we had a whole series of complicated stories for every corner of the place. Out the back, beyond the house, there was a large wild place, which was used for grazing by a local farmer and some way up from it was a wonderful crom-

lech where we went most days. It was a huge thing with a kind of sacrificial hollow in the top with the word 'Repeal' scratched deep into the stone.

Not long after their arrival in Kilternan Joe's mother sacked the nurse, Biddy Lynch, 'for impertinence' and now that she was gone the Countess was in charge of the children, something she was very unused to. She didn't know them. At this time she had not seen six of her seven children for most of a year and it would have been a year of great change for each of them, given their ages – Mimi was fifteen, Joe fourteen and Moya twelve, Gerry was ten, George seven and Fiona and Jack five and four. The Countess had no idea of the way in which Biddy Lynch had kept the children fed, dressed, organised and happy and she forgot that children grow and need clothes or just ignored it. For whatever reasons, frustration, ignorance, lack of order, she began beating her children. She expected them to be totally obedient to her without telling them what her rules were and when they got things wrong she beat them without explaining why. Each of them reacted differently; Joe always felt a duty to her and he was sufficiently used to her to be able to manipulate her but he could see it was wrong. Mimi used to stand in front of the knife drawer in the sideboard 'just in case', Fiona, who was only six, was defiant and Gerry, who already knew she hated her, was terrified. All her life she shook whenever her mother came into the room.

The Countess' violence included thumping them with her closed fists, hitting them with a riding cane or a horsewhip, but when she used this on Joe he fainted and she never did it to him again. She was not unusual for her time; it was regarded by many as normal and even necessary to beat children. 'Spare the rod and spoil the child' was a common belief and in Fitzwilliam Street they could regularly hear the judge next door beating his children up and down the stairs. Count Plunkett was rarely there to see these things and he regarded the management of the house and children as his wife's domain. He had an ambiguous attitude to her, seeing her as both the rightful controller of property and finances (including his own) although she did not have the skills for this. He also left her in charge of the children's education even though, in that area, he had so much – several good schools including a few years in Nice and studies in Art and Law in Trinity College Dublin – while her only education involved occasionally sitting with her brothers and their tutors and less than a year in a London school.

By contrast, he also saw her as 'a little girl', a child who could not be held entirely responsible for her actions. She had a rigid and tyrannical mother and a father who was never there because he was always working. She had access to considerable wealth but didn't consider herself wealthy – she used to ask her children to pray that she would find four hundred pounds by next Tuesday or 'they would all be in the workhouse.' She rarely paid her bills but she kept the management of their many houses to herself and rarely paid the maintenance. She was a very good and enthusiastic traveller and she loved and admired her husband.

From October 1901 Joe was going to Belvedere College in Dublin. From Kilternan he had a return journey there of over sixteen miles each school day. His parents went to the Fitzwilliam Street house nearly every day – by waggonette, train and carriage. Joe wasn't part of these journeys; he had to leave much earlier to cycle to Carrickmines Station, train to Harcourt Street and from there on his bicycle, to Belvedere and, of course, all this in reverse at the end of the school day. On his return journey the other children met him when they could with the pony and trap as the hill was too steep for cycling. Otherwise he had to walk the nearly two miles. Even for a healthy boy this would have been a debilitating regime, especially in winter and with hours of homework afterwards but for Joe, with a history of illness, particularly affecting his lungs, it was exceptionally difficult. That didn't stop him pottering around shops on the quays in Dublin and spending his lunch money on bits and pieces, curios, books and pet mice.

From G.N. Reddin:

> At school he was inevitably misunderstood. He was not a
> boy like the rest. His companions classed him with those
> whom they called 'queer fellows.' He puzzled them. They

joked at his expense and treated him sometimes with school-boy harshness.

Reddin also says that he was 'Cold, haughty and independent towards strangers as a boy ...' With so little structured education and such unreliable support from home he felt that he was always fighting a losing battle and Gerry records that he thought he was ignorant and was worried about not having enough education. Gerry, says of all seven of them:

> Strangers just thought we weren't much good. ... we were badly dressed, looked peculiar and it seemed as though none of us would ever come to anything.

Not only was Joe already a constant reader but it was at this time that his passion for science and technology took off and, not finding the kind of information he was looking for either at home or in school (subjects there were confined to English, French, German, Maths and Religious Knowledge) he began looking for books, chemistry books in particular, to give him answers. He found some in Webb's bookshop on the quays. He took over part of a cellar known as Robin Adair's kitchen in the basement of the Kilternan house as a laboratory and persuaded his mother to buy him some flasks and condensers and basic apparatus. He found it very difficult until he came across J. Emerson Reynold's *Elementary Practical Chemistry*. This book made things clear and progressed easily through its subject and Joe and his sister, Gerry, spent hours of fascinated enjoyment trying the experiments.

Gerry was later to distinguish herself in Chemistry in University College, Dublin. There were definite limitations on what they could do; there was no gas supply in the house to run a Bunsen burner, which made some experiments difficult or impossible, and when their mother started taking an interest, asking questions and bringing visitors down to the cellar to view her outstanding son's experiments, Joe was put off. He told Gerry that their mother seriously expected him, at the age of thirteen, to make important and original discoveries and this discouraged him completely. Joe was fascinated by Marconi's wireless from the start, probably from the time of Marconi's very first successful transmission from Rathlin Island to Ballycastle in 1898. Joe bought the weekly magazines that published all the information emerging on radio and its development and he had started building his own sets in Fitzwilliam Street and continued in Kilternan.

In 1902 the family all went to meet Miss Evelyn Gleeson, who had just moved to Dundrum, near Kilternan. She was a friend of the socialist artist, William Morris, and had similar aspirations, to make beautiful things accessible to everyone and here she was beginning her lifetime project, the Dun Emer Guild, which was to contribute that beauty to Irish society for more than fifty years. Evelyn Gleeson's arrival with her sister, Mrs McCormack and the McCormack children of similar age to the Plunkett children, Kitty, Gracie and Eddie, brought great changes in the young Plunketts' lives. These were friendships that were to last lifetimes. Evelyn Gleeson's house, Runnymeade, outside Dundrum, was a beautiful big house with a large garden, a very open house, always full of writers, painters, thinkers and talkers. Joe and Gerry joined a brush-painting class given by Lily and Lolly Yeats, sisters of Jack B. Yeats and William Butler Yeats. Nora Fitzpatrick taught them something of bookbinding and the whole house was a centre of talk and artistic creation. They loved it and spent as much time there as they could. All the young Plunketts had some artistic bent, which appeared and developed during their lives, and this time and the people they met fostered their beginnings. Most of the young Plunketts' socialising was with families known to their parents and their father already knew several families in the Kilternan area when they moved out there. The O'Morchoe family was very close by in the Glebe House, Glencullen, and their father was the Church of Ireland Rector of Kilternan. He and his wife, Anne, had seven children, four boys and three girls, and the three oldest boys, Arthur, Kenneth and Nial, were old enough to become good friends with the older Plunkett children, to roam the countryside and share games of all kinds with them. Being from different religions and traditions they went to different schools and universities and joined different armies, but one of those friendships was to have a strange last crossing in 1916.

Count Plunkett had another friend in the area who was to

prove very important to all the young Plunketts and to Joe in particular. Originally from Marseilles and then Paris, William Arthur Rafferty, a Frenchman and an engineer all his life, had run away from his family to the 1861 Great Exhibition in London, which was full of mechanical marvels. From that he realised his dream of becoming an engine driver on the London to Dover train, but he reluctantly gave this up to do what he saw as his duty, taking up his inheritance of a farm, Springfield, at The Scalp just beyond Kilternan. Rafferty got to know Count Plunkett in London and they became firm friends, both were involved in court work in the Kilternan area. He had a daughter, Lena, similar in age to the older Plunkett children and she and her father looked after Joe many times when he stayed with them to recover from his illnesses. They were also kind, in many very personal ways, to the rest of the family, right into their adulthood. Mr Rafferty and Count Plunkett shared a passion for books but in Kilternan the only books in the house available to the children, some of whom were always book-hungry, were those bought by the Count and Countess at Carrickmines Station to read on the train, light novels and detective stories, Sherlock Holmes, and magazines ideal for following developments in radio and photography. Joe and Gerry devoured all of them.

In 1903 Count Plunkett was appointed Secretary to the Cork International Exhibition, a repeat of the very successful 1902 Exhibition. He lived in Cork for most of the year before the exhibition, which ran from May to October and included a visit from the English King Edward VII and Queen Alexandra to whom he had to make a presentation. In August of 1903 the young Plunketts produced the first number of their magazine, *The Morning Jumper*, strictly for their own amusement. Mimi wrote out all their contributions with the youngest two, Fiona and Jack, being helped by the older ones with their stories, limericks and illustrations. The Table of Contents below is from that August edition:

Prologue

The Garden of Sweet Pea

Nonsense Rhymes

The Fiddling Wizard

Nonsense Verse

Charm for Dispelling Beauty

The Bad Robbers

More Nonsense

The Miller's Dog

The Tulip Fairies

Sonnet

The Magic Emerald

There are no credits or indications as to who wrote what, but in that August edition nine-year-old George Plunkett won the nonsense poetry competition with this:

When I was old and knew so much

I never cared to use or touch

A fiddle – for when I was young

I broke the strings and near was hung.

In the Christmas issue, with Mimi away in Rome, it is clear from the handwriting (this time many hands are discernible) that their mother became very involved (Gerry records that she became excited about the whole thing) and most of this 'Double Number' is written by her. There are several typed contributions and plenty of illustrations and this number includes the following:

The Editors and staff of *The Morning Jumper* tender their best thanks to the kind and sympathetic contributor who sent them the following verses:

Sing a song of sixpence, a booklet full of nous,

Seven clever authors all in one house,

When the book was opened they all began to sing,

Wasn't that a dainty treat to set before a king?

First is Philomena Editor in chief,

I know that she is saying now Oh aged bard be brief,

Sub editor is Joe, a learned man withal,

Whose scientific skill my weak mind doth appal.

Then comes helpful Moya jingling household keys

And laughing Geraldine as sweet as honey bees,

Make way for George the fifth our king by divine,

A manly little man and a special friend of mine.

Next with little frills upon her little frocks,

Fairy Fiona dances in as gently as a mouse

And last is Master Jack who though shorn of his locks
Still manages to shake the pillars of the house.

X L.C.R. (Lena C. Rafferty, daughter of Mr Rafferty of Springfield)

Mimi and Moya were now boarding in Mount Anville School, but Joe's attendance in Belvedere became very erratic and then fell away altogether as bad health took over again. He had attended the school for only two years. Now aged fourteen it was decided that the swollen glands in his neck would have to be lanced, cut open to alleviate the blockage and this was done at home in Kilternan by his uncle, Dr John Joseph (Jack) Cranny, who had a private practice and was attached to several Dublin hospitals. Nurse Keating was brought out to Kilternan to nurse Joe through his recovery and the Countess left for one of her many long holidays, this time on a cruise to Lisbon with her daughter, Moya, as chaperone, leaving twelve-year-old Gerry in charge of the household, shopping, catering management, servants – everything! The Countess saw nothing strange in this arrangement and Gerry did have some inexpert help from her father whom she loved dearly.

The earliest pieces of writing by Joe Plunkett to have survived are fragments of stories written in April and May 1904. It is very likely he was ill again – one of the pages has the score from a game of Bezique with his mother (she won) and it is also likely that *The Morning Jumper* had sparked off ideas. These fragments look like drafts or just doodling for stories, a novel, a fairy story, a thriller or a detective story … The punctuation (never Joe Plunkett's forte) is his own.

Saturday 9th April 1904

Confessions of a Murderer

Though still a young man I have committed more murders than any man living or executed by law. In fact there is or rather was only one who came anywhere near me in this matter of killing and he poor fellow (strange that

I should feel pity for anyone) – an ignominious death in the electric chair.

10 April 1904

Shady and the Fairy Bullfrog

By MJ Work

Once upon a time there was a little ghost who lived all alone with his mother in a family vault. He was six and a half years old and his name was Shady. One day he went to his mother and said 'Please Mummy will you give me a penny to buy a bullfrog?' 'What for?' said his mother 'Oh just to play with' answered Shady.

So his mother gave him a penny and he went away to buy a bullfrog. When he came to the shop he saw several bullfrogs in the window so he went in and said 'How much are your bullfrogs if you please?' and the shopman said 'A pennyfarthing'. The shopman said then seeing the disappointment of the little ghost 'If you promise to be good I will give you this little one for a penny' 'Thank you very much' said Shady as he paid his penny and took the bullfrog. What was his surprise when on looking closer at his bullfrog in the open air to see a tiny golden locket hanging around its neck. Shady immediately tried to open it when he was startled by a voice saying 'Leave that alone'. Shady looked around but saw nothing. He then tried again to open it and the voice said again, this time more loudly, 'Leave that alone'. 'Shan't' said the little ghost and redoubled his efforts to open the locket.

He had just succeeded in forcing it open and catching a glimpse of HIS OWN FACE!! in it when suddenly he saw the bullfrog become transformed. The locket slipped from his hands and he found himself confronting A FAIRY!!!!!!!!!!!!!!

Saturday 21st May 1904

'Father are you very busy, I have something to tell you' said a tall dark and very pretty girl of nineteen coming into the laboratory of Mr Lexonbridge the celebrated chemist when he was engaged in research on radium.

Joe's glands were now very swollen again and an operation was performed on them by Dr Swan, a friend of Dr Cranny.

In Gerry's account of it she says:

> He hacked poor Joe about savagely, referred to the healing tissue on Joe's neck as 'proud flesh', and burned it off with copper-sulphate crystals without an anesthetic.

The carotid artery was now just under the skin and from then on it was impossible for Joe to wear a properly fitting collar as it strangled him. The operation was performed in the Orthopaedic Hospital, 22 Merrion Street and Joe was afterwards sent to convalesce in Delaford, on the Firhouse Road, owned by Dr Swan. The whole experience was shocking and traumatic for Joe and his recovery from it took a long time.

Over these years the young Plunketts were moved around frequently; when Fitzwilliam Street was let they lived in Kilternan, when Kilternan was let they lived in Fitzwilliam Street. They were sent off to boarding schools in ones and twos and sevens and even, when their uncle, John Joseph Cranny, the doctor, died suddenly as the result of an accident in July 1904 they were sent (without the knowledge or consent of his widow) to live in Rockfield, his Dundrum country house. When their nurse left in a huff the children were on their own and seven children aged six to seventeen can do a lot of damage, albeit unwittingly, left for weeks in a strange house. The house, incidentally, had a telephone which was a new experience for the young Plunketts (they didn't have one until 1908) and Gerry records Joe making hoax calls to Harcourt Street Station on it! Dr Cranny had owned about twenty houses in Donnybrook and Ballsbridge, left to him by his father who had built them. He left seven of these, houses on Elgin Road, to his Plunkett nieces and nephews, two to Moya, who was his god-daughter, and five shared between the other six children. The Count and Countess were executors of this will, but the houses were never made over to any of the young Plunketts, even after they were twenty-one; in fact the Countess 'persuaded' Moya to sign her two houses over to her when Moya became a nun in 1914. If Joe, who was so subject to illness all his life that he could not work, had even had this legacy under his control, he might have had an income he could call his own.

In the autumn of 1904 Countess Plunkett brought the three boys, Joe, George and Jack, to St George's, the Josephite School in Weybridge, England. She had taken against Irish boys' schools and St George's, a Catholic school, had come to her attention. In December Joe wrote the following letter home to his mother whom he calls 'Mums'. George also uses this so maybe they all did.

St George's College Weybridge

Sunday 11th December 1904

Dear Mums

Only 11 days more!! How are you and Pappy? My health is quite salubrious thank you. Georgie and Jack are quite well. I am first in Chemistry after all I got 85% marks.

How are we to get home? Mr Edmund is taking most of the Irish boys home, are we to go with him? I think it would save a lot of trouble. If we did go with him we should leave London about 11 oclock am and reach Dublin North Wall about 8pm on Thursday 22nd December 1904 so please write quickly and tell me. If we dont go with Mr Edmund, how and when are we to go? Ufb. (I think this is a misprint.) When you are sending rugs for Georgie and Jack please send 3 sets of rug straps because our trunks leave the night before & therefore we will have to bring a few things such as brush and comb and nightshirts ourselves. Quite Easily Done. (that is Euclid)

I am afraid that my last letter was illegible as you don't seem to have understood that I had to pay for the photos of the football teams and also for the entrance fees for the ping pong, chess and draughts competitions which I put my name down for.

So far only one person has beaten me at ping-pong and as there are two prizes I think I have a chance for the second. Last evening I had a fight with a big boy about twice my weight, his name is Quin. He had been kicking the football at me (which hurts) up in the field where there was no-one to see fair play and then when we came down he thought he could do what he liked so he came over and called me a liar. Then I went for him. He hit me on the chest so I gave him 3 for himself. Then he hit me between the eyes so I punched his nose and after that he could not get one in. I gave him 5 on the head and then the bystanders (for this was in the study) separated us.

(NB He came over afterwards and shook hands) He didn't hurt me at all.

Monday December 12th 1904

I commenced this letter on Sunday but could not finish it.

Lots of love from us three to you and Pappy.

Your loving

Joseph

PS Have you seen the new halfpenny stamps? They are a very light green.

It must have been when they returned to the school after Christmas that scarlatina (scarlet fever) broke out and the school wrote to Countess Plunkett asking her to take the three boys home again although they hadn't contracted the illness. She brought them back to the bungalow at Kilternan as a kind of quarantine. While they were there Joe managed to persuade her that they shouldn't go back to the school because 'it was unsuitable'. How it was unsuitable is not defined, but it was usually used to mean various kinds of 'immoral behaviour' and it was enough to convince Joe's mother who said she would write to the British Government about it. They were now without schooling again and Joe wasn't well enough to be sent away to another school so Mr Greenan, the schoolteacher from Kilternan, was brought in as a tutor twice a week in the evenings. Mr Greenan was a teacher they could enjoy and Joe and Gerry derived special pleasure from his maths classes.

They could proceed as fast as they wished without hindrance and they found at last the kind of sound basis in different subjects that stood to them for years.

It was in 1905 that Count Plunkett first met Sir Roger Casement through a letter of introduction from a mutual friend, Mr Redan of the English diplomatic service in Brazil, supposed to have been the person who gave Casement his first lessons in Irish history. Casement's report on the abuse of workers in the Congo was published in 1904 and was causing considerable embarrassment to the British Government because of its indictment of the King of Belgium who 'owned' the Congo. Casement dined in No. 26 Fitzwilliam Street on a number of occasions with several of the young Plunketts there each time. There was discussion at the table of the violence and injustices to the Congo workers and, when he dined at a later date, the Putumayo Indians in Peru, and Casement was listened to with respect and admiration by all of them except the Countess who disliked him. From that time on they all followed his career with interest which helped to make them aware and inform them on international politics.

The four eldest Plunketts, Mimi, Joe, Moya and Gerry, were now aged nineteen, eighteen, sixteen and fourteen respectively. None of them had ever had formal lessons in Irish history, but they were surrounded by influences and ideas: their father's work in nationalist journals, his friendship and loyalty with Isaac Butt and Parnell, his Parnellite candidature his founding of the Society for the Preservation of the Irish Language (SPIL) and the Arts and Crafts Society, his reform of the St Stephen's Green register, and Biddy Lynch, their nurse's influence as a patriot, the poverty in Dublin and the conversation and humanitarian actions of Sir Roger Casement – all these conspired to make the young Plunketts nationalist and republican.

Their eyes and ears were open.

CHAPTER 3

• • • • •

1906–1908
Stonyhurst

One of Countess Plunkett's trips took her to London in the spring of 1906 where she visited a family friend, Tom Gurrin, who was said by the Plunketts to be 'the best handwriting expert in England' and indeed he was frequently called as an expert witness in court cases. Gurrin's sons had gone to school at Stonyhurst College in Lancashire so he probably suggested it to the Countess for her sons as a Jesuit school and college with an international reputation and so it was that twelve-year-old George Plunkett found himself starting school there on 26 September while Joseph Plunkett joined the 'Gentlemen Philosophers' course there on 1 October 1906. George was to stay in the school for the next five years to 21 December 1912 winning the class prize, a beautifully-bound book with the Stonyhurst arms engraved on it, in his first year. Joseph Plunkett was nearly eighteen now and more usually known as 'Plunkett'. On his information sheet for the College he wrote:

> Joseph M. Plunkett
>
> 26, Upper Fitzwilliam St.
>
> Dublin
>
> Born at above address on 21st Nov. 1887
>
> Educated chiefly at home
>
> Joined Philosophy 1st October 1906

Underneath this in another hand, and obviously added a number of years later, is this not quite accurate note:

> Executed by Court Martial, Dublin, May 5th, 1915, as one of the ringleaders in the Sinn Féin Rising.

In writing 'Educated chiefly at home' Plunkett was ignoring the times spent in CUS, Passy, Belvedere, and Weybridge suggesting that he hadn't bonded with any of these places, but the education that meant the most to him was the tutoring by Mr Greenan of Kilternan. Mr Greenan was obviously a gifted teacher who could make the discovery of information a light burden.

Plunkett is given in the log list as the most senior of the eleven new 'Gentlemen Philosophers' in the first year of their two-year course. Next to him in seniority was Alfred Asphar of Malta who was to become a good friend. There were nine Senior Philosophers that year.

The Gentlemen Philosophers were third-level students rather than schoolboys. The course originated in the mid-nineteenth century when Catholics were not accepted in Oxford or Cambridge Universities and although they were accepted later, it was on condition they subscribed to the *Thirty-Nine Articles* (1563) the core beliefs of the Church of England. By the time Plunkett was in Stonyhurst these restrictions had been lifted and Catholics were attending Oxford and Cambridge, but the Gentlemen Philosophers continued until 1916. The Courses included Arts, Science, Classics, Mathematics, Law and Medicine and there had been many students in all of these, but now it had dwindled to a small number, mostly foreign students from Europe and America, often from titled families who wanted a cross between College courses and an English language school. They were very separate from the main school, interaction was discouraged and even those, like Plunkett, who had brothers in the school only met them on Sundays for a walk in the many acres of beautiful grounds.

When Joseph Plunkett joined the Philosophy course he found himself plunged into a twilight world of mixed characters with widely differing aspirations, portrayed in his letter to his sister, Philomena (Mimi) less than two weeks later. Plunkett's own language often reads as an English style, but, like his siblings, his speaking voice was closer to the old Dublin accent, similar to that of George Bernard Shaw.

Stonyhurst Friday 12th October 1906

Dearest Phil

You have the address quite right. Blackburn is the nearest town but Whalley (pronounced Wallee by some walley by others and waawllli) is the nearest post town. Thanks awfully for your letter and the things. Thanks to your forethought in sending tea and cakes I have been able to give two teas to some of my friends (I dont think I can post this till tomorrow as it is 10.45 pm now)

Saturday 13th October 3.55pm

I went to bed just then as lights have to be out at 11pm. I am expecting Mums here any minute from Manchester.

At the opposite side of the table just in front of me sit 2 Philosophers; one is an Italian prince Colonna by name who is twice as English as any Rajah. He speaks English with an English accent says 'walli' (see front page) and 'well rawthah' rides a hawss, wears 'puttee leggins donchknow and looks like a Medici (Piero for choice).

The other is the ideal hero of all 'chums' serial stories the 'tall, broad shouldered genial (but not too genial) Englishman'! Taciturn except when familiar. Not too intelligent, handsome, no sense of humour except English humour. That reminds me Father Gibb (English) our Prefect asked me did I know the way an Irishman fed his pig. I said 'no how? He said 'What you dont know? To get streaky bacon feeds it one day and starves—' 'Oh' I said 'that old one' I said 'When I read that several years ago in a comic paper it was an 'English farmer'. 'An Irish comic paper?' he said

'No' I said we haven't any. Haven't any? No, our papers aren't comic, they are funny.' Then Avery who is an amurican from Noo Yoik threw me a wink and a grin and Fr Gibb changed the subject to poultry.

It is very cold and has been raining ever since Fr Gibb stuck a notice on the board saying this would be a half holiday. Such is life.

Another of the Phils is a Belgian Baron; fences, is jumpy, good-natured and has very little English. I saw Avery on Colonna's hawss yesterday, he rides just like a cowboy (I have read the Virginian by Owen Wister)

Remarkable coincidence I had just finished reading Dr Jekyl and Mr Hyde not at all what I thought.

Love from both to all

Ramises II Rex Aegypt

letter for Gerry enclosed

Plunkett was fascinated by Rameses II because, he said, the back of his head was the same shape as his own! The fascination may have started in 1905 when the magnificent and beautiful tomb of Rameses' first queen and principal consort, Nepertari, was discovered by Ernesto Schiaparelli. Plunkett's mother arriving from Manchester, would have been hugely impressed the first time she visited Stonyhurst, as she was driven up the long avenue between the two canals to the panorama of buildings accrued over four hundred years, fronted by the grandiose nineteenth-century elements, ornate and castellated. She must indeed have been impressed because she paid up quietly to have the Plunkett coat of arms included with all the others of Philosopher students in the bay window of the Great Hall, where the table on which Cromwell slept before the Battle of Preston, stands.

Plunkett's poem, *Wampyr*, is dated 1906 and could have been linked to Hallowe'en, 31 October, of that year. Plunkett was well acquainted with Bram Stoker's *Dracula* (1896) and earlier similar works by Sheridan Le Fanu and John Polidori; Plunkett's father was in Trinity College with Bram Stoker and indeed with Oscar Wilde.

Wampyr

Ruddy lips and gleaming teeth

Eyes that shine like sunset's glow

Softly swinging through the air

Laughing as they go.

Calling 'Sister with us come

Come and feast tonight with us

Fresh red blood our drink shall be

We'll regale you thus'.

Swift, dawn comes with sudden gleam

Back they hurry to the tomb

To await the shades of night

To await their doom!

JMP

Although the Philosophers' classes were in the style of university lectures, they were also regulated like schoolwork; dictation must all be kept in the same book and inspected every Saturday, punctuation left out was subject to a fine and so on. In this essay, *'People I would like to have seen',* the title was apparently set by the same Professor Gibb of the streaky bacon joke, Plunkett's whimsy on what was meant as a serious topic earned sarcastic remarks by his teacher in the margin.

Monday 19th November 1906

People I would like to have seen.

What people are there whom I would wish to have seen and have not? I mean of course 'in my mind's eye Horatio' as the other bard would say. My theme should rather be people I would wish to have known. That would suit the case better.

I think I should head the list with the illustrious name of the Mad Hatter.

Somehow the character of the Mad Hatter has always appealed to me why I cannot say unless it be that he forever seems 'let us move one place on and start again.' That is so hopeful it shows such a determination to get where there is to be got in this eccentric world. 'We're all mad here, you're mad, I'm mad, the Cheshire cat's mad' All the more reason to move one place and start again

The next two on my list are together both being famous members of the theatrical world – they are William Shakespeare esq. and Dan Leno esq. ditto

Unlike the Mad Hatter (who will never die) they are both in that period of existence which requires us to use the past tense when speaking of them.

This is a pity both for them and us. Those two great geniuses of the histrionic sphere the one creating and the other interpreting drama would have startled all others if they had collaborated.

I observe by your expression that you would like to make two remarks here – would say firstly that necessary condition of time etc. would make it difficult to carry this idea and secondly you will observe that my language is somewhat awkward.

To the first I answer what is space, time or anything else to the wanderings of a great mind. And to the second I reply that it is intentionally so, it does not do to be too explicit when dealing with such an important matter in order to allow for the danger of a misunderstanding.

All who have read Owen Wister's splendid novel will easily comprehend the wish to meet Lady Baltimore. The author's description of her is so felicitous that it is not to be wondered at that many readers of his book have desired to make her further acquaintance. This statement is most likely to be misapprehended by any who have not read the book in question.

I will stop here for I fear that if I went on the reader of this would share my fate and be overcome in a manner akin to that generally in use during the earlier part of the Victorian era by the exuberance of my verbosity.

Finis

This essay must have caused irritation if the intention was to encourage writing about heroes or people who had 'changed the world'; Plunkett, citing not just the Mad Hatter, Shakespeare and Owen Wister, but also Dan Leno (a Music Hall virtuoso whose specialities included clog dancing and playing Mother Goose) was being determinedly frivolous. He was to rescue his reputation entirely by the end of his time in Stonyhurst. Two days later Plunkett turned nineteen and one month later he went home for Christmas and records:

January 1st Tuesday. We all went in 'bus to Palmerston Road

for 4 o'clock dinner. Recitations and dancing afterwards.

Palmerston Road was where his grandfather, Patrick
Plunkett, lived with his second wife and family. The eldest,
Germaine, was ten years older than Gerry and her god-
mother, but they were all close enough to the Plunketts in
age with Gerald and Joe only a month apart. Helena, their
mother, kept an orderly and very comfortable house and
was always kind to the young Plunketts for whom she made
clothes and bought luxurious presents.

Plunkett also records his clothes sizes against the printed
list at the beginning of the diary:

> Personal Memoranda Joseph M. Plunkett
>
> Glove size 7 ¼
>
> Boots 7
>
> Collars 14 ½
>
> Hats 6 ⅝
>
> Las Palmas
>
> Weight 8st 7lbs, Height 5ft 7 ¾"

After a couple of weeks of social life and doctor's appoint-
ments in Dublin, Joe returned to Stonyhurst on 14 January
1907. He was well settled in by now and able to enjoy the
life, which in many ways suited him very well.

In his sister, Geraldine's account she says:

> Joe was the only Irish person in the class and very happy
> there as he could study as much as he liked; it had a
> splendid library and it gave him access to all the ideas

and information he had wanted for so long.

The Philosophers had a very structured day. Mass every morning was followed by breakfast at eight-thirty, lectures and study until one o'clock, sport for a couple of hours, tea and frequently Benediction or a Marian devotion, more lectures and study, supper at eight and then they could collect the evening post, read the papers, play cards or billiards or just smoke and argue like all undergraduates. The staff joined them in all these things, both in work and leisure, took part in the sports and even performed in the concert or play, the feature of each term. They had a half day each Tuesday and a whole day off each Thursday and sometimes more time off without reason. Sport was mainly football and cricket but golf, when introduced, had become the outright favourite. There were versions of hunting, shooting and fishing and those who brought a horse with them could stable it there and go hunting or trekking. Those without a horse could hire one and they all had the privilege of being allowed to have their own dogs with them. Motorbikes however were forbidden from 1904.

Plunkett's health prevented his involvement in these sports, but he had as much time as he liked for reading and a wonderful library with bays in amongst the several centuries of books. He had more independence than he had ever had before, he was in a crowd of young men whose antics and conversation were entertaining, and he had a very good friend in Alfred Asphar from Malta who was studying Law, who was nearest to him in age and who shared all of his particular interests. There were official debates on Sunday mornings in the Drawing Room and they were encouraged to invite each other to tea in their rooms most afternoons. As well as the academic elements the Philosophers were involved in the college's Officer Training Corps (OTC) often as officers themselves. The training was in drilling and musketry, including three weeks at Aldershot every year and they were overseen by and wore the uniforms of the East Lancashires but Plunkett was not enrolled in this, presumably because of his health. He advised his brother, George, to join and acquire as much knowledge as he could and although George was reluctant at first, in time he began to enjoy it and a few years later wrote a very enthusiastic letter to his mother about an exercise across local territory.

Joe Plunkett records in his 1907 Hely's Diary:

> March 11th. Monday: 1st Radio-telegram at 26 [Fitzwilliam Street] to-day

No further information!

He seems to be back home in Fitzwilliam Street from that date, perhaps because of illness. He was certainly there and ill from 6 to 16 April, in bed with 'flu and straight afterwards he travelled to the Canary Islands.

On 17 April he sailed from Liverpool for Las Palmas on the *Aburi*, which docked at Funchal in Madeira five days later where the passengers went ashore for a day's sightseeing, including a train journey up the mountain. Next morning they left Madeira and, about sixty miles out, saw:

3 whales 'spouting' also Mother Carey's chickens [stormy petrels] and a school of porpoises diving in and out of the water. A swallow has been flying round the ship.

They had a day on Tenerife before reaching Gran Canaria where they stayed in the Metropole Hotel for eleven days, sightseeing, shopping, touring and spending nights in the Casino.

After dinner went up to town square in front of cathedral. An extraordinary sight – thousands of fairy lamps, red, blue, green, yellow, purple, orange, twinkling, great crowds of people and all the grandest of bands and fireworks. Went to Casino. Never saw so many pretty girls together before ...

On 4 May:

Two three-horse carriages for Monte. Halfway had a glass of the best Muscatel I've tasted and five bananas, 4d [four pence]. On to Caldera [the volcanic crater]... simply magical.

Sun. 5th: Talked religion and politics with Holmes (a son of Lord Justice Holmes) who is an RM [Resident Magistrate] a Protestant and a unionist. He is about the only sensible man I've met this trip.

Address 3 Fitzwilliam Place, and Ballymena

Mon 6th ... to Museum ... extremely valuable and interesting collection especially prehistoric. Guanche [the original inhabitants of the island] and the anthropological sections. [Next day] – 'went to tobacco factory. Bought 100 cigarettes, 4d [fourpence farthing]...

Their ship home, the *Salaga,* was crowded and water came in to the cabin, so Plunkett slept in the smoking room for the rest of the trip, taking books out of the ship's library to keep himself amused. He was back in Dublin on 15 May, gave his last twopence to the porter at the quay and was driven home to 26 Fitzwilliam Street. He had started the month with seven pounds and his ticket.

May 25: Flew 6 yards

June 13: Arrived Stonyhurst 11am

July 10: Left Stonyhurst in brakes

[probably a day trip].

Their third term finished at the end of July and Plunkett wrote in his diary:

July 24th Philosophy exam 65%

July 29th Philosophy oral 90%

[He won the 'Next in Merit' prize (2nd place) in Mental and Moral Philosophy]

July 28 Left Stonyhurst ...

Plunkett went to Malta to stay with Alfred Asphar and his family, but he was back in Ireland and involved in the founding of The Irish Esperanto Association on 15 September 1907. The Honorary Chairman was Dr J. C. O'Connor M.A. (founder of the Dublin Esperanto Group in 1905, first of its kind in Ireland) and it was chaired by the Chemist, Edmund E. Founier d'Albe. Plunkett was one of the secretaries and drew up the brief statement of the organisation's intentions and named its officers. Major international discussions were being held that October in Paris about establishing an international auxiliary language and there was a flurry of Esperanto movements around the world. In Paris the decision taken was to reform Esperanto and make it the auxiliary language.

During that September, Plunkett wrote the following with only this crossed-out title:

TO KATHLEEN NÍ HOULIHAN

This is a song to my love peerless and beautiful

She who is rosy as the dawn and glorious as the sunset

Tender as the touch of flakes of snow falling

Sweet, sweet as the honey is my love and restful as darkness.

The harps of the bards are dumb, the poets are silent

For they are afraid to sound their poor music

Till they are inspired to sing of her worthily

Tall is she, and stately, fair-skinned as the lily.

I will deck my love with gems, all treasures I will give her

Red-gold like her hair and amethysts from the valley

*Great white pearls from the lough and rubies blood crimson and
gleaming*

When I look in the eyes of my love I see the deep ocean

Grey blue are they and limpid, mysterious and moving

Eyes to inspire great deeds and the love of our country is in them.

With their return as Senior Philosophers at the beginning
of October, Plunkett and his class now had far more responsibilities and more privileges. They could choose their rooms
by order of seniority and they had a free hand furnishing and
decorating them. On the second day committees and secretaries were chosen – a secretary for the Drawing Room, the
Smoking Room, the Games Room, each of the sports and so
on. Plunkett is listed in the year log as Secretary of the Dark
Room. Since no Dark Room is listed in the previous years
it is safe to assume that this was his own idea. The Lumiére

Brothers, Auguste and Louis, had patented their invention, 'The Autochrome Lumiere' in 1903 and marketed it in June1907. It was the first colour photography process that was easily available to the public. It was the principal process of its kind until the advent of the subtractive process in the mid–1930s. Plunkett, always interested in developments in photography ordered the kit and all the information as soon as it came out and doubtless was introducing others to it in Stonyhurst. At this stage it was a very complicated but most exciting process using eight different baths, each plate having to be washed between the developer and the firing.

14 October 1907:

SAILING WEST

Sailing west into the sunset

Now high, now dipping low

And the dancing waves with phosphorous gleam

As we glide on lit with the ruddy beam

Leaving a trail of snow.

Sailing west into the sunset

Over the Sapphire Sea

While the lapping waves make music sweet

With the engine's throb and the whistling sheet

And the salt wrack rushing free.

Sailing west into the sunset

But the sun has now sunk low

And the roaring waves with angry beat

Leap up to kiss the reefèd sheet

As we hurrying onward go.

Sailing west into the sunset

With our ship a total wreck

On the wearying waste of furious sea

With all hope gone though alive we be

A drifting, eddying speck.

JMP

An entry on 17 October in the Philosophers' diary reads 'Good deal of *esprit de corps* this year' and on 25 October it records that the new pianola arrived at 2pm. After supper they all gathered round while Father Gibb presented Mister Colonna with the key. Colonna opened the pianola with great ceremony and the Philosophers listened open-mouthed while he inaugurated the instrument with the music of Wagner. Two months later Colonna was ordered to leave the College immediately by one of the priests for refusing a punishment. The new Rector, Fr Bodkin, first allowed him to stay for another twenty-four hours, until after the pheasant shoot, and then gave him permission to stay for the rest of the year. That was typical of the variation in their treatment; sometimes regarded as schoolboys and sometimes as what they were, young men who, at their age could have been in university or work or marriage. They, of course, behaved as students do, going between earnest work, passionate thought and dangerous frivolity. Plunkett was always working on his own ideas and notes beside Dictation show that even with a question mark or an exclamation mark he contradicted the official version of English (and therefore Irish) history and literature.

Plunkett does not give the reason or context of the following poem, but in itself it shows that, as well as writing those quirky pieces he was now working seriously to master such forms as the sonnet with its rhyme and rhythm patterns. Along with the other poems from this time and through the rest of his life there is very little in the way of written changes or corrections so it seems that, mostly, he must have finished them in his mind before writing them down and they arrive both formal and complete.

12 December 1907:

SONNET

There is a sentence ringing in mine ears,

A doleful banishment mine only thought

Unheard. I cry for mercy; Heav'n sends nought

To cleanse my mind, to wash my blinding tears

And banish memories of bygone years.

My heart does shriek aloud as tho it fought

All that the powers of Evil 'gainst it wrought.

And this the dreadful cause of all my fears:

'Now ye are parted ye'll ne'er meet again'

The dread, foreboding prophesy doth toll

The death-knell of my Being; it is toss'd

Into unknown Eternity, and lost

And a great darkness falling on my Soul

Submerges it in everlasting pain.

In the Stonyhurst holidays Plunkett brought some of his friends home to Fitzwilliam Street including Alfred Asphar and Prince Marc Antonio Colonna, a descendant of one of the victors at the battle of Lepanto. Others from Stonyhurst visited at different times including Prince Adolf von Schwarzenberg.

The Philosophers' Good Day was an annual event held towards the end of their year in June or July and by this time was usually a trip to Blackpool for a fine meal in the Metropole Hotel. They left early in the morning by charabanc to Preston where they got the 9.30 train to Blackpool. The Hotel served them cold consommé, salmon mayonnaise, mixed hors d'oeuvres, saddle of mutton with mint sauce, new potatoes, cucumber with vinaigrette, asparagus, Russian salad, strawberries and cream, Peach Melba, cream cheese and caviar on toast. By the time they got back to the College in the evening it was time for dinner there, which they had with speeches and a smoke afterwards. The College had a good stock of wine, good enough for Edward VII who was a friend of the Rector's and used to dine there every now and then.

This reading list from Plunkett's notebook is probably the material for his final essay:

Revelations; Mother Julian of Norwich; St Teresa; St John of the Cross; The Psychology of the Saints, Joly Sweden- burg; R.H. Benson, Mysticism; The West Molest Lectures; The Mirror of Shalot; Tauler, Mystical Workes; William Blake, Mystical Poetry and Prose; Francis Thomson etc., Delacroix, Les Grands Mystiques; Vaughan, Silex Scintillans, Evenings with the Mystics.

Plunkett won the first prize in this, his final year for his essay on this title set by his Professor: 'The Truths, alleged as the basis of Pantheism and Deism, find their only full and com- plete expression in Theism.'

He was given a prize of five pounds and with it he bought all the poetry he could when he got home.

There is no indication of who this poem was about:

Wednesday 24 June 1908:

FIRST LOVE

Rippling ringlets palely gold

Curved lashes drooping o'er

The love-light that to me has told

What I guessed before.

Attitude of timid grace

Softly yielding to that joy

That in passing leaves a trace

Nought can e'er destroy.

JMP

They were coming to the end now, to the smoking concert on last night. They sat for their group photograph, all smoking, many holding their little dogs, most trying to look suave or cool, starting their twenties and on the fringe of their lives. This group had lost their free-day privileges once for too much dancing and once for ducks and bullets in the classroom, they had started a magazine, which created more trouble, had instituted the Top Hat Tea and the September duck shoot, their *esprit de corps* had been noted and they said of themselves 'Good humour over us all' and must have entertained the staff as much as they annoyed them. They were changed by growing older and by their experiences: Aidan Liddell, known as 'Oozy' because he loved engines and chemicals who won a Victoria Cross for outstanding valour in the World War; Reginald Primrose who had given a tea in Hurst Green and was later a Lieutenant in the same World War; Prince Adolf von Schwarzenberg who owned fantastic tracts of land and whole provinces of Bohemia, all taken away twice, first by the Nazis for his sympathy with the local Jews and then by the Czech Government; the Belgian Baron 'jumpy, good-natured with very little English'; the sympathetic Avery from New York; Prince Marc Antonio Colonna, more English than a Rajah, the musician who was nearly expelled; Alfred Asphar, the lawyer from a leading Maltese family, Plunkett's close friend whom he was to visit again in Malta and Plunkett himself, who had taken this rich opportunity to develop in every way, especially intellectually. The whole experience was to serve him well as a traveller and as a negotiator in foreign countries a few years later.

George Plunkett stayed in Stonyhurst four more years. He told his sister, Geraldine, that in his second year there he found himself 'going around in a daze for quite a long time' – some kind of depression or breakdown. He was put in charge of the pet animals to help him to get over it and discovered that he particularly liked the snakes.

CHAPTER 4

• • • • • •

1908-1910
Many-Sided Puzzle

By the time he arrived home in 1908 to Fitzwilliam Street, Joseph Plunkett was a changed person. Now used to more independence and plenty of intellectual stimulus he had to adjust to the family atmosphere at home, continual rows, violent tempers, defensive reactions, a house full of hairsplitting argument, which got worse with his return. The Count was usually out at his work as Director of the Museum or in his study and the Countess ran a continuous battle with any or all of her children, now aged from thirteen to twenty-two. It was sometimes violent, sometimes silent, often ending in a refusal to give them whatever money they needed. Plunkett found all this hard to accept being now a young man, full of opinions and missing the friends he needed to argue them. He was in poor health again – the Lancashire climate had not been good for him. On Sunday 23 August he wrote 'The Böig' based on the slithery thing which Ibsen's Peer Gynt meets in his dream and 'conquers without violence':

THE BÖIG

The boundary of darkness

                                              The Böig

Black indecision

                                              The Böig

Soft, slithery, slimey, impenetrable

The great Böig in the darkness

'Do not go through' says

                                              The Böig

'Go roundabout' says

                                              The Böig

Soft, slithery, slimey, impenetrable,

The great Böig in the darkness.

'The hill's wide enough' says

                        The Böig

'An alternative's good' says

                        The Böig

Soft, slithery, slimey, impenetrable,

The great Böig in the darkness.

Though the darkness is caused by

                        The Böig

Through the darkness develops

                        The Böig

Soft slithery, slimey, impenetrable,

The great Böig in the darkness.

The Böig had some particular resonance for him and was to remain a favourite of his over the next few years.

Because of his frequent bouts of illness Plunkett had had his own room in Fitzwilliam Street for a number of years and, following his Stonyhurst experience, where he had had a free run with the decoration of his own room, he transformed his room at home, covering its shabbiness with vivid posters, painting a copy of a H. B. Irving poster on the wall in oils and some Egyptian figures on the door. On 21 November 1908, he turned twenty-one and his mother:

> … made a tremendous fuss and public display and then presented him with a cheap and nasty gold-coloured cigarette case.

> Geraldine Plunkett Dillon

Nothing else is recorded of this birthday but the photograph from 1908 was possibly taken to celebrate the occasion. It includes the whole family: Count (56) and Countess (50) Plunkett, Mimi (22), Joe (21), Moya (19), Gerry (17), George (14), Fiona (12) and Jack (11) and is not only a record of each of them, but also the last family photograph taken.

In January 1909 Plunkett's poem, 'The Gull', was published in *The Weekly Freeman* under the pseudonym, Joseph Ó Cahan.

THE GULL

Mournful, O mournful,

As a soul ever seeking,

Sounds the cry of the gull

When it's wheeling and shrieking.

O'er the grey waste

It taketh its flight,

Without pause, without haste,

Thro' the day and the night.

Round the ship's tall mast

It circles and swings,

Never slow, never fast,

But persistently wings;

As wings the lost soul

Round this speck of a world,

From equator to pole

Since from life it was hurl'd;

Calling and crying

For rest thro' all time,

Never finding, but flying

From the curse of its crime.

Joseph Ó Cahan

It was possibly the only time he used this name and it was his first time to be published in a public journal.

To Dominic Hackett from Thomas MacDonagh:

St Enda's School,

Rathmines,

May 4 1909

I have also a private pupil for Irish, a son of Count Plunkett, he reminds me in little ways of you at times. He is great at genealogy and the like; he knows Egyptian and out of the way things and has studied philosophy at Stonyhurst under Father Maher...

There are at least three stories about how Plunkett met Thomas MacDonagh – that Countess Plunkett found him through Pearse's school, St Enda's – or that he put an advertisement in the papers and MacDonagh answered it – or that they met on a train and became friends.

Padraic Colum wrote of the meeting:

Thomas MacDonagh told me that a lady had called at the school [St Enda's] to ask him to help her son at his Irish studies. The lady was Madame Plunkett. MacDonagh consented, and his pupil, Joseph Mary Plunkett, became his admirer and his friend.

Whichever way it was, it worked. Plunkett had decided to work for the Matriculation Examination for University College Dublin and, although it was not a requirement for another four years, he wanted to take Irish as part of it.

MacDonagh calling Plunkett 'great at genealogy' is an insight into Plunkett. His father, Count Plunkett had researched their ancestry in great detail and traced the line back to the first Plunkett recorded in Ireland, John Plunkett of Beaulieu who died in 1082. Over several hundred years the Plunketts spread themselves all over Counties Louth and Meath at Killeen, Dunsany, Dunsoghly, Baltray, Loughcrew and married, repeatedly, into most of the other families of The Pale. Count Plunkett was descended from the Killeen and Loughcrew line, from the older brother of Saint Oliver Plunkett's father. In the destroying and terrible dramas of the seventeenth century Christopher, Baron Killeen, was created Earl of Fingall by the King of England, Charles I for his part in negotiating 'The Graces'. His nephew, Oliver (canonised in 1975) came to live in Killeen Castle with the Earl's family to be tutored by Bishop Patrick Plunkett. Nicholas, the lawyer, was a key founder of the 1642 Confederation of Kilkenny, which was the political opposition to Cromwell's Irish regime and loyal to the King, George Plunkett was a Captain of Foot in the horrifying Siege of Drogheda in 1641 and afterwards a colonel in the rebel army. The Earl's son, Christopher Plunkett, was captured at the 1649 Battle of Rathmines and died in Dublin Castle. Nicholas Plunkett's house at Balrath was burned down in 1642 and he was banished to Connaught, returned after the Restoration and recovered his legal practice, but was driven into exile for offering the Duke of Lorraine the Protectorate of Ireland. Lord Dunsany, a close relation, was also banished to Connaught in this period and, although he regained his house and land, his family all died on the way home.

The Plunketts were deeply attached to and worked hard for Ireland, the Irish language and its literature and (in the case of the Killeen Plunketts) the Catholic religion. Their influence was greatly reduced after the seventeenth century, but the Earls of Fingall continued to work for Catholic rights and emancipation. In all this, Oliver (1625-1681) was a central figure to Plunkett descendants, an educated, intellectual man who undertook to serve his flock despite the necessity to stay 'underground' and finished his days hanged, drawn and quartered at Tyburn on a trumped-up charge of 'treason'. Oliver died, in 1681, with great dignity and was an inspiration to many for centuries to come. All this would have been known to Joseph Plunkett and a strong factor in his passion for Ireland and his perception of justice.

> Hilaire Belloc, delighted him at Stonyhurst with a lecture on Cromwell which had no little influence upon him afterwards.
>
> Peter McBrien

By now the family had the addition of a relative from Duluth, Minnesota – Sarah Ferrall, a cousin of their grandmother, Maria Keane Cranny's – who thought she was coming over, when the Countess invited her, to mind seven 'children'. She was not expecting young adults and a bad start never really improved. She was exploited by the Countess and had no understanding of the family's passion for art and politics, but no difficulty in loudly expressing herself.

> Joe found her opinions appalling.
>
> Geraldine Plunkett Dillon

She was frequently sent places with them as a chaperone so when Countess Plunkett decided to send five of them, Joe, Gerry, George, Fiona and Jack with their friend, Theo McWeeney, to Achill for June, July and August, 1909, Sarah Ferrall, went too. They all stayed for the duration in a lodging house in Dugort.

They had freedom to wander all over the island and discover its wonders and in particular to swim in many different places. Plunkett and Theo McWeeney mostly amused themselves with the big waves on the north strand while Gerry took the younger ones to less intimidating places. This was the time when summer schools and classes for learning Irish were being set up all over the country by the Gaelic League:

> We went to Irish classes given by the Gaelic League teacher, John Langan, a fine man whom we all liked. The local group of Evangelicals lay in wait for him and beat him up because of his Irish teaching and broke the window of the room where he taught Irish dancing.
>
> Geraldine Plunkett Dillon

This letter from Plunkett must be a draft or never sent and it gives no clue as to who it is for:

> but the beginning of August should see me back in Dublin as I must get through a little work this year. This island is fascinating, all lakes and mountains and great stretches of bogland with little villages dotted all over it. I have just been to the top of the highest mountain, Sliabh na Mór, 2,200 feet. The view from about three quarters up is magnificent. I could see over practically the whole of the island which is 15 miles long by 12 broad.
>
> Unfortunately for the viewer but fortunately for his own personal appearance Sliabh na Mór wears a cap and crown of grey cloud which sometimes slips down onto his shoulders. Then he puts on a mantle of mist and like wilful majesty becomes incognito. There are caves here and cairns and cromlechs and queer sounds. He sings of little people on the mountain at night and the soft low whispering of the wind across the crannies in the rocks. The air is full of

the scent of turf fires mingled with the sea breezes and the gentle caressing rain. I have been for some distance round the coast discovering beaches of shining yellow sand and rocky strands with caverns fit for smugglers, places where drowned men's clothes are washed up at high tide and left in a melancholy line with seaweed and strange shells.

The teacher, John Langan, brought them on the big annual pilgrimage on the last Sunday in July to Croagh Patrick, but Plunkett found it too strenuous and collapsed, which meant he was bedridden again. By then he had seen the place and also the terrible poverty.

August 1909:

THE RED RED HILL

The hill has blossomed early with the bright gold furze,

And the yellow bloom is gleaming as the west wind stirs;

The sweetly scented zephyrs bring their perfume to me still,

But for me there's naught can change it, 'tis a red, red, hill.

The heather's blazing purple on the green hill's side

And the honey-bees are humming where he fought and died;

His blood that stained the heather shows its color to me still,

And the hill we roamed together is a red, red, hill.

The hill is black and desolate, the storm sounds bleak,

And gloomy are the beating waves, the sea-birds shriek;

But I hold a hope and promise from him who now is still

His blood is calling 'Freedom!' from the red, red, hill.

Seosamh Ó Pluingcéad

Oileán Acail

He was still unwell when they returned to Dublin and had to endure long periods of having to stay in bed, tedious for an otherwise active young man. He tried to build up his muscles with exercisers, weights with elastic cords and so on, until muscles 'stuck out in lumps all over him', but it didn't really do him any good. He was invited again to stay with the Raffertys in Kilternan and he stayed there most of a year.

Sir Almroth Wright, a graduate of Trinity College, Dublin, who was by then a very distinguished bacteriologist and immunologist had produced vaccines against some versions of tuberculosis and a method of measuring the immune system which he called 'The Opsonic Index'. Plunkett was sent to him in London and Sir Almroth Wright gave instructions for him to have his index taken by a doctor in Dublin and to be given certain injections. Like other treatments tried on him, it had no effect other than to be stressful and debilitating and the Raffertys invited him again to come to stay in Kilternan.

Mr Rafferty was a man of integrity and principle, kind and observant with young people, giving them space to live and think and encouraging them to consider themselves able to tackle their own problems. As Rafferty was the Coroner for South Dublin the local Royal Irish Constabulary (RIC) would bring him their reports on any violent death in the area so that he could decide whether to hold an inquest or not. He encouraged his daughter and the young Plunketts to read the reports with all their sordid details and he then asked their opinion. When they had given theirs he would give his. After the inquest, he would describe the setting, the evidence and the verdict and discuss these and whether his conclusions had been correct and especially what the social implications might be. Here was an outstanding chance to look at real life, make judgments and become aware of consequences, to grow on information and have real-life detective stories handed to you on a plate! The mountain air and the care he got from the Raffertys did Joe Plunkett a lot of good. He and Rafferty became great friends despite their difference in ages and their disagreements on politics. Plunkett felt encouraged to follow his strongest belief – 'that no intellectual decision should be made lightly'.

From his notebook (the punctuation in the diaries and

notebooks quoted throughout this book is Plunkett's own):

30th September 1909 11.30pm

Irish Times. Earthquake shocks were felt in Sicily today at or after 1 o'clock heavy rain ... condensation of water vapour, magnetic storms, Mars, density of ether and matter. Density of waves

Knights move on chess board.

Motor vacuum dust carts

Vacuum dust gatherers

Photographic senses

A new method of writing music

Inanimate prompter

I know the wind as the leaf knows it

Voice of my soul

Are you ballads of wild red weeping?

Plunkett was now writing regularly and submitting to journals. That autumn he had two poems published: *As Ye Have Sown*, written on 29 September and published in *Sinn Féin* on 8 October and a villanelle for the poet and mystic, Francis Thompson, which was published in *The Irish Monthly* that December. He also wrote 'Distant Thunder', which was published the following year in *Bean na hÉireann*. This was one of his political ballad-type poems and it begins,

Comrades are you weary waiting

For the fight to free our Land?

and ends,
Meet destruction strewn asunder

When the tramp is heard afar

When the stroke of distant thunder

Bursts the brazen gates of war.

'The Necromancers' has the touch of horror he enjoys with this first of six verses setting the tone:

The lighted gas is burning low

And silence reigns around

Within the room in ghastly gloom

Three sit without a sound

And from each place with fixed face

Each gazes on the ground.............

And in the fifth verse:

These sudden struck with terror throb

As Horror pulses through

The faces shiver, blench and sweat

They <u>see</u>, the Thing is true....

He was a constant reader; when he was ill he read at least one book a day and a 1909 notebook has a list from catalogues of about two hundred books, both a 'wish' list and books he has already read, to which he sometimes adds comments. The list shows his tastes and broad range of subjects but also, judging from the quotation at the top, 'Homo Sum humane nihil a me alienum puto', a kind of quest for an understanding of humanity that persists through the whole list. The list is given in full in the Appendix as the reading of it is an entertaining reminder of the pleasure and excitement of books.

Poems he composed in his head and wrote down when they were ready so they usually had very few changes; by contrast his prose – essays, criticism, fairy tales, very short stories, whimsy – sometimes horror – usually had many versions, corrections and crossings-out and the general effect tends to be more gauche and mannered. His work on forms – sonnets, villanelles, triolets and ballads – made the poems from this time on far more skilled and confident. Eight of them from the months of March, May and June were later published in his collection and some also appeared in journals or newspapers that year and the following year. Poems written in that productive month of June which he didn't include in the collection were 'Ariadne', 'I Dare Not Look In Those Deep Lakes, Your Eyes…' and the seventh of ten sonnets he wrote that year, 'I am as old as the eternal hills'.

But he was always inclined to be whimsical – he had tried unsuccessfully to write a prose appreciation of his hero, Gilbert Keith Chesterton, a serious undertaking, which this 'Ode to Chesterton' is not. Written in March 1910 he says it should be sung to the tune of 'The Night Before Larry was Stretched'.

Now Gilbert you know you're our man,

The only one equal to seven

Tho' you stand on the earth yet you span

With your hands the four quarters of Heaven,

Yes, your head stretches up thro' the sky

And you puzzle the angels with riddles

But they answer you back by-and-by

With the music of millions of fiddles.

So, Champion of all that's sublime,

Our madly magnificent mountain,

Now take up the cudgels for Time,

Tap the truth, let it flow as a fountain;

And when we have drunk to the dregs

And topple round tipsy as topers

Then set us up straight on our legs

We'll be merry (there's none of us mopers)

Then see us safe home to the boss.

Plunkett had by now met Patrick Pearse and the group around him who had set up the school, St Enda's on Oakley Road in Ranelagh. Plunkett is on the books as having taught there, not as a staff teacher, but probably as one of Pearse's many guest teachers, though it is not clear when or what he taught. Pearse was already committed to ideas on the drawing out of the individual and a bi-lingual system for teaching Irish and from this came his involvement in the setting up of Irish-language summer schools with the Gaelic League to facilitate teachers from the Gaeltacht whose literary skills in Irish were minimal and who had no method for teaching it. Irish still wasn't taught inside school times, but the

Chief Commissioner of the Board of Education, Dr Starkie, picked up on Pearse's ideas in *An Claidheamh Soluis,* visited classrooms in Gweedore and Clochaneely over a couple of years and initiated bi-lingualism in schools and teaching through Irish. A summer school of Irish was started in Gort an Choirce, West Donegal by an extraordinary group of mostly local activists 'to preserve the language and promote the use of Ulster Gaelic'. Those who attended were primary teachers or intending teachers and they came for July or August. Pearse visited in 1906 and again in 1907 and among other things gave a full day on continental education methods. Roger Casement paid for a new hall to be built. Classes were held on pronunciation, construction, reading, storytelling, poetry, songs and history. They used the *Módh Díreach,* the Direct Method of teaching through the language itself. There were debates – one of the most popular features – expeditions round the area and céilís in the evenings.

Plunkett's connections with Casement and Pearse and the strong connection to Donegal of his family's close friends, the O'Carrolls from Dublin, made it logical for him to go to Gortahork to improve his Irish. He also had the company of several of the O'Carrolls, who also attended the College.

Shortly after he arrived there; he heard that he had failed his Matriculation Examination for University College Dublin where he had hoped to study Medicine or Science. His sister, Geraldine sent the notice on to him and his reply was on a postcard of the Cloghaneely stone:

> Falcarragh, Co.Donegal.
>
> Fri. 21 July 1911
>
> Thanks for letter. Don't know what I'm going to do. Find out will you. I've tried thinking and gave it up. This isn't a bad little stone. I'd like to chuck it at some futile persons positioned in a recent National Institution! When are you going off? And where? Let me know.
>
> Joseph

It was obviously a huge blow! Given his considerable intellect, capacity for reading, store of information in literature and science and comfortable knowledge of several languages his failure must have been due to his very frequent illnesses and the unstructured and informal style of his education. He would not have been familiar enough with 'ordinary' information and the presentation of exam answers. On top of that he was very keen to sit the Irish exam in the Matric after only a year of study and it seems unlikely that he could have succeeded in that. By this time his younger sister, Gerry, was well established in University College Dublin and beginning to enjoy herself there which, even with their good relationship, must have been doubly galling. Of the four Plunketts old enough, she was the only one, so far, to go to university, perhaps because of a mixture of determination and commonsense, going to the Loreto on the Green pre-university centre and following all their advice. Later George and Jack both went to University College Dublin.

This letter to his mother implies that he already had heard his bad news; he mentions Nuala O'Carroll's results but not his own.

> Falcarragh Co Donegal Friday 15th July 1910
>
> My Dear Mummy,
>
> (as the Ka said when he found himself locked into the Pyramid) Thanks for the watch which at last arrived...
>
> ...If I drink any more cream today I'll burst which would be sad. The food is more than plentiful, it is obtrusive. They give me lamb (& salad) chicken and green peas, salmon on Fridays, eggs for breakfast, an egg with my tea, soda bread and yeast bread, they bake every day (I mean in the house I'm in) jam (two kinds) (every other day but I refused two-pence a week) biscuits, cider and cocoa. Well are you satis-fied? The water comes from a well but is quite pure as there are no drains!
>
> The Sweeneys do everything possible for me and a lot of impossible things. They have handed the whole shebang over to me, given me a dark room, a piano, a library, a grey-hound to course with, a tame solicitor for breach of prom-ise cases (one of the sons of the house, they were educated at Blackrock College) meals every hour of the day and night and they see to my laundry!!!! Oh, I forgot! They also supplied me with an alarm clock as I hadn't my watch and made the O'Carrolls free of the piano! These (the O'Cs)

are only about ½ a mile away, (3 minutes on the bike) and are very well (Nuala passed <u>her</u> matric thank goodness) and send all sorts of messages by this to you. I see them every day (at least several times) and we all go to Cloghaneely College which is about 2 ½ or 3 miles away. We get there at ten am and work till 12 noon then lunch quite beside it (very good – 4 pence) till one pm then lectures again till 3pm then back. The weather has been perfect this whole week and very hot so we work outside. There are about 50 students at present and all decent people. The teaching is excellent, the fee one guinea. Needless to remark I paid the fee (& as there was about £2.0.0 to come up on account of ticket to Letterkenny 30/- or so & then bicycle ticket & then excess fare for going on limited mail & then ticket & bike ticket on from Letterkenny to Falcarragh, I have less than £2 left, so you might send me some.) Tomorrow Charlie & I are going to Tory Island (pronounced Torry) in a boat and very good company, the P.P. Fr Boyle & the best oarsmen in Ireland, as it's a great chance to see it being such a curious place all by itself & 400 inhabitants & a King. We have had three ceilidhs at the College, songs, recitations & dances. Latter very good & with beautiful names e.g. the Waves of Tory, the Bridge of Athlone and the Walls of Limerick (which Gerry knows). I've to go to bed now and be up early so Good Night.

Love to all the ____ & other wild beasts. Iósep

There is a beach here, 16 miles of hard sand and about 40 rivers

All the people round here speak Irish so I'm getting on.

This ballad in honour of the Irish College looks like something for an evening's entertainment there:

COLÁISTE ULADH

Cloghaneely Irish College

Has a wealth of wit and knowledge,

Not to speak of health and beauty

Grace and graciousness go leór ,

But among its charms entrancing,

Men and maidens, songs and dancing

There is nothing so delightful

As yourself mo mhíle stór.

….When the moon is shining palely

On the evening of a céilidhe

And the purple stars are peeping

Through the open College door

There is music on the night

Of the dance and voices laughing

But tis laden with the music

Of your voice mo mhíle stór.

And this, on a serious subject is dressed up in comedy, of which his sister, Geraldine says:

> is an extremely good imitation of the old topical ballad, with all its beautiful badnesses. It is sung to 'The Groves of Blarney'.

THE BALLAD OF THE FOOT AND MOUTH

As I walked over to Magheraroarty

On a summer's evening not long ago,

I met a maiden most sadly weeping,

Her cheeks down streaming with the signs of woe.

I asked what ailed her, as sure became me

In manner decent with never a smile,

She said I'll tell thee, O youthful stranger,

What is my danger at the present time.

On my father's lands there are man mansions

With sheep and cattle, and pigs go leor,

Until the Saxon came over the border

With detention orders that raked him sore.

His herds they plundered and killed five hundred,

And the rest they sundered north, east and south,

Saying, keep the hides all the woolly fleeces

For the beasts have disesses of the foot and mouth !........

This ballad appeared in the *National Student*.

Falcarragh

24 IX 1910

A Mhathair Dílís

I believe you're home now. Are you? You'll have noticed (probably!) that I stayed on here. I didn't write before because it is too hard work and my bike is laid up and I have to walk to the College (or anywhere) because I'm tired mending it and it's never entirely tired getting punctures and by the time I've walked three miles there and three miles back (after 3oc) and had my dinner (about 5oc) I think I deserve a rest especially as the people I get most letters from are the O Carrolls and I work hard to answer their letters as well as having answered Sallie's and postcards to you but if I don't end this sentence soon you'll be getting mixed. That's better. Now.

1 Thanks very much for the dixionary, it's miles beyond any I ever saw.

2 I haven't time to write an English Grammar for anybody or I'd start now.

3 No suits necessary. It's not cold and anyway I can wear the four I have if it is.

4 About Irish: I never heard of anyone learning to speak it or understand it properly in less than two years and I've only been a few months altogether (counting Achill). Also Northern Irish is quite different in pronunciation and often in idiom to Munster or Connaught Irish but still I have learned a good deal & I've got the pronunciation well enough for anything. I could give elementary lessons in the *Módh Díreach* (Direct Method).

The College Session is over tomorrow so what about getting back sometime? Also some money. I paid Mrs Sweeney three pounds out of the four pounds you sent a month ago and since that Sarah sent me one pound of which I have ten shillings left. I now owe Mrs Sweeney £4-£5 (yesterday 23rd IX 1910)

I'm going to lose this post if I don't hurry

Love Joseph

It was only a month later that he found himself in love with Columba O'Carroll, deeply in love, maybe for the first time, but Columba was only seventeen and the following is almost certainly the revelation and the beginning of that unrequited love, which was to continue for the next five years:

The seventeenth day of October in the year nineteen hundred and ten

God drew aside the veil that hangs within the windows of my soul

I saw you as you were, as you are and as you shall be

I see you now but with my bodily eyes

The eyes of my soul are again veiled yet the bare memory is over-powering

You are young. There are seven veils yet between your real eyes and the things of this world but at the moment of my vision my soul was bare and luminous with lamp of God. Something you saw, I know not what, nor do I know the force of your young memory, I cannot tell when I shall see you again, but I pray God it may be soon for though I have but to see you as you are you must look upon the original work of God, you must see me as I could be.

On 21 November he was twenty-three and the following Christmas card took him several revisions over pages of his notebook to create. The words are beautifully crafted for simplicity and the circle with wings design which he uses so often – upturned wings now and a cross within the circle – decorates the poem.

To greet you with the winter's sunlit snows

To greet you with the flaming green of spring

To greet you with summer's reddest rose

To greet you with the autumn's colouring.

Greeting with all the year's best gifts I sing

And send my song to you o perfect rose

From whose pure heart a subtle perfume blows

A wafted breath of the eternal spring.

May joy be yours this Christmas and New Year.

CHAPTER 5

• • • • •

1911
A Social Life

Plunkett kept a diary for most of 1911, his entries mainly noting where he had been and who was there. There are days with no entry, mainly when he was ill, and there are a number of items that have no explanation, but what is there is a vivid picture of the life of a well-off young man enjoying himself in Dublin and on the continent, often interrupted by illness. Members of the O'Carroll family are frequently mentioned, the Plunketts and the O'Carrolls grew up together and Joe was now in love with Columba. One year after the Plunketts moved into 26 Fitzwilliam Street the O'Carrolls moved into 43 Merrion Square, a five-minute walk away and much of their social life was in the back and forth between the two houses. Joseph O'Carroll, senior, was a bright, innovative doctor who published a number of medical papers and caused many advances in medicine in

Ireland but as a father he tended towards the overbearing. Of the eight children, his daughters, Nuala, Columba and Blanaid were in school and university at that time, but were also doing their best to get away from home. His sons Charlie and Frank were destined for the British Army and Joseph, who had been born within a month of Joe Plunkett and, like him, baptised in Westland Row Church, was banished to the USA at seventeen for unstated crimes.

The Asphar family also features prominently; Plunkett had kept in touch with his friend Alfred Asphar of Malta from his Stonyhurst days and became firm friends with his sisters, May, Helen and Agnes, regularly corresponding with them and visiting the family in Malta with his mother in the spring of 1911.

(Editorial clarifications are in square brackets. As before, all punctuation is Plunkett's own.)

JANUARY 1911

SUN. 1ST at the O'Carroll's

WED. 4TH Mums At Home Mrs O'Carroll and Miss Mac Loone [Mrs O'Carroll's sister]

[An 'At Home' was a general, but formal, invitation to callers to a private house, usually in the daytime.]

Moy Mell Ball ['The Plain of Delight'] at the Gresham [Hotel] Very Good

THURS. 5TH to Mrs O'Carroll's At Home. James MacLoughlin from Cloughaneely there. Good time with the kids.

SAT. 7TH Rink [Rollerskating rink, Earlsfort Terrace]

SUN. 8TH Henry Cotton and Dudley White to lunch. I hit Henry and hurt my hand. To Sheridan's in evening.

MON. 9TH To rink with Charley O'Carroll. Nuala and Columba [O'Carroll] there & Ed. Ward.

TUES. 10TH In bed all day with 'flu' and cough. Couldn't go to [Frederick] England's dinner. Read John Mitchell's **Jail Journal**. Great!

WED. 11TH In bed all morning. C & N [Columba and Nuala]

THURS. 12TH In bed all morning. PM James MacLoughlin in. Also Thomas MacDonagh. Talk.

FRI. 13TH Cahirdaniel Ball at Gresham. Didn't go. Moya went. Saw Columba and others in afternoon at their house. Told N. Tears. Was I right?

[note added] 19th Sept. 1911 Yes.

SAT. 14TH Hand still bad. To rink. Very tired. To confession with Henry

SUN. 15TH To Cotton's in evening at Clontarf. PM called on England [Palmerston Rd., Rathmines] Met Dick. Mercedes Dalton there.

MON. 16TH [Dudley] White to go Wednesday. Fiona [Plunkett] went back to school at Holyhead. Hand still bad.

TUES. 17TH. Couldn't go to Mrs Salkeld's. [Blanaid

Salkeld was a poet, critic and actor, known for her artists' soirées]. Thomas MacDonagh in in evening. Work.

WED. 18TH Cough. Clongowes Ball. Didn't go. Theatre of Ireland. 'Cello lesson. Typewriter. Didn't see White. Bertie got his Littlego [repeat exam – Bernard Sheridan was then a medical student in TCD.].

THURS. 19TH Cough. In bed morning. Got up very late. Typed poems. Finished reading **Charles Dickens** by G.K. Chesterton. Read **L'Eté de St Martin** [1896, by Henri Meilhac] for Franco-German [Club].

[The Franco–German Club was a social club run by two German teachers. Meetings were held in members' houses and tea and music was offered. Members would read a play in French or German.]

FRI. 20TH Cough. Franco-German rehearsal in evening at Cadic's.

[M. Edouard Cadic, Professor of French and Romance Philology National University]

Got up late. Typed. Read at rehearsal. Cadic pleased. Columba and Nuala there. Also Mrs O'Carroll. Walked home with them.

SAT. 21ST Cello, 12 O'Reilly's. Didn't go. Cough. Rink. Sheridan's.

SUN. 22ND Cough. In bed all day. Read **Traffics and Discoveries** Kipling and played fiddle. Began Bergson's **Time and Free Will**.

MON. 23RD Franco-German at 26 Fitzwilliam St.

Very Good. About 60 or 70 people. Mollie Cronin played harp. Columba and Nuala and Mrs there. We danced afterwards. Matt Brennan stayed the night.

[At that meeting in Plunkett's a row of harps played Irish airs. The Count went down to the basement and got a piece from the Irish music collection he kept there and Mollie Cronin transposed it for the harp. The Countess herself also played.]

TUES. 24TH Cough. Got up late. Mums cold bad. Sylvia Sheridan in bed too with bad cold. Dessie (Nelson) McHugh very ill. N F's letter. Tears.

WED. 25TH Cough. To Irish Self-Government Alliance. Elected on Young Ireland Branch UIL.

[The United Irish League (UIL) was the official Irish Parliamentary Party organisation and Tom Kettle had founded the Young Ireland branch which contained younger intellectuals like Frank Sheehy–Skeffington and Rory O'Connor. After a couple of meetings Plunkett was convinced that it was just a part of the Party machine and he gave up on it. The Young Ireland branch was eventually suppressed by the mainstream Party]

Theatre of Ireland rehearsal. Met Ginger (J.J. O' Connell BA) twice. Rink with Moya. Talked to N. The Others went to pantomime.

THURS. 26TH C and N. Rink with Moya.

FRI. 27TH To Sheridan's. Electric wiring with Bertie. Stayed on to supper. Denis and May O'Donoghue and Mrs Morrogh.

SAT. 28TH O'Reilly cello 11.30. N. No rink.

To Post Impressionists with Henry.

[The Art critic, Roger Fry, brought an exhibition to London of a Paris group of painters he called 'The Post Impressionists'. He believed it to be the most important new movement but it was disliked or despised by many and critics. The artists included Gauguin, Seurat, Signac, Van Gogh, Cezanne and Matisse. Some of this exhibition was brought to Dublin in January 1911 by Ellie Duncan (Lady Drogheda) and the United Arts Club. There were similar huge discrepancies in its reception; AE (George Russell) considered to be a fine critic, wrote in his review in *The Irish Times*: '... the only conclusion I could come to ... was that the painters were not decadent but merely decrepit.'

Joseph Plunkett revered AE as a poet and may have been influenced by him, but it may just have been youthful arrogance that made him write on his exhibition programme of a Cezanne, 'poor', of Signac's *St Tropez,* 'looks like coloured chalks', Matisse 'hopeless', Vincent van Gogh, 'ought to be shot', but Gauguin, he says 'can draw' and of a Georges Roualt landscape he says, 'great light effect and distance'. Count Plunkett was a serious, talented and respected art historian, but his area of expertise was the European

Renaissance so his children had been brought up surrounded by that period's paintings and prints. Katherine Tynan, the poet, said of Plunkett:

He was a tall delicate youth with something misty about him, very full of theories and with a somewhat opinionated air.

But according to Norman Redden:

...this frigid exterior was only a cloak which he employed to conceal his innate shyness.]

[The diary continues:]

Confession with Henry and Sheridans and back with them to Pembroke Road. Stayed late.

SUN. 29TH Columba and Nuala. 11.30 Mass Westland Row. Drove to MacKay's with Bertie and Hilda. Violet sang. Brought B and H back to supper and then went with them.

MON. 30TH Cough. Theatre of Ireland. Last night had a long talk with Daniel O'Connell the Liberator. Mums still in bed.

TUES. 31st Columba and Nuala. Royal Zoological Society Lecture R.D.S. All the O'Carrolls there. Mums in bed. Thomas MacDonagh 8pm.

FEBRUARY

WED. 1ST Theatre of Ireland Committee and rehearsal. 9pm then lecture, RDS 'Stone Age in Ireland' by R. A. S. MacAllister. 2pm N. Eccles St dance at Gresham. Henry took me. Met Miss Cruise O'Brien there. Talked a lot (I did).

THURS. 2ᴺᴰ Cough. Bought **National Student** for my sonnet 'To Ireland'

[Not one of his best, this poem has a rabble-rousing style beginning with –

Mother and daughter of dead kings of death

Erin, tire ever-living; we have sworn

To raise again thy banner..............

– but it is largely tongue-in-cheek as so many of his ballads are.]

They shall devour the vomit of their scorn

And cringe, and 'Mercy' shriek with rattling breath.

FRI. 3ᴿᴰ Lecture R.D.S. 'Radiant Matter' Went to Theatre of Ireland. No rehearsal. Awake late and wrote a poem 'I sit and beg beside the gate'
[later renamed 'YOUR PRIDE']

I sit and beg beside the gate,

I watch and wait to see you pass,

You never pass the portals old,

The gate of gold like gleaming glass.

Yet you have often wandered by,

I've heard you sigh, I've seen you smile,

You never smile now as you stray

You can but stay a little while....

...And you have still your regal pride

And you have sighed that I should see

Your gifts to me beside the gate,

Your pride, your great humility.

SAT. 4TH Cello lesson. 5.30 MacDonagh. Met Charlie O'Carroll and Ginger O'Connell.

SUN. 5TH Hand still bad. Cough 9.30 Mass Westland Row. Walked back with Columba. Henry and Mrs Cotton in. Dudley's dog Dooley died. Brought books to Arthur Barry and Enie [Helena Plunkett Barry].

MON. 6TH Franco-German Club at Mrs Baker's. Did not go. 8pm Theatre of Ireland Rehearse. Met Bertie. Music Recital R.D.S. Wind Quartet VG

TUES. 7TH Thomas MacDonagh. Theatre of Ireland rehearse.

WED. 8TH Cough. Starkie's Dance. Went with Moya. Home about 4am. Went to see National School in Hardwicke St.

THURS. 9TH cough. Stayed in bed Bertie came. Bad headache. Played fiddle.

FRI. 10TH Slept late. Rehearsal.

Talked to Jack Morrow about Post Impressionists.

[Plunkett does not record how this conversation went. Morrow was an artist and political cartoonist from Belfast and this note suggests that Plunkett was still looking for an insight or wondering had he been wrong about them.]

SAT. 11TH Went to White. In O'Carroll's. Céilidh at Rutland [Parnell] Square [No. 25] of Students' National Union. Met again Miss [Kathleen] Cruise O'Brien and talked to her for about six hours.

SUN. 12TH 11.30 Mass Westland Row. N. Rested. To O'Carroll's at 7.30. Danced.

MON. 13TH Hans Wessley Quartet Recital at RDS. Very Good. Kreutzer Sonata etc.

TUES. 14TH Cough. French play at Theatre Royal. Le Gendre de M. Poirier [Emile Augier and Jules Sandeau, 1854] Well done. Walked home with Columba and Nuala. Rehearsal at 8. Cough very bad.

WED. 15TH Rehearsal. 2 days before, letter from Dublin

Theatre owners saying they would take legal action if they opened without a license.

THURS. 16TH Rehearsal. Telegram from Dublin Theatres threatening to stop the play.

FRI. 17TH Rehearsal (dress) George Simpson's brother very ill and he had to go to Belfast. Trying to get license for play.

SAT. 18TH Theatre of Ireland play **The Storm** by Ostrovsky produced at Molesworth Hall. License obtained. Simpson's brother scraped through and he came back. I played Kuligin in **The Storm.**

[Kuligin is a watchmaker trying to discover the secret of perpetual motion. He opens the play singing lines in praise of the Volga. Plunkett used 'Luke Killeen' as his stage name.]

SUN. 19TH Wrote poem 'The Stars sang in God's Garden'.

The stars sang in God's garden,

The stars are the birds of God;

The night-time is God's harvest,

Its fruits are the words of God....

...For many live that one may die,

And one must die that many live

The stars are silent in the sky

Lest my poor songs be fugitive.

Went to O'Carroll's to say 'Good Bye' as I am going to
Malta.

MON. 20TH Play again

TUES. 21St Cough. **The Storm** again

WED. 22ND Went to Petite O'Hara's recital. Molesworth
Hall. Afterwards to tea at United Arts Club. At 8 to first
public meeting of Irish Self-Government Alliance.
Kathleen Cruise O'Brien.

THURS. 23RD Bought a few things and packed. Went
to **Priscilla Runs Away** [Elizabeth von Arnim, 1910] with
Moya, Gerry, Sarah and Arthur Barry. Afterwards supper
at 26, Fitzwilliam Street. Jim Hogan came over.

FRI. 24TH Took 1.15 train to Kingstown [Dun Laoghaire]
then L & N.W.R. [London & North Western Railway] boat
to Holyhead. Train to London. Arrived 11p.m. Cab to West
Central Hotel. Mums and Pappy there.

SAT. 25TH Mimi came [his sister]. After breakfast cab
to station for special P&O train to Tillbury Dock. Gerald
Gurrin there. Bought books. Mums and I to Tillbury Dock.
Boarded P&O SS Sicilia. Loading cargo all day. Walked out
to Post Office. Loading cargo all night. SS Sicilia is 4,174
tons register 7000 tons gross – capacity 309 all told.

SUN. 26TH Left the dock about 11pm. Butted out from innumerable barges and lighters by squat, fat steam tugs, sea choppy but quiet. Grey sky and grey sea. At our table are a Mr Bell (an engineer) and Mr and Mrs Boycott. There are 19 First Class passengers. The Captain's name is Watkins. Wrote to Columba.

MON. 27TH Still choppy. Quiet and grey in morning. Letters went with last pilot at midnight when we passed the Isle of Wight yesterday. Started rolling in the evening when we hit the Biscay swell. Read **Rewards and Fairies** [1910 short stories] by Rudyard Kipling

TUES. 28TH Very bad headache. Stayed in bed. Ate nothing. Rolling abominably all day. Mums helpless. Worser and worser in afternoon. Evening worst. Nearly everyone helpless. Slept at night!

Read **The Forest** [1904] by Stewart White.

MARCH

WED. 1ST Better. Still rolling. Took an Ash Wednesday breakfast but forgot when they brought soup at 11. Threw Lent to the winds at lunch. The fiddle on the tables. The sun came out and it was hot! Lay on upper deck. Good dinner! Though still rolling. One of the officers came to me and said that his name was Meredith and that he met me at Earlsfort Rink with my sisters!

THURS. 2ND Rolling ceased. Good weather.

Read **Actions and Reactions** [Rudyard Kipling stories]

FRI. 3RD Hot. Read volume I of **From Sea to Sea** by Rudyard Kipling.

SAT. 4TH Read vol.II of ...[above]

SUN. 5TH Coolish. African mountains visible. After dinner sang choruses. Read **Halfway House** [novel 1908] by Maurice Hewlett. Church parade. Rather funny.

[The missing pages here include their arrival in Malta and meeting with the Asphar family.]

MALTA

FRI. 10TH At 2.30 went with Mr Asphar to Valetta to the Palace. Saw the Council Chamber with great tapestries, the Armoury and all the armour of the Knights, the Ballroom with frescoes, the State Reception Room, lovely furniture, frescoes and hangings. Then went to a café and had chocolate and on to the Barracca [Gardens]. Next to the Opera House and recovered my cigarette case. Saw another church, bought and posted cards and back by ferry and carrozin. After supper went to Rocklands and played Bridge with Affie, JK and Helen. Saw Agnes. Came back to Limpopo's and found Fr O'Reilly talking to Mums. Then Fr O'Grady came in and talked also. Met Blue-Sister Frances.

SUN. 12TH Wrote to Columba in answer to her letter read this morning.

MON. 13TH To Notabile (Citta Vecchia) Lunched with Mrs Galea and the Misses Asphar. Took train there from

Valetta. Mr, Mrs and Aggie also Mrs Denaro. Went to churches and the catacombs. Coming back in the train played games with Aggie (anagrams etc.)

[The end of their time in Malta and leaving there is missing. The next entry is their arrival in Sicily seventeen days later.]

THURS. 30TH Arrived at Siracusa, Sicily at 10.20. Saw grotto and Greek Theatre. Train to Catania. Large city, rather dilapidated. Churches closed. Saw Duomo and St Nicholas also museum. Many good pictures ancient and modern. We went to Hotel Bristol. After dinner took electric tram through the city. Fireworks going off under my window when I went to sleep or perhaps its drums and cymbals. Saw Vincenzo Bellini's tomb. Monument, manuscripts, piano and other relics.

FRI. 31ST Lost 10.10 train. Took 3.15pm and arrived Messina 6pm. Boarded the Citta di Siracusa which left at 7.45. Large comfortable boat. Sea quite calm. Saw a good deal of Sicily from train and then something of Messina. Earthquake ruins.

APRIL

SAT. 1ST Arrived Naples 7am. Went to Hotel Metropole. Took 11.25 train to Pompeii. Lunched. Saw the city. Took 4.20 train back. Dined. Went to opera Theatro San Carlo. **I Pescatore di Perle [The Pearl Fishers]**. Wrote to Agnes. Wrote postcard to May. Weighed myself. 8st.11 lbs. Ridiculous for my height and age [5ft. 9", 23 years old].

SUN. 2ND Mass 11.00 at the Duomo. Then to museum, pictures and statues. After lunch siesta and then walked the fashionable promenade gardens. Tram to Pozzuoli and back, a good distance. After dinner to opera at Theatro San Carlo, Aida, Verdi, magnificent. Back about 1am.

MON. 3RD After lunch we went to the museum and saw the same and more. Then walked through the town for miles and bought a few trifles. Had coffee in a café.

TUES. 4TH Left by 10am train. Reached Rome 2.15 pm. Left Rome 2.25pm. Arrived Orvieto about 4pm. Went to Palace Hotel. Good but dear. Very good wine. Went to Duomo. Frescoes by Luca Signorelli and Beato Angelico. Pieta by Ippolito Scalza. Chose a few photographs. We were shown round the Duomo by the custodian, Veluti, who had copied many of the frescoes very finely. Orvieto is altogether charming, a beautiful medieval town. Funicular railway from station to town.

WED. 5TH Rain. Went again to Duomo and saw the picture Madonna di San Brizio and other fine things. I bought a picture for 15 francs or at least Mums did. Bought some pipes and tobacco. After lunch went to museum and saw many pictures and treasures taken from the Duomo, also statues, marble, of the 12 apostles. Bought photographs and postcards. Left Orvieto by 4.30 train. It was late. Arrived Firenze about 9pm. Went to Hotel Helvetia. Very full it being the season. Got one room and were thankful.

THURS. 6ᵀᴴ Slight rain. Went to Post Office for letters and then round the city. It's delightful and I feel as if I knew it always. Went looking for quarters and found Berchielli's. Lunched there and decided to come as they just had two rooms. Went over the Ponte Vecchio and looked at shops. Called at Dr Dunne's 9 Via Tornabuoni to see Mrs Dunne who was Mary Redmond. She was out but we saw him. Back to Helvetia and changed over to Berchielli's, Lung' Arno, Acciaiaoli 16. The shops are full of gorgeous things. Very good Asti Spumante.

FRI. 7ᵀᴴ Rain. Wrote to May. Went to Duomo. Saw doors of Baptistry. Went to Post Office and back to lunch. At 1.30pm Mrs Dunne came and drove with us to Palazzo Vecchio where we saw a magnificent collection of portraits by all the greatest artists of Europe. Also huge frescoes by Vasari and splendid tapestries. The portraits are a special exhibition (Italian). Then to tea at the Albion tearooms full of fashionable English and back. Very heavy rain.

SAT. 8ᵀᴴ Went to Post Office. At 2pm Mrs Dunn and Charlie with motor and drove us to Certosa where we saw the convent etc. Many great pictures, Perugino, Angelico and della Robbia, their work. Then drove to Fiesole. Explored amphitheatre and museum. Saw a church, had tea and drove back. Magnificent views. After dinner went to the Folies Bergeres some of it good.

SUN. 9TH 9 oclock Mass. Letter from Agnes. At 10 Mr Dunn and Charlie came and we went to the Accademia di Belle Arti. Saw Botticelli's Primavera and thousands of others. Charlie and I to Uffizi. More Botticellis and millions of others. Took tram to beyond city and walked to the Dunn's. Lunched and had music and played games and walked round. Drove back for dinner 7pm. Met Brunetti Selvi. William DDS Villa Aliveri, Pian dei Giulliari, Firenze, Italy.

MON. 10TH Postcard from May. To the Uffizi. Talked to a man finishing a gorgeous copy or rather facsimile of the Magnificat. After lunch to the shops. Bought **The Man who was Thursday** G.K.Chesterton and **What is wrong with the world?** GKC, then reproductions of Botticellis and coloured postcards. Had bad tea in a bad café. Read **The Man who was Thursday** for the fourth time. Cough still bad.

There is no more from Plunkett until after he gets home to Dublin probably because of illness, which so often dominates his life. His mother writes to the Count:

14th April 1911 Florence

We leave here on Tuesday for Bologna and Milan then home. Weather fine.... D is taking me round the Medici chapels and Palazzo Davanzati. Lunching with Carmichael

Monday …

On 19 April from Hotel San Marco, Via Inghleterra, Bologna, she writes:

> Crossed the Appenines. Lovely and hot. Had another look at Primavera…Today we go to Suphatua and if not too tired to Milan in the evening.

MAY

[Back in Dublin]

FRI. 5TH In bed. [His handwriting is very shaky].

SAT. 6TH Tomás MacDonnachadha came and told me that **The Irish Review** had accepted 'The White Dove'.

[Thomas MacDonagh was usually referred to by the Plunketts as 'Tomás'. Plunkett constantly experimented with Irish versions of his own name and his brothers, George and Jack, changed their names to 'Seoirse' and 'Sean' respectively.]

SUN. 7TH Still in bed. More temperatures.

MON. 8TH Slightly better. In bed.

TUES. 9TH Read proofs of sonnet 'I saw the Sun' for the **Dublin Review**. Still in bed.

WED. 10TH Will I ever get up?

THURS. 11TH Yes, soon.

MON. 15TH Up and out.

TUES. 16TH Out again.

WED. 17TH Sent 'Love-Lullaby' to the **Atlantic Monthly,** Boston.

O Love, my song

Is sung to the trembling string

Of Love's own lyre. O Strong,

Thy strength I sing.....

THURS. 18TH Out to Rafferty's. Springfield, Kilternan.

FRI. 19TH John Naylor in to play Chess with Mr Rafferty. He looks exactly the same as when I saw him last 16 or 17 years ago.

[Plunkett's note] 25 MAY 1911 Doctor's prescription: Dr De Szendeffy, Treatment for tuberculosis. Repeptonized Iodine. 0.75 c. grms. Menthol .06 c.grms. radium Barium chloride .1 drop in a solution of Ether. 1cc to be injected daily for 30 days.

[The high success rate claimed by this Hungarian doctor caused widespread interest and news of it was sent by Marconi's wireless telegraph from Clifden to the USA on 28 May 1911.]

WED. 31ST Theatre of Ireland General meeting 8pm 6 Harcourt St. Reorganised. Kitty and Gracie [McCormack] in there and Miss [Evelyn] Gleeson, Mrs McCormack, Mrs O'Connell, Miss Nairn, Jack and Fred Morrow, James and Mrs Stephens, Seumas O'Sullivan, George Nesbitt, George Simpson, Justice Bride Foley, Countess Markievicz, James Cousins, Frank Walker. Went in by train for meeting.

JUNE

THURS. 1ST To 'Uí Breasail' at RDS buildings Ballsbridge. Sheridans there and lots of others. Took Nuala and Mary Frances Ward to tea and then on hobby horses. Mary Frances took us to Punch and Judy. Met Kitty and others.

FRI. 2ND To Gill's for Gaelic books and then to Ponsonby's. Drove out to Springfield with Mums.

Irish Review for this month published with my poem 'White Dove of the Wild Dark Eyes'.

WHITE DOVE OF THE WILD DARK EYES

White Dove of the wild dark eyes,

Faint silver flutes are calling

From the night where the star-mists rise

And fire-flies falling

Tremble in starry wise,

Is it you they are calling?

White Dove of the beating heart,

Shrill golden reeds are trilling

In the woods where the shadows start,

While moonbeams, filling

With dreams the floweret's heart,

Its sleep are thrilling.

White Dove of the folded wings,

Soft purple night is crying

With the voices of fairy things

For you, lest dying,

They miss your flashing wings,

Your splendorous flying.

Gorgeous weather.

SAT. 3ᴿᴰ Moya, Gerry, Jack, Nuala, Columba, Maeve, Frank and Mary Frances drove out for picnic. We all and Lena went up the Scalp and lunched. I gave Columba a brooch. Nuala a pendant, Maeve a crocodile pencil. Back to tea, talk and tennis, also boat on the pond.

MON. 19ᵀᴴ McKay's and Fred Lucas. Moya and Gerry. Tennis.

TUES. 20TH Inoculation. Wrote to Nuala.

WED. 21ST Nancy Maude, Bean Mhic Uí Cathmhaoil & Seosamh Mac Cathmhaoil came to tea. Gave him the June **Irish Review**. He told me about his play **Judgement**.

THURS. 22ND Weight 9st 9lbs. Mums came out and stayed the night.

FRI. 23RD Sent 'Jimmy the Bawler' to **The Nation** Mums went back to town with Lena to stay the night. Naylor to chess. Played very late.

SAT. 24TH Letter from Nuala. She and Columba may come out here tomorrow.

2 a.m. Saw the dawn and wrote two verses. Tri-riming tetrameter quatrains. Lena and Mums drove back here. Played Bridge. Lost 1d!! [one and a half pence] Stormy and showery.

SUN. 25TH To 12oc Mass Enniskerry with Mums and Mr Rafferty. Brendan Crichton came. Then Columba and Nuala. After tea walked to Scalp then rifle shooting. Mums drove them to the train at Carrickmines. After dinner played Bridge. Won two rubbers. (2/3d) [two shillings and three pence].

MON. 26TH Measured height 5ft.9ins. (in slippers)

TUES. 27TH Meeting of the S. P. I. L. [Society for the Preservation of the Irish Language) 5.30 at 6 Molesworth St.

WED. 28TH Today Columba goes to Cliff Lodge, Rossnowla, Ballyshannon, Co. Donegal for the holidays.

JULY

SAT. 1ST My poem 'The Task' published in today's **Academy** (Your Pride)

MON. 24TH inoculation

TUES. 25TH Sent poem 'The Eye-Witness' to the **Eye-Witness** paper.

THE EYE-WITNESS

…Tell what you see and know

Of the tree of death and love.

Lean from the golden bars

And if what we seek you find,

Shout what you see to the blind,

Shout down from the stars.

FRI. 28TH The **Eye-Witness** sent back my poem.

SUN. 30TH Letter from Harrie Smyth returning book I lent her.

MON. 31ST Wrote to Columba and to Charlie. Wrote to Harrie Smyth.

AUGUST

TUES. 1ST To town with Lena and Gerry. To An t-Oireachtas

with Mums. Met Mrs Salkeld and her mother Mrs French Mullen, Thomas MacDonagh James Stephens and his wife, May Kerley, Seosamh MacCathmhaoil, Douglas Hyde, Charlie Power, Aodh O Dubhthaigh, Cadic and saw Louisa Kenny, the Hon. William Gibson, Eoin MacNeill, Madame Markievicz, Padraic O Concubar, Hugh Kennedy and many others. After dinner back to Springfield.Sent sonnet: 'Love' to the **Academy.**

LOVE

I am as old as the eternal hills

Yet younger than the ever-youthful moon,

Younger than Hope, upspringing all too soon

On fields of Death: I as the blood that spills

On those same fields, am spent for many ills:

Though I sleep hid, my very name a rune,

My deeds are chanted to a battle tune,

And I am sown and reaped, whoever tills.

I am the Sun that slays with blinding light,

I am the easeful darkness, soothing pain,

I am the dawn of day, the dusk of night.

I am the slayer and I am the slain,

The toiling gleaner and the golden grain,

I am Life, Death, Hell's depth and Heaven's height.

Weight 9st 12lbs. Violet MacKay married to Fred Lucas at Sandyford Co. Dublin.

THURS. 3ᴿᴰ Mimi Moya Gerry and Fiona went to Jack's Hole [County Wicklow] for two weeks.

FRI. 4ᵀᴴ Lena went to Wexford. Seosamh Mac Cathmhaoil [the poet, Joseph Campbell, from Belfast] came to teach me Gaelic.

SUN. 6ᵀᴴ Mums & Pappy, Sarah and Nellie Fitzsimon came out to tea.

MON. 7ᵀᴴ Photography. Chess, won two.

TUES. 8ᵀᴴ Sent photographs to Columba. Sent June **Irish Review** to Helen [Asphar].

WED. 9ᵀᴴ Seosamh Mac Cathmhaoil. Veto Bill through the Lords.

[This Bill reduced the veto powers of the British House of Lords so it was supported in Ireland and by the Irish Parliamentary Party as it would enable the passing of the Home Rule Bill.]

Weight 9st12lbs.

WED. 16TH Sal to stay here. Also Hans Breitmann.

[A nickname probably – Hans Breitmann was a fictional character from C.G. Leland in German/English nonsense ballads]

THURS. 17TH The Raffertys left for the Continent. Seosamh Mac Cathmhaoil

FRI. 18TH I went up to Glencullen to see the MacCathmhaoils. Talk and tea. The Duncans came just as I was leaving.

WED. 23RD The girls back from Wicklow. I went in to Horse Show. Saw Sylvia and Bill. Letter from Columba,

SAT. 26TH Mrs Cotton came out to stay a short time. Brenda and Mrs Crighton called.

MON. 28TH Twenty pages of a letter from Helen. Seosamh MacCathmhaoil.

THURS. 29TH Mums and Pappy drove out with Fr Joseph Keating SJ.

WED. 30TH The MacCathmhaoils came down to tea and shooting.

THURS. 31ST Columba comes back to Dublin. Went into town with Mimi. Decided on 5.46pm train. Went to Broadstone, there at 5.45. Wrong station. Went to Amiens St got there at 6 but in time. Met Columba Nuala and the rest. Walked back with Frank. Bought Coleridge's poems, **The Case for Home Rule** [Stephen Gwynn, 1911] and **Home Rule Finance** [An Experiment in Justice by Tom Kettle,

Maunsel 1911].

SEPTEMBER

FRI. 1ST Rita and Charlie Cotton came. Georgie and Willie Fogarty had us all over to tea at the camp.

[The following piece on Symbolism is simply dated 'September 1911' and is one from a collection of sundry writings and pages of Irish exercises.]

Symbolism – the meaning of symbols. Need for an essay on the common misconceptions. Symbols are two kinds, primary or real, secondary or arbitrary, analogical and metaphorical. Choice of Symbols, Christian or non-Christian – no real distinction. Symbols are part of nature – Intuition, vision and prophecy, that is interpretation. Language is symbolic so, frequently, is thought. Images, tools, symbols of art, the nature of the case, pictorial, in poetry the reason for using symbols apart from words. Symbols in religion, the necessities, examples, some common symbols - God, the Church, wisdom, Seraphim and Cherubim, angels representing... wisdom, apostles etc. Isaac etc Dante, the Mystics, a note on numbers, bibliography. Primarily symbols have a resemblance to the thing symbolised ... associated in the mind with that symbolised. [JMP]

TUES. 5TH Biked into town [probably motorbike]. Met Columba and Nuala. Theo in. Mums and I went to **The Arcadians**

WED. 6TH Long talk with Joseph Geoghegan about his theory of decorative arts. Went to Dr Meenan. He says I must go away for the winter early in October. I don't want to. Bought Fiona MacCleod's **Poems and Dramas.** Met Ginger O Connell.

THURS. 7TH Went to our Hall at Hardwicke St. Mums is to entertain members of the Eighty Club and others at a garden party at Springfield on the 16th. Rode out from town and wrote a ballade.

SAT. 9TH Tennis. Mums and Pappy drove out and stayed.

SUN. 10TH 12oc mass Enniskerry. Met John Griffin and Miss MacCarthy. Theo MacWeeney came out. Also Dr and Mrs MacKay and Henry Reggie and Charlie Cotton. Tennis. Card from Thomas MacDonagh.

WED. 13TH Drove in with Moya. Left revolver at Garnett's [Gunshop on Parliament Street]. Went to Hardwicke St. (our hall) Met Columba and Nuala and drove them to Grafton St. Bought **The Ballad of the White Horse** by G.K. Chesterton and read it. Met Brenda Crighton who asked me out on Sunday. Met Molly Cronin. Fetched Joe Geoghegan and brought him to tea and there found Tomás. Miss Gleeson and Kitty and Mrs MacCormack to supper and then on to Theatre of Ireland [play] at our hall.

THURS. 14th Met Maeve [O'Carroll]. Tomás MacDonagh came to supper and stayed well into the night working at my poems to get them in order which we did at last thank goodness. Left my gold watch at Moulang [Joseph Moulang, watch case maker & metal gilder]. To be ready in a week.

FRI. 15TH Gave Ponsonby my manuscript. Got back the Smith and Weston and cartridges.

SAT. 16TH Reception of the Eighty Club at our house. A lot of them came. Some were nice, the rest were extremely funny and appallingly ignorant of Irish affairs. Mollie Cronin played the harp. Confession. Saw Dr and Mrs O Carroll and Maeve.

SUN. 17TH 9oc mass Westland Row. Language procession. Jerry Cronin drove me out in his car to Kilternan with Mollie and Vicky. Lunch and tea at Springfield and drove back in a quarter hour to town. Columba, Nuala, Maeve and Blanaid with Mrs O Carroll came in evening. I saw Columba and Nuala home. I was right on 13th January

MON. 18TH Caught 11.45am train to Carrickmines. Moya and George met me at Foxrock.

TUES. 19TH Lena and Mr Rafferty should be back. Moya and I drove into town. I took back my manuscript from Ponsonby's. Bought Columba a birthday cake inscribed **Multum in Parvo** [Much in little] **Ad Multus Annos** [For many years.] 20th September 1911 and **The Innocence of Father Brown** GKC and gave her **The Ballad of the White Horse** GKC. Met Columba and Nuala. Drove back. Mr

Rafferty returned.

WED. 20TH Columba's birthday. I packed. Lena returned.

THURS. 21ST Moya, Sara and I drove in from Kilternan. Met Kitty at Dundrum and left her at station. Pappy suggested that he and I should leave next Saturday for Algiers. I met Tomás and brought him in. He is to see about getting my poems printed. I had a letter from Bernard Smith from Fermoy. He'll be here on the 28th [his classmate from Stonyhurst].

FRI. 22ND Saw Columba and Nuala. Met Willie White, letter from Columba thanking me. I answered it.

SAT. 23RD Pappy has to stay another week. Wrote to Bernard Smith. Lena in to lunch. Sent four of my poems to Thomas Keohler [poet and critic].

SUN. 24TH 9oc mass Westland Row. Met Bessie in a tram. Did not speak to her. Frank O' Carroll in.

MON. 25TH Mary White [a cousin] in.

TUES. 26TH Went to Theo. Tomás came to supper. He had seen Roberts [George Roberts, publisher] and asked me to ring him up. I did. Roberts asked me to send him my manuscript for estimate. I did.

WED. 27TH Tailor's pm. To see George Roberts 12.30 pm. Saw him and talked. Got estimate and copy of agreement. Met Columba. When Life. Read **The Wild Knight** GKC in National Library. Met George Simpson. Went down to say goodbye to the O Carroll's. Talked to the doctor and

Columba, Nuala others etc. met Frank, Charlie O Carroll.
...

THURS. 28TH Bernard J. Smith did not come. Dr and Mrs O Carroll with Nuala and Frank leave for London. Frank going to school at Shrewsbury. Wrote poem 'I see his blood upon the rose' in the small hours.

[He made one small change: line 3 read 'His body shines ...' and he crossed it out and wrote 'gleams' over it instead]:

I SEE HIS BLOOD UPON THE ROSE

I see his blood upon the rose

And in the stars the glory of his eyes,

His body gleams amid eternal snows,

His tears fall from the skies.

I see his face in every flower;

The thunder and the singing of the birds

Are but his voice and carven by his power

Rocks are his written words.

All pathways by his feet are worn,

His strong heart stirs the ever-beating sea,

His crown of thorns is twined with every thorn,

His cross is every tree.

Tomás came in. showed him estimate etc. letter from Bert Smith and wire saying he comes tomorrow.

FRI. 29TH Mimi and Moya leave with Rita Fitzsimon for London. I signed agreement with Maunsel to publish my poems. I met Bert at Kingsbridge and brought him here to stay the night. Talked for hours. Italy has declared war with Turkey on account of Tripoli.

SAT. 30TH Must send **Fairytales** to May Asphar for her birthday on the 15th Bert went off by 7.30 pm boat North Wall.

OCTOBER

SUN. 1ST Unveiling of the Parnell Monument. Went with Tomás. Tremendous crowd. Saw John Redmond. Out with Tomás to Houston's [David Houston, founder of **The Irish Review**]. Met Miss Alderton and Molly Maguire. Tea there. Brought Tomás back to supper.

MON. 2ND Bought **Celtic Wonder Tales** for May. Went to see Columba at 43. She was gone to school. Packed my things and went to meet her. Did not meet her. Met Molly Cronin. Pappy and I caught 1.15pm train, Westland Row. Mums saw us off. Georgie saw us from Kingstown. Arrived

London before midnight and went to Grafton Hotel, Tottenham Court Rd. Comfortable, new and moderate. Saw the Meade Coffeys crossing.

CHAPTER 6

• • • • •

1911–1912
Algiers

On 6 September Plunkett recorded that he had gone to Dr James Meenan who told him that he must get away from the beginning of October for his health and he records that he doesn't want to go. According to his sister, Gerry, it was his mother's decision that he should go to Algiers, although Algiers would not have been the place to send someone with chest and lung problems; Egypt was by far the best for this and those who could afford it went there. Count Plunkett was going on a tour of continental museums as part of his work as Director of the Dublin Museum so it was decided they would travel together. The Plunkett family were all very relaxed travellers, particularly in Continental Europe where the first ports of call in each city were the art galleries and theatres. They could afford this lifestyle and the set of people they met were similarly wealthy causing a general assumption that they couldn't be nationalists. This, of course proved a useful cover for Joseph Plunkett later on.

OCTOBER

TUES. 3RD

LONDON

Went to Exhibition of Old Masters at Grafton Gallery. Lord Curzon & Duke and Duchess of Connaught. Then to Royal Society [Dining] Club: lunch there. Out to Gurrin's. Mimi and Moya there. Dined at Gianello's in the Strand. Who should walk in but Dr and Mrs O'Carroll and Nuala. Talked to them and said 'goo'bye'. Then to Coliseum. Saw Cissy Loftus and Sarah Bernhardt. Latter in 3rd Act of Fedora. Wrote to Mums and Columba.

WED. 4TH Letter from Seosaimh Mac Cathmhaoil. Postcard from Moya. Took Moya from lunch then to **Fanny's First Play** [George Bernard Shaw] at the Little Theatre, then tea. Pappy and I dined at Gatti's and went on to Hippodrome. Saw Réjane in **L'Alerte** and Leoncavallo conducting **Pagliacci.** Wrote to George Roberts choosing paper cover for my book and to Tomás. Read. Delayed letter from Bernard Smith. There is no authentic news in London re Italo-Turkish War.

THURS. 5TH Leave for Paris 11am Victoria. Left Dover 1.15 pm. Arrived Calais 2.30. Lunched and left Calais 3.30. Arrived Paris (Gare du Nord) before 7. Taxi to Hotel

Terminus opposite Gare du Lyon. Moderate and good cooking.

FRI. 6TH Breakfast at hotel and walked the Boulevardes. Good lunch in open air. Went to the Louvre. Saw wonderful pictures. Italian the best, Botticelli, Lorenzo di Credi, Ghirlandaio, Angelico. Then round the shops at the Palais Royale. Dined also in the open. More Boulevardes and went to **La Femme Nue** at the Theatre Porte San Martin. Jane Hading was wonderfully good (back to hotel 12.45 am) but Berthe Bady was superb, a great actress.

SAT. 7TH Saw the Church of St Severin. Lunched in the Boulevard St Germain. Walked the Boul'Mich. Went to the Luxembourg Gallery. Sculpture. Pictures by Manet, Monet, Degas etc. Coffee and drove to the Jardin des Plantes. Dined near our hotel (Restaurant Massilia). Well and not too wisely. Then to a cinema, funny, and audience most entertaining. Wrote postcards.

SUN. 8TH High Mass at the Madeleine. To the Louvre. Italian School, modern French, Rubens, Van Dyke and the Flemish painters, El Greco, Ribera, Zurbaran, Velasques, Murillo and heaps of others. Lunch at Duval's then Nouveau Cirque. Coffee amid the Madding Crowd. Tuileries Gardens before Louvre. Dined at hotel. Wrote to Helen. Violent toothache.

MON. 9TH Toothache. Auto to Grand Poste. Caught

2.30 train to Lyons. Bought **Les Marriage de Paris** par Edmond About. Long journey. Ate at Dijon. Arrived at Lyons 10.48pm. Snowing! Went to Hotel Bordeaux. Noise and toothache. But slept.

TUES. 10TH Dejeuner at 11am. Walked to centre of town. Bought **Révélations de l'Amour de Dieu** Julienne de Norwich. Drank a bottle of wine and went back to hotel. Caught 5.23pm train. Dined on board. Too dark to see Avignon or Tarascon. Arrived Marseille 10.40. Drove to Hotel Noailles et Metropole, Rue Noailles. Got a room. Streets very bright.

WED. 11TH Went to Cook's and booked passage to Algiers. Also reserved room in Hotel Continental. The boat Ville d'Algers leaves on Friday. Went to Post Office. Lunch at restaurant. Population very various and southern. Streets very busy and crowded. Walked about the town. Wrote to Alfie. Sent book to May. Sent postcards to various people. Wrote to Wilfrid Ward. Dined at very good but cheap restaurant.

THURS. 12TH Wire and money from Mums. Went to Post Office then to Cook's. Lunch at Rst. Walked round. To Post Office again. Dined at Rst. Walked to Museum des Beaux Arts in the evening (shut). Great crowd. Pappy talked for hours mostly family. Went to Church of St Vincent de Paul (late) Toothache.

FRI. 13TH Left hotel at 12 noon. Boarded the SS Ville

d'Algers and left Marseilles at 1pm.

Sea smooth. Read and talked (or rather Pappy did) and slept.

'At nos hinc alii sitientes ibúnus Afros'

SAT. 14TH Toothache. Talk and sleep. Cabin very hot and too small for three berths. Tartaria occupied the third. Arrived Algiers about 4pm. Drove to Hotel Continental at Mustapha Super Ceu. It was building another wing so we went down to Hotel de la Regence, Place du Government in the heart of Algers.

Wonderful! Walked round and watched things.

SUN. 15TH Very hot in church! Jack's birthday. May's birthday. Mass at the Cathédral (St Phillippe). Mgr Bollon preached extremely well on Faith and reasonable certitude. Walked round. Violent toothache all day. Tried laudanum on it. No use. Bought a blistering remedy which gave a certain relief or rather a different pain.

[His postcard home]

ALGER Hotel de la Regeuse Oct. 15th 1911

Here at last. Beautiful place, very lively crowd in all sorts of costumes and faces and attitudes. Arrived last night after a perfectly smooth passage, not a bit tired and quite well.

Love Joe

MON. 16TH Hot. My face terribly swollen and aching all day. 'How charming is divine philosophy'. Big thunderstorm with heavy rain. Lovely effects of lightning.

Slightly feverish. Took 0.5 grammes Quinine. Hot weather but cooler. Face still badly swollen and very painful. Took 0.5 gr of Quinine. Walked to Post Office. Ache better. Took tram to Champs de Manoeuvres. The Post Office is the most beautiful modern building I've seen, specially inside.

WED. 18TH Hot sun. Went to Post Office and saw some shops. We have spent most of our time watching the people who are extremely dignified (except the young ones) and fascinatingly artistic faces. Swelling gone down a little and hardly any pain but very difficult to eat. Finished Les Marriages de Paris and bought **Napoleon Intime** par Artur Levi.

THURS. 19TH Face better. Received galley proofs of my book from Maunsel. Corrected them and sent them back. Letter from James Stephens full of extravagant praise of my poems. Letter from Wilfrid Ward giving permission to republish the sonnet I sent to the **Dublin Review**. Bought a sword for Georgie or Jack for 5 francs. Wrote to Columba.

FRI. 20TH Bought books on speaking of Arabic. Went looking for hotels or pensions at moderate prices. Walked a lot and asked at many but got no satisfaction. There is talk of Moya coming but no certainty which makes arrangements difficult. Went to a [roller skating] Rink in evening and skated. Just like Dublin! (I.D.T.!) [I don't think!]

SAT. 21ST Hot! Round the town and up to gardens to Notre Dame des Victoires which was once a Mosque. This is Mum's birthday. Letter from Mums. Frank Cruise O Brien is married. Took tram to Belcourt. Great crowds! Streets and shops very gay.

SUN. 22ND Hot! 11oc mass in the cathedral. Another good sermon by Mgr Bollon. Wrote to Agnes. Sent post-cards. Wrote to Mums. Letter from Moya asking me is she to come out here. Wrote part of an article on Bernard Shaw. Letter from Tomás enclosing proofs and suggestions.

From Thomas MacDonagh]

Grange House

16-10-1911

Brother Bard

I send you your proofs. You are at such a safe distance now that I can venture to send them to you. The book will be fine, better than I thought. The poems are better to me, so printed, though I do not know why it should be so but it is. 'The Epitome' is splendid. Title? I thought of *Signs and Wonders* ... and now in reading the proofs felt that there is the germ of a suggestively fine title in *The Sword* and a title with the word 'Circle' in it. Could you make a design with the circle and the sword in it and give the name to the book. On the whole after having considered it fully there is much in what Roberts says of Jimmy and 'The Böig'. They are full of ingenuity but not as good as any of the rest and out of tune, ... I think I do not like 'The <u>whispers</u> of my soul' as the last line of the book but I see 'The Epitome' now in new light; it is wonderful. The printing is carefully done. Of course it is in rough galley pull. With this I send to you a circular letter we are getting out. Both names are on the list.

I hope you can read this crabbed scrawl.

With best wishes to Count Plunkett.

Yours ever

Thomas MacDonagh

MON. 23ᴿᴰ Hot! Corrected proofs and wrote to Tomás. Wired to Moya to stay for her work. Wrote to Moya. Took tram to Boulevard Brn and back.

TUES. 24ᵀᴴ Tram to Station Saintaire. Walked. Tram to Les Deux Moulins. In evening went in search of a drink. Had to invent one. Lemonade and Benedictine! Sent postcards.

WED. 25ᵀᴴ Train to Mustapha and spent the afternoon at the Musée des Antiquites. Good Stone Age collection and Roman and Christian remains. Fine Moorish things. Heavy rain. Went to rink in evening.

THURS. 26ᵀᴴ Tram out to Maison Carrée. Cattle and sheep fair on. Very fine. Walked. Tram back. Wrote to Mums and to Alfie. Listened to some good music in a cafe.

FRI 27ᵀᴴ Municipal Museum closed so we took tram to Ruisseau. Then to Rink ('Grand Skating Park') and back.

Above: 1884. Marriage of Count Plunkett to Josephine Cranny.
Photograph taken on steps of Muckross Park, the Cranny home in Dublin.
Below: 1892. Joe Plunkett holding the donkey for his sisters, Mimi and
Moya.

Above: 1893. Plunkett Family. From left: Moya, Joe, the Count, the Countess with George on her knee, Mimi, Gerry.
Below: 1896. Lord Mayor's Party: Gerry as the Duchess of Savoy, Moya in a Kate Greenaway dress, Mimi in an Irish costume, Joe as a Gallowglass.

Above: 1897. Joe Plunkett aged ten.

Above: Stonyhurst College. The Philosophers' Drawingroom.
Below: The 1908 Stonyhurst Philosophers. Plunkett, seated, centre right, A. Asphar, seated, second from left.

Right: 1908. Joseph and his father, George Noble, Count Plunkett.
Below: 12 August 1908, (Back l to r) George, Gerry, Joe, Moya, Mimi, (Front l to r) Fiona, Count, Countess, Jack Plunkett.

Left: 1909. Joseph and George Plunkett at Springfield, Kilternan. **Below:** 1911. The Cronins' 1908 Mors with the Plunketts and the Cronins.

Top left: 1911
Moya Plunkett and
Fr Attard of Malta
in Algiers.
Top right: 1912,
Algiers. Joseph
Plunkett in Arab
costume.
Left: 1912, Algiers.
Joseph and Moya
Plunkett dressed for
a fancy dress party,

Above: 1912. Thomas MacDonagh with his wife, Muriel (Gifford) and son, Donagh.

29th October 1911

My Dear Mums

Thanks very much for your letter and the enclosure which was highly humorous. Did you read it? I'm sure Mr Conmee meant very well but there was nothing practicable in it. This place is very hot and lazy. It's difficult to explore in the daylight because of the heat but the trams at night are rather nice only you can't see much. I got the proofs, read them, corrected them and returned them the same day. Have they sent any page proofs since? I would like to see how the titles look. I have had no letter from Tomás, I mean MacDonagh, though I wrote to him. James Stephens sent some of the proofs and wrote me a letter of extravagant praise saying also that I was up against him and that he was clinging tightly to his own private laurels in trepidation. Wilfrid Ward also wrote saying that I might republish the sonnet I sent the *Dublin Review* so that's all right. Did you see the October number of the *Dublin Review*? If my sonnet is in it please send it on to me. I have taken no photographs because [it is impossible] to get films for the Ensignette on this side of the world and my other camera must be still in Marseille. I wrote for it the other day.

Is Moya coming? If she is, send her my roller skates to bring me. I don't know enough about this place to tell you whether it would be any use or no (I don't mean the skates but Moya). I might send you some prose manuscript but not unless I knew what you were going to do with it. It is always better for the author to send a thing to an Editor than a third party. Also for instance I wouldn't write for a Healy-ite rag like the Murphy Independent. [The *Irish Independent* was owned by William Martin Murphy, patron of Tim Healy, close associate of Charles Stewart Parnell's, who then opposed him.]

I am perfectly well and my waistcoat is bursting though it's the new one. I will weigh myself as soon as I find a machine. The food at this place is uniformly excellent, sometimes it bangs Banagher and you know who Banagher bangs. It is not easy to do much owing to the heat but the weather is expected to cool down shortly.

Love Joe

[Letter from Joseph Plunkett to Thomas MacDonagh, November 2011]

Grand hotel

Samhain 1911

A Chara,

I think I forgot to say anything about a title in my last letter. *The Circle and the Sword* might be very good but there are several points to consider about it. First, I cannot judge whether the connexion would be sufficiently obvious. If it would (to an outsider I mean) it would be admirable. But secondly, I made no provision with Roberts for any device on the cover except the title. Also, though I know the sort of design I would like I cannot draw it, anyhow with sufficient exactness. I don't even remember what a Crusader's Sword is like – though indeed I think it ought to be an ancient Irish sword after the enclosed blot, in which the blade is leaf shaped (cf blades in National Museum) and the circle and hilt together for an Irish cross. My sister, Geraldine, could probably draw the thing very well. It should of course be printed in gold on the cloth covers and in black (I suppose) on the paper. Roberts would want to charge for a stamp or dye for the gold for which my mother would have to pay so be forewarned. But you can deal with her I know. Anyhow I like the title and my father (judging more or less as a critic) approves of it, but you will be able to judge better than I would whether it would be satisfactory and an expressive label for the book. I know that is horribly coldblooded but I have learned to distrust my fancies. I see very plainly that other people have to be thought of and I have to remember that too ... Of course I know that it is easy to shirk my responsibilities and put the onus on you, but the weak always oppress the strong in our country!'...

SUN. 5TH Went to rink. Wrote to Alfie. Quarter to 11 mass at the cathedral. Fr Attard said it. Another fine sermon from Fr Bollon. I wrote a lyric in short measure last night and this morning **The Bread is Mine.** Wire from Mums asking whether I wished Moya to come.

Wired back 'Yes'. Bought a pipe for Georgie. 9 francs. Real Turkish. Letter from Mums. Tubes from White's. [Moya wanted to go there to mind him if he got ill]

MON. 6TH Reading Dame Juliana's 'Revelation de l'Amour de Dieu'. Wrote a long letter to Mums. Wrote to Columba.

TUES. 7TH Letter from Pappy from Marseille. [The Count had left Joe to begin a work tour of museums] Letter from Gerry. Note from Mums. Also **Academy** with review of Seosamh Mac Cathmhaoil's things. Also Oct. No. of **Dublin Review**. Fr Attard came. Offered to teach me Italian. I rejoiced. Bought a nice cane for 2 francs 75. Another letter from Pappy from Marseille. Wrote to Pappy to Lyon and to Paris. Wrote to Tomás.

WED. 8TH Wrote two poems; 'A Battle-Song' and 'From the Rim of the Shield'. Cards from Lena and from Sara. Fr Attard came to see me in the evening.

THURS. 9TH I went to see Fr Attard at his rooms in the presbytery. He lent me the life of the B. Curé d'Ars. I lent him the **Dublin Review**. Bought the **Mercuré de France**. Wrote to Gerry.

FRI. 10TH Rain. Chilly. Letter from Alfie.

SAT. 11TH Wrote to Mums.

SUN. 12TH Hot. Messe des Hommes at the Cathedral. Mgr. Bollon preached. Fr Attard came and I kept him to dinner and talk. Weighed myself. 9st. 8lbs. Card from

Mums saying that Moya leaves Southampton Tuesday next.

MON. 13TH Cooler. Fr Attard came and took me up to Notre Dame d'Afrique. On the way down we met Madame d'Malglaise and her son in a motor. They drove us down. He has the Anglo-American Garage. Freeman's Journal. Wrote to Mums.

TUES. 14TH Cool. Wrote to Alfie. Went to Fr Attard and with him to L'Ecole Lavigerie where we arranged with M. Stackler to give me lessons in Arabic (3 per week, 50fr per month) then to the market where I bought a beautiful bi-lingual Virgil in 5 volumes for 1Fr 20c. Finished the **Revelations of Dame Juliana of Norwich.**

WED. 15TH Letter from Pappy from Avignon dated 12th inst. M. A. Stackler came and gave me the first lesson in Arabic.

[From Peter McBrien:

... Stakler, the tall dark cosmopolitan who taught him Arabic (it was Stakler's habit to go out of nights amongst the different tribes of the hinterland disguised as one of themselves and be hail-fellow-well-met with the strange guardians of the fringe of the Sahara).]

Letters from Georgie and from Mums also from Aggie with snapshot. Fr Attard came.

[Fr Attard was a Maltese Catholic priest who was probably introduced to Plunkett through Alfred Asphar.]

Had a talk with a Tyneside shipping man about all sorts of things. Joseph Nicholson his name. Stayed up late and finished my essay on 'The Sanity of Shaw'.

THURS. 16TH Read Italian Grammar also St Thomas' **Summa Theologica**. Took photographs. Fr Attard came. Talked to Nicholson. Read Virgil (**Eclogues** and **Georgics**).

FRI. 17TH Took snapshots. Arabic lesson. Fr Attard came and we went out and found that Moya's boat comes in on Sunday next 9pm. Then to the presbytére and looked at cameras and stereo views. Read Italian and Theology. Stackler offered to take me to an Arab marriage feast on Sunday evening.

SAT. 18TH Letter from Columba. Letter from Moya saying they are coming to take rooms. Letter from Mums. Proofs from Maunsel. **Freeman's Journal.** Went out for a walk with Fr Attard and saw pictures. Wrote to M. Stackler. Another letter from Mums. Card from Pappy. **Irish Review** for November. Paid hotel bill to 15th. Wrote a poem 'The Planets Seven that Swing through Heaven']

SUN. 19TH Rain. Messe des Hommes at the Cathedral. M. Bollon preached. Went to Fr Attard and talked. Then he came with me to meet Moya's boat and met Moya and Mrs Carberry [of New Zealand] and brought them to hotel. Wild jokes. Got wet waiting a long time also tired as I slept badly. In morning wired to Mums about my book. The little blue flower was sold today for the benefit of the sufferers of the floods.

MON. 20TH Took them to Post Office and wired to Mums. Arabic lesson. Fr Attard came and after tea we went to the Jardins M... and down through the Arab part of the town. After dinner Moya played the piano and sang and I danced cakewalks and sang. Letter from Helen. Present from May for my birthday, a prayerbook.

TUES. 21ST Wrote the Jewel-Sonnet.

OCCULTA

Crowns and imperial purple, thrones of gold

Onyx and sard and blazing diadems

Lazuli and hyacinth and powerful gems

Undreamt of even in Babylon of old

May for a price be given, bought and sold,

Bartered for silver as was Bethlehem's,

And yet a splendour lives that price contemns

Since five loud Tongues a deeper worth have told.

Braver is she than ruby, far more wise

Even than burning sapphire, than emerald

Anchored more strongly to impalpable skies;

Upon a diamond pinnacle enwalled

The banners blaze, and 'Victor' she is called,

Youthful, with laughter in her twilit eyes.

Slept badly. My birthday. Card from Mums. Wrote to Mums:

From the Grand Hotel de la Regence, Algiers
Place du Government, Prop. Bruggemann and Flumn
Algiers
Date, Feast of the Presentation 1911 [meaning his birthday – 21 November]
My Dear Mums,
Thanks for your letter of the 13th which I got with the proofs, also for your letter of the 15th and card of the 16th which latter came this morning. Moya is here, of course you got her wire. I hope you got my wire correctly.
You might have remembered that the book was to be dedicated 'To My Mother' if Tomás had any reason for not wanting it dedicated to him, as I thought he might have – it would be ridiculous for him to refuse it on account of the book being better without a literary sponsor.
[Countess Plunkett paid for the publication and the book was dedicated 'To Thomas MacDonagh']

Of course I wrote the 'note' for Maunsel and of course I did it properly, also the contents though that may need some emendation. There are some bad mistakes in the proofs, especially when the second page of the *Eye-Witness* is titled 'Doom' as if it was another poem – there is a 'u' for an 'n' in the second word of the title on page 19 – but I'm sure Tomás will have seen those, besides other misprints as in 'The Böig'.

We, that is Fr Attard and I, met Moya and Mrs Carbery on the boat when they arrived – a day sooner than the schedule, as they did not stop at Tangiers so they arrived on Sunday evening. Too late to wire. Mrs Carbery is a very good sort and I laughed more since she came than in the past year! Yesterday I showed them the French part of the town and Fr Attard came and took us over the Arab quarter in the evening before dinner. They are delighted with the place. Today Fr Attard is to bring us up to a Hotel 'Meublée' kept by secularised nuns & in a beautiful situation and we will try to make some arrangement. Otherwise the three of us will take an appartement near where the Régiuse is.

I have started Arabic with a teacher and I'm to give him 50 shillings a month for three lessons a week. It is very good. I have not ridden as a horse would cost ten shillings for half a day or seven shillings if I took it often. I am much better altogether than when Pappy left and putting on weight. May sent me a beautiful prayer-book for my birthday and I have had several letters from Alfie and others. Please thank Sara and Jack for their presents and say I will write as soon as I can. I would be glad to get a registered letter as I paid my hotel bill and have only a little left.

Cheers for Tomás!

Love from two

Joe

[TUES. 21ˢᵀ CONTD.]

Wrote to Tomás and congratulated him on his appointment as lecturer in English Literature in National University of Ireland. Fr Attard came and brought us to see apartments where we took three rooms. Also out to Villa des Oranges at the Colonne Voiral kept by secularised nuns. Then back and arranged for meals at a gambling club! A sort of private hell! But used as a restaurant!!! V.G. Wedding party in Hotel and piano all night!

WED. 22ᴺᴰ Storm. Letter from Tomás telling me that he is going to be married and thanking me for my book which is dedicated to him. Letters from Mimi, Gerry and Fiona and card from Mums. Arabic lesson. Went to see Fr Attard at his rooms. Reading Arnold Bennett's 'Clayhanger'.

THURS. 23ᴿᴰ £5 [five pounds] from Mums. Finished Clayhanger. Walked round the shops with Moya and Mrs Carberry. Tea at Marchand's. Fr Attard came to see us and we kept him for dinner. After dinner music, I mean piano and a cheery youngster named Marcon played rather well. His father has a silk shop in Tunis.

FRI. 24TH Arabic lesson. Paid bill and left hotel. Went into our new rooms opposite. It is Gallery Duchassaing 2 Place de Government. Lunched at Gruber's then went to the Marebé de Chestary and bought necessaries. After lesson Fr Attard came and we gave him tea. Dined at Gruber's. Stayed up late talking.

SAT. 25TH Breakfast at 9 (coffee and roll in my rooms). Wrote to Gerry for her birthday. Lunch at the club. It poured rain but we went to the Post Office and Fr Attard came in after tea. Dined at the club. Wrote to Columba.

SUN. 26TH Messe etc as above. After lunch to circus in the Rue Constantine beside St Augustin's. Slightly tedious. 2.30 to 6pm. My camera arrived at length from Poste Restante, Marseille.

MON.27TH Gerry's birthday. Arabic lesson. Then went out with Stackler to see a native carpet factory run by Europeans. **Magnifique et pas cher**. Brought Stackler back to tea and Fr Attard came in. After dinner Rev. C. T. Whitwell found us by good luck at the Cercle Republicain but had very little time so we saw him off at the boat.

TUES. 28TH To the cemetery at Boulevard Brn. Smoked Kif [Hashish] to try it. Absolutely no effect.

WED. 29TH Arabic lesson. To Rink in evening. **Irish Times**. 17 Italians crucified by the Turks (or Arabs) in Tripoli.

P.S. Perhaps.

THURS. 30TH Had the Irvings to tea then brought them to The Cathedral, then to the Mosquée des Femmes. Fr Attard gave us an Italian lesson. Re-wrote the lyric 'The Bread is Mine' begun on the 5th November.

DECEMBER

FRI. 1[ST]Arabic lesson. Fr Attard came. The 'Patron' of the Cercle stood us a good bottle of wine. Benediction twice at the Cathedral. Singing accompanied by guitars and mandolins, of the youths. Mgr Bollon preached.

SAT. 2ND Went round the Arab Quarter with Stackler. (he was in uniform). Confession at St Augustin's. Benediction at the Cathedral. Arab Quarter very gay. Fine clothes. Curious women unveiled. An Brionglóid nó an Aisling.

SUN. 3[RD]Pappy's birthday (1851)

8oc mass at the Cathedral, Perp. Ador.[Perpetual Adoration.] then Messe des Hommes. Mgr Bollon preached. There was a banquet at the Cercle with Admirals and things and the Mairie. Tram to Maison Carrée. Vespers there. Tram back. After tea wrote a poem 'Muktoub'. Ma-Haa (Mrs Carberry) gave us reminiscences. Started a letter to Pappy.

[Letter to Count Plunkett]

I am a great Poet

But unfortunately very few people know it

And to be forced to bring out a second edition

Is my ambition.

Not an Aisling

Algiers

3rd December 1911

Me Dear Da

Hoppy Birdie!

The enclosed chant to the gallery is a present for you. Also the introspective poem above. Muktoob means literally 'it is written' they don't say 'kismet' here they say 'muktoub' Have you ever <u>eaten</u> couscous? If not it is made of Semolina rolled and rolled and etc. in small little round spherical balls (not square) like shot – but it isn't – or I will be if it is. When you've got through the last sentence they serve it with boiled (not really – but stewed) meat and vegetables but they haven't any meat so they just use weeds and things to give it a flavor but they don't so they have to bring up reinforcements of red peppers in the form of sauce. We had some. It was very good & it had all three in it. (Not us.) I have to stop here. Finis.

Love, Joe

THE HILLY HOT SANDS OF SAHARA

El Arabi has walked the sand

The hilly hot sands of Sahara

He has left the green and fertile land

For the hilly hot sands of Sahara

Though every day the sun beats strong

The nights were blue and gold and long

And his heart sang loud a low sweet song

Of the hilly hot sands of Sahara.

Of the color of sand was his buff burnous

The hilly hot sands of Sahara

His meal was made of coarse cous-cous

And the hilly hot sands of Sahara

Five times a day he made his prayer

(bowed towards Mecca he wished him there)

On a little carpet he spread on the bare

And hilly hot sands of Sahara

El Arabi has walked to death

On the hilly hot sands of Sahara

The sands have stifled his living breath

The hilly hot sands of Sahara

'Muktoub' he said and bowed him down

A small dull speck on the wide light brown

And the stars shone out like a golden crown

On the hilly hot sands of Sahara.

Smoked Kif.

MON. 4ᵀᴴ

Poured rain. Letter from Rev Charles T. Whitwell from Tangier. Arabic lesson. Kept Stackler to tea. He gave me two 'sand-roses'.

[A 'sand rose' or 'desert rose' is a rosette formed of minerals such as gypsum or barite.]

Another letter from Whitwell from Lisbon. Brought Fr Attard back.

TUES. 5ᵀᴴ Poured rain. £5 and two letters from Mums. At 4pm Stackler came and brought us to see the house of an Arab friend of his. The friend's mother was making a blanket on a hand loom. Then to the friend's cousin's house where he gave us coffee sitting on cushions on the floor. His wife also came in and had coffee and was very shy. Her silver anklets were in pawn. Fr Attard came to see us. Benediction. Wrote sonnet 'The Circle and the Sword' ('Long have I waited by the Gate of Gold')

WED. 6TH Arabic lesson. Kept Stackler to tea. Benediction at Cathedral 8.30pm as usual. Moya and Ma-Haa went to Les Deux Moulins.

THURS. 7TH Bought a fiddle and two bows in a beautiful (!) case for 22 francs!

FRI. 8TH Immaculate Conception BVM. Arabic lesson. Procession and Benediction at the Cathedral at 8. Brought Fr Attard back and had a furious argument about the Empire of Death (The 'British'). Posted **The Dublin Book of Irish Verse** to Helen.

SAT. 9TH Helen's Birthday. Long letter from Mr Sheridan. Letter from Mums saying that Georgie is ill (dated 5th inst.) enclosing half of a £5 note and saying that my book may be published today. Benediction at Cathedral at 5pm. After dinner went to the opera **La Vie de Boheme** par Puccini. Fairly well done. Bits of it really well rendered.

SUN. 10TH 8oc mass at Cathedral. Also Messe des Hommes. Mgr Bollon preached extra well. [We] Were up with the organ. Wrote to Mums and finished the letter to Pappy commenced on the third. Sent a postcard to Georgie. Moya and Ma-ha went to the cathedral and brought back Fr Attard to tea. After dinner went to the theatre and saw a wild and woolly melodrama **Le Bossa** which had 5 acts and 10 scenes and ended after twelve.

MON. 11TH Rain. Arabic lesson. Kept Stackler to tea. Fr Attard came in also. He has been forbidden to smoke by the doctor but can't stop.

TUES. 12TH Letter from Mums. Georgie a little better. Other half £5 note. Moya and Ma-Ha went to the Requiem Mass at the Cathedral for French soldiers and sailors. I wasn't feeling very bright so didn't go. Was with Stackler who came to take me to the National Library. Moya and I went to a small Rink owned by the Patron at the Club. Fr Attard looked in but had to bunk.

WED. 13TH Arabic lesson. In the middle of it the post came. 3 notes from Mums saying that Georgie had a big operation for appendicitis and was recovering but that it was a miracle that he was alive. MacArdle did it. Also 2 copies of my book **The Circle and the Sword** posted on Saturday. We had a champagne supper on the strength of the news.

THURS. 14TH 33 copies of my book came from Maunsel. Sent one to Columba and also a letter. Wrote to Mums. Moya and I to Rink with Ma-ha. Wire from Mums for news. Answered it. Postcard from Mums saying that Georgie is still improving.

2 Gallirie Duchassaing

14–12–1911

My Dear Mums

Just a line to tell you that I received your letter with second half of the five pound note and also your three other letters which came together last night full of news and excitement.

Don't give Our Lady Of Lourdes all the credit for Georgie or Notre Dame d'Afrique will be jealous and I'm sure it was N D d'A that did it. We would like all the details unless it bothers you. Also I received the Book – first two copies from you and this morning 33 copies from Maunsels. Allow me to congratulate you on it – you can't say anything because self praise is no praise. Also (if I may so express myself) – please congratulate Tomás on it for me and say I am writing to him. You might ask Roberts to send me a copy of the list of papers he is sending it to for review (and did you remember to tell Durrant to send me cuttings?). I will write a list for you to send it to as soon as I can. I think that printed slips 'with the Compliments of the Author' might save writing and postage.

I would like the *Irish Review* for December <u>and</u> the next number.

Love to Georgie and all

Joe (Author of the *Circle and the Sword* Maunsel and Co. £1,000,000,000 net.)

FRI. 15TH Arabic lesson. Stackler to tea.

SAT. 16TH Wrote to Mr Whitwell. Wrote to Georgie. Sent Whitwell a copy of the book.

SUN. 17TH Messe des Hommes. A lady sang! Ma-ha went out by herself to Maison Carrée by train and walked back. 11 km. And she is 73. Tattoo [seems to be a nickname for Fr Attard] came in to tea. Played Euchre and Bridge. Letter from Mums with £5 note.

MON. 18TH Arabic lesson. Paid Stackler 50 francs. Kept him to tea. Tattoo came in. Bought **Anthologie de la Poetes Francais Contemporains** in 3 volumes, leather, for 15 francs.

TUES. 19TH Tattoo came at 10.30am and brought us to see the Archbishop, Mgr Combes, at the Archevéché. He was very nice and talked to us. The Archevéché is beautiful – indeed perfect. After tea went to see Tattoo. On the way got a grand letter from Tomás. Tattoo had hurt his tongue at the dentists. He gave us 6 relics of Martyrs. The Dec. No. of the **Irish Review** came. I wrote 8 lines against Yeats.

WED. 20TH Wrote to Mums. Sent copies of my book to Charlie (O'Carroll) G.K. Chesterton, Alfie, Aggie and Helen [Asphar]. Arabic lesson. Stackler stayed on. Tattoo came in. Stackler lent me a book on the Kabyle language.

THURS. 21ST Letter from Mums. Went to the Rink (Casino de la Plage). Hurt my left knee. Tattoo came in.

FRI. 22ND Very little sleep on account of knee. Arabic lesson. Gave Stackler a lesson in English.

SAT. 23 Very little sleep. Christmas cards from Mary

White, Rita Doyle and Seamus MacLochlainn. Read the French poets. Tattoo came in. Confession. Juanita dined at our table.

SUN. 24TH Knee bad. Birdie's [Bertie Sheridan] birthday. 11.30 mass at Cathedral. The Patron stood us champagne and strudel. Tattoo came in and brought Issanchou who did card tricks. Said he'd get us places for midnight mass. We dressed and went. Met the Demecks (Maltese). Waited in the street a long time but got in.

MON. 25TH Good weather. Midnight mass at The Cathedral. Went in evening dress. Slept late and rested. No post today. Tattoo came in. we dressed for dinner and astonished the natives.

TUES. 26TH Good weather. Letter from Columba and thanking me for my book. She says Mrs O'C. is giving a dance for Nuala in January.

WED. 27TH Arabic lesson. Tomás to be married to Muriel Gifford at the University Church, Stephen's Green.[1] Inoculation (I think this must be yesterday). My knee is a lot better but occasionally painful. Wrote 8 lines for Moya. Called it 'Murder'. Cooler. Letter from Mums £5. Paid the Patron at the Cercle. Card from Theo. Card from Aunt Helena and Oliver [Plunkett] with congratulations on my book.

MURDER.

The clatter of blades and the clear

Cold shiver of Steel in the night

Blood spurts in the strange moonlight—

The pattering footsteps of fear,

A little thud and a sigh—

The babbling whispers are still,

Clouds come over the hill,

Silence comes over the sky.

JMP For Moya   *28th December 1911*

THURS. 28TH Cards from Aggie, Helen and May. Wrote to Mums.

FRI. 29TH St Thomas of Canterbury. Tattoo in. Translating Victor Hugo's **Le Legend de la Nonne.** Arabic lesson. Into the de Costas. After dinner we stayed on at the Club and danced. I taught Juanita a cakewalk step. The Patron treated us.

SAT. 30TH Walked round in the crowds. Shops very busy. Went to see Tattoo. Tired. Yesterday got **The Irish Monthly** for January with review of my book.

Extracts from Press Comments on *The Circle and the Sword* by Joseph Plunkett (Maunsel. Paper, 1s. net; cloth 2s. net.):

Academy Here is the spiritual life indeed. The powers both of expression and of thought in this slender volume make it worth any half dozen collections of modern minor singers. There is a religious mysticism which is often amazing though occasionally somewhat obscure as in the poem entitled The Sword... Always there is something arresting and forceful while in several metrical experiments real mastery is shown. We sincerely hope to see more of this poet's work for it is full both of achievement and promise.

Irish Review It is sincere mysticism

The Poetry Review The thought is keen, the expression vivid and occasionally there is real magic.

The Irish Monthly All poetry-music, exquisite diction, refined feeling

The Times (London) Mystic force and that kind of imagination that belongs to the Irish School.

Morning Leader Love poems and nature poems which show deep feeling and fine diction. . . . . . curious individual distinction.

Evening Standard Strong and finely imaginative

Freeman's Journal There is an exquisite blend of imagery and tenderness, a glow of religious fervour and a love of country that combine to make the poems appeal strongly.

Cork Constitution Beauty of diction and imagery

Tuam Herald Young though he be, he shows clearly that he

has the divine gift.

From Peter McBrien:

> And for example of his time-sense read the first poem in *The Circle and the Sword*, a gigantesque, which a critic in the *New York Evening Post* considers one of the great sonnets of the world:

> *THE GLORIES OF THE WORLD SINK DOWN IN GLOOM*

> *The glories of the world sink down in gloom*

> *And Babylon and Nineveh and all*

> *Of Hell's high strongholds answer to the call,*

> *The silent waving of a sable plume.*

> *But there shall break a day when Death shall loom*

> *For thee, and thine own panoply appal*

> *Thee, like a stallion in a burning stall,*

> *While blood-red stars blaze out in skies of doom.*

> *Lord of sarcophagus and catacomb*

> *Blood-drunken Death ! Within the columned hall*

> *Of time, thou diest when its pillars fall.*

Death of all deaths ! Thou diggest thine own tomb,

Makest thy mound of Earth's soon-shattered dome,

And pullest the heavens upon thee for a pall.

SUN. 31ST Messe des Hommes. Gave a sugar bowl to de Costas and Benedictine Aux Quatre Visaires. Very tired. Great crowds of people.

Wish I was home.

This was a queer year.

CHAPTER 7

● ● ● ● ●

1912
Algiers, Dublin, Limbo

From a review of *The Circle and the Sword* by Joseph Plunkett in the *Irish Review*, January 1912 by Thomas MacDonagh:

> ... He is perhaps the youngest of published Irish poets. He will come to a more concentrated power ...

> ... Mr Plunkett ... is amazingly accomplished. Yet it is safe to prophesy that he will never produce work of what may be called Art for Craft's sake. He will come rather to see that craft and technique and all the creatures of prosody are only the hand maidens of poetry. He has probably come to see it already ...

> ... It is, as I have said better that the reach should exceed the grasp. 'What else is a heaven for?' This poetry aspires. It is sincere mysticism.

THE LIAR AND THE LUTE

A piratical poetical parochial paradoxical periodical

The liar has lifted the lute

And his prize is the pirate's pay;

He has busted the back of his boot

As he bunked with his booty away.

He has busted the back of his beauteous boot

And the sleuth hounds scoot after to slay.

The bosun is brazen and bald

(His left eye is swung on a swivel)

He never comes back when he's called

And though drunk he is seldom uncivil;

But he swore a dark oath when through Hell he was hauled

That he'd drink hotter grog than the divil.

The Cap'en is crazy and curst

(His left leg is only a wattle)

Though frequently ready to burst,

He always has room for a bottle.

When the boilers exploded he left the ship first

And for why? 'Cos he stood on the throttle.

JMP

JANUARY 1912

MON. 1ST No good resolutions. Resolutions no good. The Patron (Caseneuve) gave us Rink tickets so we went. Went to Tattoo [Fr Attard] in evening and danced cakewalk.

TUES. 2ND Sang at Club. Translated the 'Chanson de Joffroy Rudel' from **La Princesse Lointaine** by Edmond Rostand.

'LA PRINCESSE LOINTAINE'

It does not seem so rare

To love one only Fair

Of brown or chestnut hair

Or golden tress,

If but for you she gleams

With gold or shadowy beams

But mine is of my dreams

The Far Princess....

Translated 'Le Cantiléve de la Pluie' par Auguste Gaude:

I have drunk the rain

In the holly shade

My eyes are fain

Of a lovely maid…

WED. 3ʳᴰ Wrote to Mums. Arabic lesson.

THURS. 4ᵀᴴ Alfie's birthday. Wrote to May. Letter from Tomás.

FRI. 5ᵀᴴ Wrote postcard to Fiona. Arabic lesson. Great excitement in Madame de Costas over the catching of a big rat. At the Cercle. Hippolyte fainted.

This is the end of this diary. He doesn't mention that he wrote to MacDonagh congratulating him on his marriage to Muriel Gifford, that he was offered the job of manager of a skating rink after the then manager ran away with the owner's wife. Neither does he mention that he had a piece of jewellery made with an Arab and Celtic design for confusing future archaeologists and that (according to legend in the MacDonagh family) he learned to ride a camel at speed and smoke a Woodbine cigarette at the same time!

A notebook he used from January to March, 1912, survives with the version of his name, Ioseph Ó Pluinghcéid, on the cover, the one he particularly favoured of many. In the notebook there are experiments in words and number values, Arabic alphabets and pronunciations guides, lettering, Arabic vowels with English equivalents, codes, drawings, doodles, a rough, unfinished verbal caricature of W.B. Yeats, French translations and a poem of his own in French, Irish words here and there including a prayer/poem in Irish with a version in French and an 'Ancient Scandinavian alphabet'.

From the 1912 notebook:

THE IMPRISONED PRINCESS OF A THOUSAND TOWERS.

I was walking by the river the other day when a speckled salmon put his head out of the water and said 'Oh King's son and Ollamh, lean down to the water and listen'... and I heard the voice and the singing of Aengus of the stories and this is the story he sang: Once, in the olden days when all beautiful things were true, there lived in Ireland a princess more beautiful than the summer night. Her hair was dark as the deep dark hollows in the waves on a day of drowning ...... Her eyes were as brown as the brown bogland pools when all the stars danced in them when shaken by the breath of her thoughts. ... and when she sang, grass and the leaves and the growing grain and the shaken rushes stood still as death to listen while the birds of the branches, the beasts of the woods and the pastures and the fishes of the streams and the lakes and the rivers came to hear her song.

JMP 1912

Translations by Plunkett of 3 poems by Ahmed Bey Chawky:

They have beguiled her by telling her she was beautiful

The Beautiful Ones always let themselves be enticed by flattering phrases

Her admirers are many; nevertheless She has not forgotten my name.

But when She sees me She turns aside as if nothing existed between us two....

One day that we were − Oh ask me not how we felt! − we were exchanging love tokens.

Chastity watched over us: our wishes sought not to prevail against it.

The Beloved, to draw nigher, plucked at my burnous which resisted her disobeying.

Then She said to me 'O Poets, you who are most truly men, tempt not the maidens.

Fear God in your acts; for however comparable with the shifts of the veering wind are the impulses of a woman's heart, yet temptation will always have its way in the end.

Do you remember my tears – tears of blood – that once I shed for my forsaken land? Do you remember how jealous I was of the birds that flew back to it? …

O my Beloved come to me in my dreams and let mine eyelids kiss your image!

A FABLE

There was once a man who used to work very hard all the week and then get very drunk on Saturday. One day his wife came to him and said: 'Why do you work very hard all the week and then get drunk on Saturday?' The Man replied: 'I work very hard all the week, then I get very drunk on Saturday so that on Monday I will be sufficiently ashamed of myself to earn the price of another booze.'

Moral: some people work on Saturday and are then drunk all the week!

JMP Algiers Jan 27th 1912

THE ORDER OF TIN BASINS:

Flames H. Handbill,

Surgeon Toady, Colonel Broken Down, Sir Careless Crammerin, Lady Darnit,

Lady Shadow, Captain Seoil Sinkinsun, Sir Mistoffers Styxinliver, Laird Skirlpipes of Gaberdine, Mr T. Doublemuscles, Sir Shedblood Arson, Captain Plague, Lord Heigho,

Lord Beery, Lord Muddypuddle, Sir Joblot of Baltherskite,

The Eleven Grades of Love

1. Istihassan	Satisfaction in presence
2. El Monadda	
3. El Holla	Affection lasting open
4. El Mehabba	Perfect accord (affec)
5. El Khaona	Pure unchanging
6. El Acheg	Intensive amour
7 El Chegef	Ardent passion (hurt)
8. El Tataioum[i umlaut]	Exclusive blind (haunting)
9. El Onalata	Delirious passion
10. El Iktibal	Madness
11. El Djenoun	Possession Djinn

SONNET

Though our lips can only stammer we yet chant

High things of God. We do not hope to praise

The splendour and the glory of His ways,

Nor light up Heaven with our low descant,

But we shall follow thee, His Hierophant,

Filling with secret canticles the days

To shadow forth in symbols for their gaze.

What thrones and crowns await His militant

For all his beauty showered on the earth

Is summed in thee, O thou most perfect flower.

His dew has filled thy chalice and His power

Blows forth the fragrance of thy mystic works,

White blossom of his Tree: Behold the hour,

Fear not. Thy fruit is Love's most lovely birth.

JMP Thursday February 22nd 1912

A white-bird lit upon a withered bough

And sang a song of battle and of birth

The dead branch woke to life on the earth

JMP

Yet you shall understand for I will speak

First to your soul then to your heart in song.

JMP

The laughing stars fell silent and a flame

Shot from the moon, stabbing the wakeful night

To sudden sleep – and by its wavering light

Crept stealthy winds a-groping as they came.

They crawled beneath the Idols towering frame

And snapt the pillars of its arrogant height

Then at its fall leapt forward to the light

As roaring Hell burst loose in maddened shame.

The bloody stars hung sullen in the sky

Enviously watching, till a welcome word

Loosed them their tethers – Like a wounded bird

They dropped: earth rocked beneath their battle-cry.

Great screaming flames flung up and Heaven heard

'Hell's beaten back, by seven that could die.'

JMP Saturday February 3rd 1912 Algiers

[Those last lines have a curious prophetic ring.]

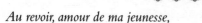

Au revoir, amour de ma jeunesse,

Fleur de ma vie, du jardin ou l'espoir

Est mort, mort sous les baisers de tristesse.

Au revoir!

Au revoir, beaux yeux de mon amante

Beaux yeux si doux si brillantes et si noirs,

O levres roses! O bouches odorante!

Au Revoir!

Je vais ou va toute choses de la vie,

Les fleurs de matin dormirant le soir

Etoiles, amours, et coeur de mon amie.

-Au revoir!

Samedi 16th March 1912

A poet is his own recording angel.

James Stephens must judge James Stephens. This is just as well for he has no peers.

One of their last invitations in Algiers was to a masked ball for which Joe and Moya, dressed up in hired costumes, took each other's photos with Joe's camera in their apartment at No. 2, Gallirie Duchassaing; the glass negatives still survive. Their visit came to a rather abrupt end. The weather was now the worst for years with heavy snow and Moya, on local advice, was trying to arrange to get them to Egypt, but their mother told them to come home straight away instead so they left Algiers, arriving home just before Easter.

It is ironic that Plunkett, who was very expert in the culture of Ancient Egypt, should have been so close to going there and seeing for himself the real objects which he knew from the books of his extensive Egyptology collection. He had not wanted to go to Algiers but got wonderful value from it; however it must have been very hard for him to miss seeing his first book of poetry through the printing and to miss MacDonagh's marriage to Muriel Gifford. MacDonagh had done so much for him; theirs was a friendship noticed by many as being rare and close.

Fragment from 19 January 1912:

These eyes that seek and this tongue that sings

Have also seen and sung unhappy days

And should they hold the vision-haunted ways

An earthy vapour still about them clings:

Yet you can clear them, give them leave to praise

And lo! The beauty of immortal things.

Back in Dublin, it was a 'cold raw Easter' (7 April) and a few weeks later he, 'founded The Columba Press'. He bought a small printing handpress from Thomas MacDonagh and used it for publishing poetry, calling the publishing house after Columba O'Carroll who was still the love of his life. He wanted to be able to control the look, format and place of the poem on the page, and he published two of his poems written in Algiers, 'The Seven Stars' and 'When Satan Laughs' as the first venture of the new press. In those months he was being regularly published including 'Leila' in *The Irish Review*, in June, 'I Sought Him' in *Studies,* also in June and 'Signs and Wonders' also in *The Irish Review* in October.

On a wet day in June Dr James Meenan found Plunkett walking home in the rain because he hadn't the money to pay for a tram, soaked through and with a temperature of 103. He was put in the Merrion Street Orthopedic Hospital where he had his first really major lung haemorrhage. His sister, Geraldine, who had begun as a medical student in University College Dublin, but changed to Chemistry, had kept many good friends in Medicine who were now doctors and interns and she kept up with information at a time when there was huge ignorance about health in all sections of the population. She was now in a position to intervene on Joe's behalf and she says:

> We got Dr Crofton to look after him; this was a concerted plan between (Dr) Harry Meade, (Dr) James Meenan and myself. Dr Crofton had one really good point: he treated his patients as being ill. He put them to bed and fed and nursed them instead of the usual procedure then, which was to treat them harshly and make them take too much exercise.

Plunkett and MacDonagh had started working on setting up a new theatre which would specialise in international contemporary plays by writers such as Chekhov, Ibsen and Strindberg and Irish plays which were not 'peasant' plays. The Theatre of Ireland had been in existence since 1906 and MacDonagh made approaches to the well-known actor, Frank Fay, offering him the position of leading male actor and he offered the musician and nationalist, Arthur Darley, a partnership in the theatre. This required letters and visits to Plunkett in the nursing home for comments and agreement ...

MacDonagh to Plunkett:

> What do you say of Arthur Darley for a co-man? He is artist he is enthusiastic, he is wealthy, he is Fay's friend, he is my friend, is he yours? He is a splendid man ...

MacDonagh to Frank Fay:

> ... We would not be the Theatre of Ireland. We do not want to begin with a past. We are not against the Theatre of Ireland

or against the Abbey, though I think we are necessary only because of the failure of those two in different directions...

In this letter MacDonagh mentions Plunkett's illness as one of the problems facing them at the time. In a note to MacDonagh regarding Fay, Plunkett says:

… he certainly is a wonderful man, knows a tremendous lot and has great enthusiasm but I suppose his sense of humour is reposing, neatly folded, in the proper basket.

Plunkett had now been moved from the hospital at No. 22 Merrion St to the Convalescent Home at No. 28.

Sráid Mhuirbhthean Uachtar a 28 [28 Upper Merrion St.] an lá seo 20 IX 1912

Dear Mums

I won't get up till this evening so if anyone wants to see me let them come here. Perhaps though I will be with you for supper and stay till 9.30. The local demon said I might if my temper was normal at 7pm so you'd better put my name in the punchbowl. But I would be obliged if some decent person would ask at Ponsonby's for two books I ordered, they are the *Wild Night* by Chesterton and *The Unknown Eros* by [Coventry] Patmore.

I have the money for them (about 7/6) they may either be paid for or put down to my account. This elegant script is being executed in a more or less recumbent position which no doubt accounts for its regularity.

Mise Pluinghcéad

He was in the hospital for several months going home to Fitzwilliam Street at times when he was well enough, but he had another haemorrhage while he was there and was severely restricted in every way. When his mother began complaining of the cost of keeping him in hospital for so long Dr Crofton allowed him to go home which created a new set of problems.

Despite the size of the three-storey over-basement Fitzwilliam Street house there was little enough in the way of separate bedrooms for the number of people living there so, in order to create one for Joe, Sarah Ferrall, their fifty-year-old American cousin, was moved into one of the return rooms with Geraldine and Moya while Joe was installed in the room behind it. At that time Mimi was in London, Moya and Geraldine, both studying, were living at home; George was in Stonyhurst, Fiona in the Bon Secours School in Holyhead and Jack in Clongowes College. Geraldine's account of an incident from this time gives a flavour of the atmosphere in the house and Joe Plunkett's place in it.

> Moya, concerned about Fiona's lack of warm clothes, asked Ma to give her a winter coat. Ma began to scream at her that there was no necessity for a winter coat as the convent Fiona was going to was French (as though the nuns brought the climate with them) and as she screamed and worked herself into hysterics she started hitting Moya, who was standing on the stairs, with her walking stick. Pa, hearing

the racket, came out of his study, saw Moya with her hands over her head and thought that she was attacking Ma so he also began to hit Moya with his walking stick. Joe arrived in the hall to this appalling scene, took the stick from Pa and broke it over his knee. Ma took this as a personal insult and redoubled her screaming. Joe comforted Moya while Pa, realising his mistake, stood helplessly patting her on the head to show he was sorry. By the time I came in, Pa had retreated to the study, Ma to the dining-room, and Joe was still trying to soothe poor Moya. Joe, as always happened after an affair like this, was boycotted by Ma but she did give Fiona the coat.

Another incident after this in which the Countess tried to hit Geraldine, who was by now too strong for her, resulted in Joe telling his mother she shouldn't do such things to which she replied, 'Do you mean to say that I should apologise to my own children?' Joe said it would be the right thing to do. 'Well, all I can say is . . . I'm sorry.' Geraldine says:

> … that was the last physical violence on any of us. I was twenty-one. Joe was twenty-four.

Their mother obviously took stock and her solution 'in order to give Joe more room and comfort and the possibility of being properly looked after' was to give him the use of a house in Donnybrook and whichever of the girls would look after him could live there too. Geraldine was not only delighted to take this up, but she was the only one available at the time. She had been operated on for appendicitis and was still recovering so she had had to postpone her final chemistry exams. They moved to 17 Marlborough Road, Donnybrook, just as 1913 swept in, the beginning for her and for Joe, despite his illness, of a time of liberating intellectual freedom and political action.

CHAPTER 8

• • • • •

January To July 1913
The Good Life And The Review

When the third Home Rule Bill was finally published in January 1913 after the many problems associated with its enactment, Joe and Geraldine Plunkett were deeply disappointed with its provisions. John Redmond's campaign for an Irish Parliament for purely Irish affairs had only resulted in a hands-tied institution with no power over anything that mattered. A large number of departments were to remain permanently in English hands, including Customs and Excise (about three-quarters of the country's revenue), Income Tax, National Health Insurance and Old-Age Pensions, the Post Office, the Board of Works, land annuities, road boards, factory and workshop control, the police and the army. These last were not surprising given that they were the instruments of control by London. An English-nominated senate would have the power to delay Irish legislation and Irish Members of Parliament were to remain in London. Joe Plunkett believed that taking part in the London Government made Ireland part of the propagation of injustice throughout the Empire and that the Irish Parliamentary Party's imperialism equalled that of the British Government. Joe and Geraldine and her fiancé, Thomas Dillon, were now regularly in the company of people with similar political concerns who took the trouble to read the Home Rule Bill and assess its provisions. Irish Parliamentary Party (IPP) MPs stated that their leader, John Redmond, had been assured that the Bill would be interpreted in a 'friendly' way and would be much better than it appeared, but this was hardly reliable.

Joe made many friends at this time, literary people whom he met through Tomás MacDonagh, and Geraldine's university crowd, scientific, medical, political and nationalist. Joe and Tommy Dillon got on very well with on-going arguments about everything, especially socialism and social equality – Joe thought it would work but Tommy thought it wouldn't. Dillon's relations included John Blake Dillon, Valentine Dillon, Myles Dillon, James Dillon and John Dillon of the IPP, strong Mayo landed gentry with education and a sense of the contribution they made to society but unable to trust that society. Socialism was regarded by much of the Establishment as an evil disease.

The house Joe and Geraldine were living in from just before Christmas of 1912 had become a drop-in centre, a friendly and interesting place, a political and literary hub.

17 Marlborough Road in Donnybrook was a two-storey redbrick built in the 1880s by Joe and Gerry's grandfather, Patrick Cranny. He had built about forty houses at the Donnybrook end of the road including his own family house, Muckross Park, on over two acres. Joe and Gerry had easy access, walking or on the tram, to the University at Earlsfort Terrace, Thomas Clarke's shop on Parnell Street, the Literary Society céilís at 25 Parnell Square, the Moore Street market, the National Library and Thomas and Muriel MacDonagh's in Ranelagh. There was very little furniture in the house, which was tough on Joe when he was ill, but each of their bedrooms had a good bed, there were plenty of shelves put up for Joe's books and there was one 'not uncomfortable' armchair. Mary Bolger was a general domestic servant employed by their mother who could 'cook' just brown bread and scrambled eggs, but she was devoted to Joe and made him comfortable as much as she could. Geraldine was already a skilled cook and took a lot of trouble to buy and cook the kind of food Joe liked. At the time having weight was equated with good health and being thin a great source of worry. He was still frequently so severely ill that Geraldine never got back to her final degree exams and although she had not expected it to be that difficult there were great compensations in their new lifestyle.

They had been good friends since they were children in Kilternan and had found themselves in agreement on many things including the artificial and unreal social life around Dublin Castle and Joe had supported Geraldine when she announced to her mother that she did not want to be 'presented at court'. From that time on they and most of their siblings were moving into separatist nationalism in their beliefs. Joe also allowed Geraldine to look after him with more tolerance than he had with others. Geraldine, who was then twenty-two, also says:

He told me that he used me as a person to talk to about everything that happened.

Joe was now twenty-five and Geraldine's description of him from this time gives a view of the physical man which will hardly change in the next few years:

He was about five foot nine but looked rather less as a rule as he stooped in repose and was very thin and muscular. He was dark-haired but his beard did not grow strongly. His skin was white and he had a good deal of colour in his lips and cheeks. His eyes were very large, his nose thin, high-bridged and delicately cut and his mouth was finely drawn and mobile.

He was noticeable in Ireland, where clothes tended to be conservative, for his somewhat extravagant dress and appearance. Meeting others on his travels with a similar flamboyant style made him very at home with this, but sometimes there was another reason for it; in one of the many battles with their mother over clothes the family had tried, unsuccessfully, to get her to give Joe a light overcoat, but when a cloak was suggested she was delighted and made him a circular unlined cloak of royal blue faced cloth with a velvet collar. He may even have had a hand in the making of this himself. He liked strong colour and fine craftwork, especially in jewellery. Geraldine said that he would have been very much at home in medieval Italy. This aesthetic sense was part of his interest in theatre and design, particularly that of Gordon Craig whose sets, costumes and lighting revolutionised theatre. This was the modernist view of drama which Joe Plunkett and Thomas MacDonagh hoped to create in the theatre they aimed to set up.

When Joe was well enough he loved food, wine, uproarious parties and dancing – his party trick was dancing while sitting on a chair. He went with Geraldine to the National Literary Society céilís and the Society also used to organise debates on Sunday nights with such titles as '*That the policy of Wolfe Tone is the true policy in Irish national affairs*'. It cost a half-crown to get in to the céilís and they started at eight–thirty continuing until six next morning when they went home in a cab. Joe would dance until about midnight when he tired and spend the rest of the night in 'intellectual flirtation'. The National Literary Society was a cover for the secret organisation, the Irish Republican Brotherhood (IRB) and Geraldine, in later years, reckoned that the company at those céilís included at least forty people who were to be presidents, taoisigh, politicians, diplomats and upper civil servants in post-independence Ireland. Along with the Gaelic League it became an important venue for argument and discussion for and against political systems, for devising constitutions and for assigning blame for existing evils. Joe and Gerry Plunkett were well aware of what a wonderful life it was, enhanced by their physical and philosophical independence.

Plunkett was writing very regularly now with more than one finished poem a month, many of them published and, as can be felt in these extracts, gaining in strength.

PROTHALAMION [a bridal song]

...Then this magic dusk of even

Shall give way before the night—

Close the curtains of delight!

Silence is the only song

That can speak such mysteries

As to earth and heaven belong

When one flesh has compassed these.

21st February 1913

DAYBREAK

As blazes forth through clouds the morning sun

So shines your soul, and I must veil my sight

Lest it be stricken to eternal night ...

...But I beneath the planetary choir

Still as a stone lie dumbly till the dark

Lifts its broad wings— ...

THE SPLENDOUR OF GOD.

The drunken stars stagger across the sky,.

The moon wavers and sways like a windblown bud,

Beneath my feet the earth like drifting scud

Lapses and slides, wallows and shoots on high ;...

—I have burst the grape

Of the world, and let its powerful blood escape

Untasted — crying whether my vision durst

See God's high glory in a girl's soft shape—

God! Is my worship blessed or accurst?

March 1ˢᵗ 1913

YOUR FEAR.

…Your name that's known

But to your heart, your fear has flown

To mine: you've heard not any bird,

No wings have stirred save yours alone.…

1st April 1913

He intended most of the poems with which he was satisfied to be part of his next collection, *Occulta,* but history was to interfere with this plan.

When he had to stay in bed it was often for weeks at a time and he used to study anything and everything, philosophy, biography, mysticism, history and military history. He read great numbers of novels of all kinds and he loved good detective stories. He had a huge admiration for G. K. Chesterton, his novels, especially *The Man who was Thursday,* the Father Brown stories and his weekly articles in the *Illustrated London News.* Chesterton was an original thinker who used ideas from metaphysics, religion, the occult, science and anything else; his contradictions, absurdities and paradoxes appealed to Joe who used them in his own philosophy to interpret national and international news and politics, to read the real story behind the words. He continued to write poetry when confined to bed, nonsense verse, ballads, triolets, lyrical poems and he was working on several long philosophical poems which were in a red folder he had with him up to the start of the Rising and which disappeared, presumably lost in the fires. He also collected street ballads. Sometimes the handwriting in his poems has the look of illness or exhaustion about it. He also sat up in the bed playing the fiddle which he had never studied formally – presumably the 1911 cello lessons never came to anything. He played music-hall and café tunes, 'Two lovely black eyes', 'Just because I happened to be there' and, after his 1915 trip to the USA, 'Ragtime Cowboy Joe'.

Joe used to get his brother, George and friends, Theo McWeeney, Colm O'Lochlainn and anyone else he could find to play *Little Wars* with him, a game which came out that year. H.G. Wells, author of *The Invisible Man, The History of Mr Polly, War of the Worlds* and many, many more works, had already brought out a book of floor games in 1911, but his *Little Wars* came out complete with toy soldiers made by W. Britain. Pieces of string gave the distance infantry, cavalry and so on could move, and each move had a set time, all supervised by an umpire. The four-point-seven-inch spring breech-loader gun could fire a wooden cylinder about an inch long. Wells was a pacifist and his philosophy comes through in the extensive rule book for the game. With the whole floor of one of the rooms in No. 17 as a battlefield covered in toy soldiers there was endless excitement and arguments for hours and Joe learned a lot about tactics and strategy and it led him to read up on real battles.

NO SONG

...I have no way to make you hear,

No song will echo in your heart;

Now must I with the fading year

Fade. Without meeting we must part—

No song nor silence you will hear.

Joseph Plunkett 3rd June 1913

From *The Irish Review* January, 1913:

> *The Irish Review* was founded to give expression to the intellectual movement in Ireland. It publishes poems plays and stories in English and in Irish and deals critically with every Irish interest
>
> Literature, Art and Science, Politics, Economics, and Sociology. In politics, *The Irish Review* aims at making an adjustment by promoting free discussion.
>
> The subscription is 7/6 per year and 3/9 per half year, post free.

In the editorial of the first issue, March 1911, they explain:

> We do not see the intellectual movement ... as purely liter-
> ary; we think of it as the application of Irish intelligence to
> the reconstruction of Irish life.

The Irish Review had been co-founded in 1911 by Padraic
Colum and his wife-to-be Mary Maguire, James Stephens
and David Houston, who funded the journal. It seems they
were all editors over the next two years with Thomas Mac-
Donagh as an associate editor and, 'after an interregnum',
Joseph Plunkett became the editor in June 1913. It was Mac-
Donagh who brought Professor Houston to 17, Marlborough Road to ask Joe Plunkett if he would take over when
the *Review* got into financial trouble and Padraic Colum and
his wife were moving to the USA. Plunkett had been interested and quite involved in the journal from the start and
had had some poems published in it. The *Review* had been
losing money for some time and Houston had paid out more
than he could afford. They did not want it to go to strange
hands so if Joe could find about £200 to pay the debts he
could have it with their blessing. Padraic Colum did have
reservations about Joe; in a letter to MacDonagh he said:

> I do care about [the *Review* as] an organ of free opinion in
> Ireland. I have a great respect for Plunkett but I know that
> he is a delicate young man and may have to put the whole
> thing aside on a doctor's order.

This was true enough, but underestimated Joe's determination. He was pleased at the offer and took it as a compliment to his standing as one of the better young poets. He knew, personally or by reputation, most of the contributors and admired most of them, it was work that interested and stimulated him and ownership would be a real privilege. However there was a practical problem. As usual, having no income of his own, he had to apply to his mother for the two hundred pounds needed to clear the debts and continue publication. As she was on holiday he wrote to her explaining the situation and in her reply she told him to 'offer one hundred pounds' so he had to write again and explain that it wasn't that kind of settlement. It took time, but she liked the idea of a magazine, gave Joe the money and he became the owner of the *Irish Review* on 16 June 1913. His work as editor didn't take effect until the August edition as June was already out and July fully planned.

Towards the end of June Countess Plunkett organised a picnic in a hayfield at her latest acquisition, Larkfield in Kimmage, eight acres of land, a house and garden, two cottages, a bakery and some sheds, a two-storey barn and a three-storey mill with mill stream and wheel on the Poddle River. Geraldine was on the picnic and took the time to examine the land and buildings in detail. Joe doesn't seem to have been there that day, but he and Geraldine had been there before. Kavanagh's, the Dame Street gunsmiths, rented part of the land for customers' target practice on butts and Joe,

Geraldine, Phil and Willie Cosgrave had gone there to try out revolvers.

Joe Plunkett's conviction that Ireland must be separated from England had been certain for some time now, appearing in poems from 1907 on and in June of 1913 this poem is published:

THIS HERITAGE TO THE RACE OF KINGS

This heritage to the race of kings

Their children and their children's seed

Have wrought their prophecies in deed

Of terrible and splendid things.

The hands that fought, the hearts that broke

In old immortal tragedies,

These have not failed beneath the skies,

Their children's heads refuse the yoke.

And still their hands shall guard the sod

That holds their father's funeral urn,

Still have their heart's volcanic burn

With anger of the suns of God.

No alien sword shall earn as wage

The entail of their blood and tears,

No shame price for peaceful years

Shall ever part this heritage.

Joseph Plunkett 22 June 1913

His nationalist poems are more ballads than poetry, but that made sense as it was often the earliest form of nationalism encountered by children, and the children of the wealthy, like the Plunketts, were sung such ballads by their maids and nurses.

Countess Plunkett had bought the Hardwicke Hall in Hardwicke Street 'for a song' in 1910 and provided the Dun Emer Guild with a home there in the rooms at the back, but Joe saw the theatrical possibilities of the hall and, once more, persuaded his mother into spending money on a venture. This time she took it up very enthusiastically, rolled up her sleeves, had a stage made, brought in curtains, decorative serpents and furniture from auctions. Her taste was not the same as her children's; they were reading and hearing about the Moscow Arts Theatre, she liked *High Life Below Stairs*. The first play staged by the Plunketts in the hall (now being called the Hardwicke Theatre) was *The Dance of Osiris* written by Joseph Plunkett under his stage name, Luke Killeen. Performed on 26, 27 and 28 June 1913, as a benefit for the Connemara Islands Fever Fund, the current famine which Roger Casement had called 'An Irish Putumayo'. The 'islands', linked by a road to the mainland, constituted one of the worst congested districts, but the Congested Districts Board had done little about them. Three thousand people on nine thousand acres of bog and rock trying to live from a diminishing seaweed market, a failing fishing industry, few animals and tiny patches of potatoes or oats and high rents for small cramped housing meant that just staying alive was a near insoluble problem.

The play was experimental and used Gordon Craig's ideas on a small scale. The script seems like an attempt to make a large-scale theme (an attempted coup by the Lords of Justice and Administration in the King of Egypt's court) come to life on a very small scale, five actors, casual language, drinking wine and smoking, hints of seduction and the King of Egypt himself wearing a dress and veil as a disguise for the entire (short) length of the play! Definitely not a great work, but it entertained most people there.

The July *Irish Review*, included among other items, a ravishing picture by Harry Clarke: *The Silver Apples of the Moon, the Golden Apples of the Sun*, poems by James Cousins, a story by Lord Dunsany and the article: 'Ireland, Germany and the

Seas', by Shan Van Vocht. Many writers in the *Review* and other journals used a *nom de plume* and it sometimes makes the writer untraceable, but Joe recognised the style of this article and others which had appeared in the *Review* as that of Sir Roger Casement whom he had met a few times in their Fitzwilliam Street house and greatly admired. He wrote to Casement and asked him to continue to write for the *Review* not realising that Casement had asked Padraic Colum not to reveal his identity and now believed he had. Joe reassured him that no one had told him, that he had worked it out from the style and text and Casement not only accepted it completely, but went on to write some of the most important articles published in the *Review*.

The front room of No. 17 Marlborough Road was turned into the office of the *Review*, which became a central part of both Joe and Geraldine's lives. MacDonagh used to bring people who were interested in the *Review* round to meet Joe there and MacDonagh stayed involved in the editing, making it more of a joint venture with Plunkett. The publisher was Ernest Manico of Temple Bar who published other papers and journals and the printer was Mr Latchford who had consummate taste in layout and printing, the poems centred on the page and each page a separate picture. Geraldine was as fast and voracious a reader as Joe and they both read all the books sent for review. As a result Joe developed a dislike of sloppy thinking and writing and became much more critical of his own work. He found writing prose very difficult despite MacDonagh's encouragement to continue with it. Plunkett and MacDonagh usually agreed with each other vehemently after plenty of argument, layered with humour, at great length on literature, politics, taste, printing styles, layout, bindings and everything else.

ORTHODOXY

In Ireland one can only disagree with one's own side. We do not disagree with AE's irreproachable Buddhism, we admire, nor with Stephen's paganism, we wonder, nor with George Moore's eroticism, we laugh. All these perfectly orthodox according to their canons...

The only thing not perfectly orthodox is orthodoxy for that is always to embrace all new knowledge and vision and consequently cannot decay.

Orthodoxy means 'of the right opinion' no matter what comes up. To the orthodox nothing can come amiss. To be orthodox is to have an open mind. To be a heretic is to be bound to take the wrong view...

JMP 8 July 1913

This extract from a fragment, also from that July, must be more real than fictional:

Chapter eleventy eleven

...When she had come to see him on Monday afternoon he

had made an effort to say to her what he had in his mind about his not taking any steps for the present. To put his wishes, his hopes, his desires into any kind of action that would tend to forward them on account of the probable cost to her peace of mind and her frank friendliness to him. He had tried, he feared unsuccessfully, to tell her that he would, till further notice, as he might have put it, not do anything in the nature of paying her attentions or making love to her, or in any way to influence her affections or her ideas in his favour and moreover that he would not even hold in his mind as an intention of purpose the hope of gaining her love and her consent to marry him.

JMP 1913

And this meditation on beauty is also unfinished:

There are three more or less distinct stages or steps in the development of the sensitiveness of the human soul to beauty and three distinct activities of the soul aroused at these stages by the perception of the beautiful. The stages are the classic, the romantic, the mystical and their respective activities take the form of art, philosophy and love...

...it may be as rare to find one who is solely an artist or a philosopher or a mystic as to find one who is all three and all perfectly. ...Each of these three steps of development and evoked activities is contained in the third where all sensitiveness of the soul to beauty is a kind of love, love is both intuitional and rational and both the testimony of expression and contemplation or discourse implicit in worship, the mystic is artist, philosopher and lover.

...The classic is looked upon as being genius swayed by ideas and the romantic as genius swayed by emotion, whereas the classic is the production of the heart moved by direct perception of beauty and the romantic is produced by the effect on the heart of ideas of purpose. This can be immediately confirmed by referring to the great works of art or literature.

JMP 11 July 1913

CHAPTER 9
• • • • •

August To November 1913
The Lockout And The Peace
Committee

Plunkett's first edition of *The Irish Review* came out in
August 1913. The front cover, as usual, gave a list of the
main items and information on their agents in London,
Edinburgh and, in Boston, The Four Seas Co. for the whole
of the USA. The picture was *The Seaweed Gatherers* by Jack
Morrow and the rest of the Contents read:

> Poetry by Thomas MacDonagh and Katherine Tynan,
> 'Social history, Women in the Middle Ages' by Mary
> Hayden, 'Economics, the Transit Problem' by Justin Phillips,
> 'Gaelic literature, *Dánta Griosúighthe Gaedheal, Slíocht Dua-
> naire Gaedhilge*: Songs of the Irish Rebels' ... A Page from
> an *Irish Anthology* by P.H. Pearse, 'Criticism, Walther von der
> Vogelweider', by Nesta de Robeck, A serialised story: 'The
> Soul of Kol Nikon', by Eleanor Farjeon, Reviews: *Oliver*

Goldsmith by Padraic Colum, *The Ripple* by Miriam Alexander.

An advertisement on the back cover announced the publication the following October of *Lyrical Poems* by Thomas MacDonagh, 'six shillings net. 12 D'Olier St, Dublin'

With all of this safely in to the printers Joe Plunkett set off for Cloghaneely in Donegal to join the O'Carroll family, especially Columba, staying with his younger cousin, Aidan McCabe, in Swellan, Cavan town, on the way, a journey he made more than once that month.

22nd August 1913

17, Marlborough Rd.

Donnybrook

Dear Aidan,

How are you since I left? I had an easy journey on Monday, [18 August] only one thing I regret, I might as well have had no ticket because I was never asked for it. Last night I rang up Amiens St Station to inquire about the mobike but as they said there was none there I hope you haven't dispatched it. I forgot to tell you that it should be sent 'carriage forward' if that is the technical term for not paying for it before it arrives. – but they may keep it shunted for weeks on a siding or something. If it is not gone do not send it till Monday. If it has gone, drop me a postcard. If is still there and the back tyre will stay up you could take it to mass on

Sunday. I am sure it would be good for its soul. Early mass would be the best. I will now telephone to see if the railway company have it.

Au revoir I've to try and catch this post.

Yours

Joe Plunkett

Royal Arms, Omagh

Saturday August 23rd 1913 7.30pm

My dear Aidan

Don't be surprised if you get this letter on Sunday morning or if you don't. I leave here by the 9.09 train on tomorrow and will try to be in time for the 11 o'clock mass in Bally-shannon. I did not intend to stop here (and so let you know of my whereabouts) but the temptation is irresistible. As I am so near and I have a spare tube with me, I may as well take the bike back to Dublin.

Always your friend

Joseph Plunkett

Plunkett came back from Donegal still in love with Columba O'Carroll, who was, by now, a medical student in University College Dublin, but he was depressed about it and couldn't see that it was going to get anywhere. Geraldine tried to encourage him to give her up – it was now three years of unrequited love – but he wasn't ready for that either. Columba – was, of course, his muse as well as his love and his love poems tend to be his best work, well crafted and technical, but stitched through with beauty from the natural world, often a surprise from a man whose natural world seems to be the city. There is no sense of him cynically using his love and her denial in his writing, rather the poems seem to be more real, more expressive of depth and self-perception as time goes on and there is a long way to go before any resolution happens, partly because they really are good friends and, even though she does not return his love, she always treats him kindly. Columba had many devout admirers, one of whom was the same cousin, Aidan McCabe, to whom Joe was writing, and sometimes mentioning his Columba sadnesses:

17 Marlborough Road

Donnybrook

Wednesday August 27th 1913

My dear Aidan

You will be pleased to hear that I arrived (seeing that such was one of my reasons for setting forth) even if you're not more pleased than I was at having to leave (which was not at all). They (meaning in this instance the railway company) evidently did not intend to let me get so far (why I know not, they can hardly have had an inkling of the true state of affairs) or if they did they thought of a curious way of showing it (this method of writing is slightly involved, but, as will probably appear if you can succeed in deciphering this epistle, it is the only possible way of partly expressing myself just at present) because they (the aforesaid railway co.) took pains to detach the van containing Freya (the motorbike) so called because of her habit of losing her garter (*On y soit qui mal y pense*) at Dundalk, to which unholy spot she had to be wired from Amiens St and did not turn up for some three hours after I'd arrived there. Eventually we were reunited and brought each other home.

Now, I am where I started this letter; that is to say here.

As to the reasons for the concatenation of convolutions forming this literary style (save the mark!) They are or seem to be

I. Supper including beer and tea

II. Pipe and tobacco and the absorption of smoke therefrom, which smoke includes disintegration products of oil of tobacco, nicotine and formaldehyde.

III. A state of – shall we say grace? At any rate, a state of the mind resultant on being here and not there and correcting proofs etc. Instead of 'a taking of his *dolce far niente*'

Wouldn't I like a walk to the strand or to the point of the links to clear my brain! And telepathy is a far more restful and certain means of communication than correspondence. However, what's impossible can't be and never came to pass, so I've got to grin. Grinning is a peculiar form of human activity. In spite of numerous asseverations to the contrary I am prepared to hold that it is a unique accomplishment proper only to man. A good and proper habit of grinning cannot fail to affect a permanent modification in man's natural inclination to seriousness (the 'evil' of genesis). Curiously enough, grinning, contrary to the popular superstition is not so much done with the face as with the feet. It is known to the erudite (that's me) as putting one's foot down with a heavy hand. It is thus chiefly an activity of the soul (mind the spelling!) The iron heel of decision must be placed with unerring accuracy on the rubber neck of fatuity. Therefore I surcease.

Here endeth the first lesson.

I hope you're all having a good time. Will you give my love to Aunt Fanny and the rest?

There is a tram strike on and a horse show and a general migration of the Babylonians so that the promised city appears not only sated but slightly seasick. That's all. The September number of the *Irish Review* will be out on Saturday barring the will of god or the king's enemies.

Yours ecclesiastically

A slightly bluish

Plunkett

In this September *Irish Review* pieces by Eleanor Farjeon, Mary Hayden and P. H. [Patrick] Pearse were continuations from the previous issue and the picture was 'Summer Sketch' by Dermod O'Brien. There was a story, 'The Threepenny Piece', by James Stephens, 'Irish History and Dogma' by Patrick J. Little, '*Druimfhionn Donn Dilis*' translated from the Irish by Thomas MacDonagh and *Lux in Tenebris* by Joseph Plunkett, his first and only long poem published – an essay on despairing love.

Extracts from *Lux in Tenebris* [Light in Darkness], one of the many poems to or about Columba:

If the dread all-seeing stars

Ringed Saturn and ruddy Mars

And their companions, all the seven

That play before the lord of heaven,

Each blossoming nebula and all

The constellations, were to fall

Low at my feet and worship me,

Endow me with all sovranty

Of their wide kingdom of the blue—

Yet I would not believe that you

Could love me—

…If every flower and beast and bird

In God's great earth and splendid sea

Should live and love and fight for me

And my sweet singing and sad art—

Yet could I not conceive your heart

Stooping to mine, nor your wild eyes

Unveiling their deep ecstasies,

Your tenebrous hair sweep near my lips,

Your eyelids bring your soul eclipse

For fear that I should be made blind

By love's bright image in your mind….

Ending with:

…Only your passion-haunted eyes

Interpreting your mysteries:

These are to me and my desire

For pillar of cloud and pillar of fire,

A gleam and gloom of heaven, in hell

A high continuous miracle.

In that last letter to Aidan McCabe he says:

There is a tram strike on and a horse show ...

William Martin Murphy, owner of the Dublin Tramways Company, had sacked nearly 350 of his workers whom he suspected of membership of the Irish Transport and General Workers' Union (ITGWU), and the remaining tram workers response, on 26 August, was to pin on their union badges and go on strike, leaving their trams where they were, on the first day of the Dublin Horse Show. There followed a series of meetings, marches, arrests, protests and police baton charges during which people were knocked to the ground and beaten. Two people died as a result, James Nolan and John Byrne, and inquiries and investigations ensued. By now William Martin Murphy had persuaded over four hundred employers to create a prohibition on unions (supposedly only the ITGWU, but effectively all unions) and a huge proportion of workers, particularly of the unskilled, found themselves locked out. James Larkin, who had already been jailed once, appeared on a balcony of the Imperial Hotel (owned by William Martin Murphy) helped by, among others, Nellie Gifford, Thomas MacDonagh's sister-in-law. Another sister-in-law, Sydney Gifford, was outside in a cab with Countess Markievicz trying to raise support. Larkin was arrested immediately with more police activity and Thomas MacDonagh, who had gone there to see if he could help, was appalled at the savagery of the baton charge and later he described to the official Inquiry, as he had earlier to Joe and Gerry, the horrible sound of batons on people's heads. Five hundred were wounded and poured into the hospitals. The army was called out.

Shortly after the beginning of all this Joe and Geraldine went home for the family Sunday dinner in Fitzwilliam Street. The usual Sunday dinner there was an enormous roast of beef with large dishes of vegetables followed by equally large apple pies with custard. They drank claret or Graves with this and sometimes brandy with the coffee. Joe gave his opinion about the lockout, assuming it was the same as the rest of the family's; he saw justice as being the same for everyone. His mother, Countess Plunkett, in Geraldine's account:

> … attacked him with fury, screamed and roared, flouncing about the place, in and out of the dining room, wanting to know how her own family could actually tell her that the men were right.
>
> 'I never heard of such a thing! They demand work! Well the world is coming to an end!' she said.

She had always expressed kindness to any men who worked for her, but paid them very badly. Her children thought this was 'only natural meanness'. They tried to tell her about the pay and the conditions suffered by both men and women workers but it was no use, she would not listen. Joe and Geraldine left 'after a silent dinner' and did not go

215

back for some time. They were mystified at her 'unusual personal interest' in the situation; they didn't know that she had bought a slum property in Upper Abbey Street and James Larkin was denouncing slum owners. She had bought the Abbey Street house, let in single rooms, and a block of six flats down the lane at an auction. When two tenements in Church Street collapsed killing seven people there was a renewal of campaigns against landlords. Countess Plunkett kept the Abbey Street property a secret from her children so, with no inkling of it, Joe went down to James Larkin with a subscription for the workers and in a speech the following day Larkin mentioned this and added 'His people have rotten tenements'. Joe was terribly upset and thought it must be something belonging to his grandfather, Patrick Plunkett, but Patrick Plunkett's property was only in well-off suburbs. Joe never did know about Abbey Street.

John Redmond, John Dillon and the Irish Parliamentary Party (IPP) were, in effect, the leaders of the people so it was assumed that they would come home when the Lockout and Strike began. Joe, watching events thought that the IPP would support the workers in Ireland but now he began to think that Alderman Cotton, who was in the Employers' Federation, locking workers out, and in the IPP, prevented them from doing this and that the IPP's default position now was to 'wait for Home Rule'. The United Irish League had become the official IPP organisation and was dominated by the very conservative Ancient Order of Hibernians but the Young Ireland Branch (YIBS), founded by Tom Kettle, contained many of the younger political intellectuals, among them Thomas Dillon and his friend, Rory O'Connor and, most admired of them, Francis Sheehy-Skeffington with his reputation for deeply-held convictions, integrity and strong opinions on women's equality and politics.

Tom Kettle himself was a lecturer in Economics in University College Dublin where he and Thomas Dillon got to know one another, both joining a small dining club called *Cui Bono*. Kettle had been IPP MP at Westminster for East Tyrone, re-elected with a bigger majority but resigned when appointed Professor of Economics in University College Dublin. He called a meeting at the Mansion House where his suggestion that a Peace Committee be formed was agreed on and Kettle elected Chairman. He asked Thomas Dillon to act as secretary and Dillon, in turn, asked Joe Plunkett to be his assistant. This was a practical idea – Joe had a motorbike with a sidecar and with a transport strike on, getting around was a problem but Dillon was also aware that Joe wanted to be doing something useful. The Peace Committee invited the clergy of all creeds, public officials and anyone relevant to join them. Those who did included the Lord Mayor of Dublin, Lorcan Sherlock, Rabbi Herzog and Rabbi Gudansky, Charles Thomas Ovenden, Dean of St. Patrick's Cathedral, some of the Capuchin monks, the lawyer, James Creed Meredith, Thomas

MacDonagh, Professor Charles Oldham, William Butler Yeats and Francis Sheehy-Skeffington. One employer, Edward Lee, with shops on Abbey St, Jervis St, Kingstown and Rathmines, joined the Committee. The rest of the employers denounced the committee as pro-labour and spoke of 'interfering professors'. The Dublin Industrial Peace Committee held more public meetings in the Mansion House but few besides the actual members went to them. They were theoretically neutral but in fact their sympathies were with the workers. Dillon and Plunkett called on the Catholic Archbishop of Dublin, Dr Walsh, to ask him to join the Committee and Dr Walsh told them that he considered the workers were only demanding their rights, but he did not think he should join the Peace Committee or speak in public, because he was concerned that the employers would not accept his decision. Later he did make public statements on the side of the men but the employers ignored him.

The Peace Committee then invited both sides to arbitration and the workers agreed, nominating their leaders to speak for them and asking the Committee to find a basis for peace, but the employers refused to have anything to do with it and there was a complete deadlock. Having met the Dublin Trades Council the Peace Committee finally met the Irish Parliamentary Party MPs for Dublin, known as the 'Dublin Six'. Tom Kettle had arranged this for himself and Thomas Dillon and Joe Plunkett but didn't turn up so the other two were left to deal with the MPs who, except for William Field, were very annoyed with the Peace Committee. Field stayed to discuss the situation properly with Plunkett and Dillon but he had no Party support for action. Dillon and Plunkett also went to see John Dillon but he would do nothing.

The following, written in September 1913, is Plunkett's idea of the necessity for a just and egalitarian state:

> It should be (but unfortunately isn't) obvious that the sole objects of government should be the peace and prosperity in the fullest sense of all the individuals composing the nation – that all other objects, such as the furtherance of law and order, the cultivation of relations with other powers and peoples, the extension of boundaries, the building up of trade, the development of resources, the subjection of enemies, the pursuit of the arts, sciences and philosophies, the promulgation of ideals, should entirely and completely subserve those first named. It should also be evident (but here there is more difficulty) that the destinies, the habits of life and labour, the ideals and religion of the individuals composing the nation should as far as possible be their own free choice. This alone is liberty. It was not only the great Emperor Otto whose mind wavered between *'l'etat, c'est moi'* [I am the state] and *'Ich dien'* [I serve] The Fabian Society does the same. The collectivist theory of government makes the state (as embodied in the government) more important than the governed – which is precisely the

fallacy of oligarchy and aristocracy.

Put in these terms the absurdity is manifest therefore these terms are never used. The nearest approach to them is the statement of the position one logical step back. One is permitted to say that the difference between the democratic theory of government and all the other theories is that the former supposes that the opinions and desires of the governed should prevail even when they run counter to the ideas of those in power, while all other theories of government assume as axiomatic the proposition that only those possessing power know how it should be used.

There is always, moreover, the double subsumption that those who know how power should be used will thus employ it and that those who do not know could not be trusted to find out.

JMP 1913

James Connolly had been a labour organiser in Scotland, the USA and Ireland and had written extensively about socialism and workers' rights. It is likely that Plunkett already knew him from his writings, but Connolly had come to Dublin to help in the Lockout and Strike and became, when Jim Larkin left, the articulate and inspiring Labour leader. Plunkett asked Connolly to write about the Lockout and Strike for the October issue of the *Irish Review* so they must have met or at least corresponded at this time and it may have been their first encounter. Connolly's article appeared in the prime space in the October issue so full of wisdom, erudition and fascinating writing that it would be tempting to reprint it all but here is a taster which is as much as space allows.

It begins:

> HAVING been asked by the Editor of the *Irish Review* to contribute for this month's issue a statement of the position of Labour in the present crisis in Dublin, and having gladly consented, I now find myself to be in somewhat of a difficulty in setting the limits and scope of my article.
>
> ...When the English peasantry revolted against their masters, did not all English aristocrats join in sympathetic action to crush them? When the German peasantry rose during the Reformation, did not Catholic and Protestant aristocrats cease exterminating each other to join in a sympathetic attempt to exterminate the insurgents? When, during the French Revolution, the French people overthrew kings and aristocrats, did not all the feudal lords and rulers of Europe take sympathetic action to restore the French monarchy, even although doing it involved throwing all industrial life in Europe into chaos and drenching a Continent with blood?
>
> Historically, the sympathetic strike can find ample justification. But, and this point must be emphasised, it was not mere cool reasoning that gave it birth in Dublin. In this city it was born out of our desperate necessity. Seeing all classes

of semi-skilled labour in Dublin so wretchedly under-paid and so atrociously sweated, the Irish Transport and General Workers' Union taught them to stand together and help one another, and out of this advice the more perfect weapon has grown ...'

From 'Labour in Dublin' by James Connolly, *The Irish Review*, October 1913.

Joe felt he could support every word that Connolly said; he admired and respected him for his honesty, for the way he listened to others and for his intellectual freedom. Sadly, when Thomas Dillon, who was keen on the Labour movement, wanted to join it, Connolly said, 'We are not yet prepared to take people with education', although by then he had educated himself to a very high degree.

17 Marlborough Road

Donnybrook

Oct 16th 1913

To our right trusty and wellbeloved cousin Aidanus Maccabeus Cavananensis.

My dear Aidan

Any news from your part of the world? When are you coming to Dublin? There is only one piece of news from hereabouts and I am sure you know that already – about Charley O'Carroll coming home. I have been working myself blue as one of the hon. Secretaries of the Dublin Industrial Peace Committee and am now laid up with a cold. I have also had a few collisions with various vehicles etc. on the motorbike and got toppled over two or three times but came off very well on the whole. The bike is still going strong.

Salute ernan dorus and let us know when we shall again have the happiness of beholding you.

Your affectionate cousin,

Joe Plunkett

Joe's motorbike was frequently borrowed by friends, who were not necessarily good at managing it, and they often left the belt loose. Joe took the motorbike out after it had been borrowed and the bike's belt caught when he was running with it to start it, flinging him on the ground. He got synovitis – inflammation of the joint – in both knees, which were also badly cut, and had to stay six weeks in bed. Dr Crofton took the chance to try an injection of tuberculin, an antitoxin, but Joe's temperature went up to 104 degrees for eight or ten hours and Geraldine couldn't find Dr Crofton. She says, 'Joe was flattened after this.'

17 March

Oct 29 1913

My Dear Aidan,

Can (and will) you and your brother come in on Friday evening, Halloweve, to 26 Upper Fitzwilliam St to help us to burn nuts? (or do you consider that too personal?) about 8 oclock. The O Carrolls are coming as well. Court dress not compulsory. SPQR

You affect. Cousin (forcibly removed)

Joseph O Pluingcead

PS of course if you are free tomorrow Thursday evening come out to here 17 Mar without prejudice as usual JMP

YOUR SONGS

If I have you then I have everything

In One, and that One nothing of them all

Nor all compounded, and within the wall

Beneath the tower I wait to hear you sing:…

…You come rejoicing all the wilderness,

Filling with praise the land to joy unknown,

Fresh from that garden whose perfumes have blown

Down through the valley of the cypresses—

O heart, you know not your own loveliness,

Nor these your songs, for they are yours alone.

JMP 30ᵗʰ October 1913

This poem, one of the many probably addressed to Columba, seems to have some importance for him above most of the others because it appears in rough versions in a number of places. His poetry had acquired a flavour of death in those months, death of love, death of the heart, making a new emphasis for an old theme:

WHITE FEATHER

I've watched with Death a dreadful year

Nor flinched until you plucked apart—

A feather from the wings of Fear—

Your innocence has stabbed my heart....

9th September 1913

Moriturus Te Salutat

(He who is about to die salutes you)

...And yet I love you that you say

You will not love me—truth is hard,

'Twere so much easier to give way

And stay the death-stroke, my reward—

Courage, brave heart! 'tis Love you slay.

16th September 1913

November's *Irish Review* carried an article by Tom Kettle entitled 'The Agony of Dublin', which set out his and the Peace Committee's attitude, but while it begins in moderation to discuss both sides his tolerance for the employers becomes less as the article progresses:

> ... Certain citizens of Dublin ... met together and formed the Peace Committee. They were told that the time was not ripe. If they put their noses in – to employ a historic phrase – the noses would be chopped off. At any rate, who were they but a set of academic busybodies? When I myself, on one occasion, mildly suggested that there was such a thing as public opinion, the combatant to whom I made the suggestion merely said: 'Damn public opinion!'
>
> The time is always ripe for peace. It was ripe when the tramway-men were locked out, and riper still when the first strike was proclaimed...
>
> The Peace Committee asked for a truce, on terms to be fixed by a conference, which would then proceed to formulate a scheme of final settlement. We never touched upon the merits of the dispute. So far from meddling with business details, we said deliberately that the adjustment of

these must lie with the representatives of the two parties to the dispute. This programme was greeted in some quarters with ill-concealed hostility and unconcealed derision...

... The workers have talked wildly, and acted calmly; the employers have talked calmly, and acted wildly. The workers have, during the dispute, expressed their willingness to enter into conference on the basis of the Askwith Report, or on that of the Peace Committee programme, or on that of the Lord Mayor's memorandum. The employers broke off the Shelbourne Conference, and have declined to take part in any since proposed.

Countess Plunkett cancelled her generous allowance to Joe and Geraldine after the row about the Lockout at dinner in Fitzwilliam Street and insisted on Mary, their domestic help, bringing her the household bills to pay. Geraldine could no longer look for special food for Joe to try to keep him nourished but she had an income as a laboratory demonstrator and was giving chemistry grinds so she could create a certain amount of independence and comfort for them but, of course, he was still frequently ill:

Very occasionally I would find when I came home that Joe was looking upset and annoyed which always set back his health. It was caused each time by Ma who had dropped in for literally a few minutes. I did not ask him what she had said, he would not have told me, but I was pretty sure she had been complaining about how much it cost to keep him alive and saying that she could not afford it.

Geraldine Plunkett Dillon

The employers succeeded in their plan to starve the workers back to work, and they gradually returned as desperate necessity forced them. By the end of January 1914 most of them were back, the last (in March) being the women workers in Jacob's biscuit factory. The workers appeared to lose the fight, but a year later all the tram men belonged to the union, and trade unionism had to be accepted.

On 19 November the Irish Citizen Army was founded for the workers to protect themselves from the kind of police violence they had experienced during the Lockout. The only weapons they had to protect themselves were short white staves, but the employers, who allowed their own protectors to carry and use guns were terrified, Gerry Plunkett says 'this was the forerunner of revolution, of the workers' republic...' At the age of twenty-five Joe Plunkett had gained first-hand experience of public and private conduct on the Dublin Industrial Peace Committee. Although the Committee was not able to do very much, it would have been worse without it; there would have been an impression that no 'respectable' person sympathised with the workers in their appalling hardship but more and more were shocked when the workers' pay and conditions were published in the newspapers. For some it was a radical turning point, among them Patrick Pearse, Thomas MacDonagh and Joseph Plunkett

CHAPTER 10

• • • • • •

November 1913–July 1914
A Long-Awaited Force

It was on his twenty-sixth birthday, 21 November 1913, that Joseph Plunkett saw this newspaper announcement:

> A public meeting for the purpose of establishing a corps of Irish Volunteers will be held in the large Concert Hall of the Rotunda on Sunday 25th at 8 p.m. Eoin MacNeill, B.A., will preside.

Another notice appeared that Saturday saying that the venue had been changed to the Rotunda Roller-Skating Rink, and that a manifesto from the Provisional Committee would be read.

Plunkett, like thousands of others, was immediately drawn to the idea of a voluntary army, a response to the country's sense of vulnerability with an approaching war and talk of the Ulster Volunteers 'marching to Cork' and setting up a provisional government for four counties of Ulster when Home Rule became law. Edward Carson had said to his Ulster Volunteer supporters:

> Drilling is illegal. The Volunteers are illegal and the govern-
> ment know they are illegal and the government dare not
> interfere with them. Don't be afraid of illegalities.

and Professor Eoin MacNeill had written as a response to
the Government's tolerance of Carson's activities:

> … the British Army cannot now be used to prevent the
> enrolment, drilling, and reviewing of Volunteers in Ireland.
> There is nothing to prevent the other twenty-eight counties
> from calling into existence citizen forces to hold Ireland 'for
> the Empire.'

Patrick Pearse, in even stronger terms:

> For if there is one thing that has become plainer than
> another it is that when the seven men met in O'Connell
> Street to found the Gaelic League, they were commencing
> … not a revolt, but a revolution.

The previous year Roger Casement had suggested the
raising of a volunteer force to defend Ireland's neutrality if
war broke out. Now the time had arrived.

Plunkett, painfully aware of his physical limitations, asked
Geraldine whether he would be any use to the Volunteers
and she encouraged him to go to the Rotunda meeting. He
called on Professor MacNeill, at his Herbert Park house very
close by; he had not known MacNeill before this except by
reputation, but he had read his article, 'The North Began', in
An Claidheamh Soluis and MacNeill was kind and encouraging and told Plunkett he should come to the meeting. Plun-

kett did not expect to have a real part to play in all this, but he underestimated his public profile as a poet, editor and activist for peace in the Lockout and strike which was still in progress. He also knew several of the organisers, Patrick Pearse, Thomas MacDonagh and Seosamh O Cathmhaoil (Joseph Campbell) and most of the others were known to him and he to them in some way, Seán MacDiarmada, Éamonn Ceannt, The O'Rahilly, Bulmer Hobson and Piaras Beaslaí, so when he arrived at the meeting that Sunday night he was invited on to the platform with the Provisional Committee.

The meeting adopted the project of a Volunteer Organisation as set out in the organisers' Manifesto and the enrolment of Volunteers began there. The crowd not only filled the Rink, but two overflow meetings were held in the Concert Room and in the grounds with several thousand out on the street who could not get in at all. A crowd of the Dublin strikers burst into the packed hall to declare their sympathy. There were speeches by Eoin MacNeill and Patrick Pearse, which were enthusiastically received. Both stressed that the Volunteers were for the defence of the rights and liberties of all the Irish people and that there was no intention of any aggression towards the Ulster Volunteers, rather, it was hoped there would be a connection between the two organisations. A far more guarded speech by Michael Davitt followed, but when Laurence Kettle stood up to read the Manifesto he was drowned out by Larkin followers because of a labour dispute in his father's business. The noise was eventually reduced by Captain White, the chief organiser of the Citizen Army, getting up to speak, commanding great respect. Over three thousand joined on that day and immediately afterwards the enrolled men were divided into district corps and, within days, drilling was begun in various places throughout the city. The three thousand became ten thousand by Christmas.

Plunkett came back from the meeting full of enthusiasm and delighted by his selection to the committee and next day set up the Volunteer *Manifesto* to print in the *Irish Review*. It was now that he changed the sub-heading on the cover from 'Irish Literature, Art & Science' to 'Irish Politics, Literature and Art'. In fact in this edition the *Review* articles still had a broad range even with the political emphasis: 'The New Land Bill and Compulsory Purchase' by Justin Phillips; 'The Revolt of the Middle Class', by J. Justin Dempsey; 'The Problem', by An Ulster Imperialist; 'The Re-Discovery of the Celts' by Eoin MacNeill; 'Wagner's *Parsifal,* or the Cult of Liturgical Æstheticism' by Edward Martyn; Plunkett's poem: 'The Vigil of Love' and the continuation of Eleanor Farjeon's story and Patrick Pearse's '*Dánta Gríosuighde Gaedheal'*. The picture was 'Portrait Study', by Gabriel Gifford. With all this there appeared the Volunteers' *Manifesto* showing the organisation as non-sectarian, voluntary, nationalist and democratic, the Company and Half-Company officers being elected by the men:

The object proposed for the Irish Volunteers is to secure and maintain the rights and liberties common to all the people of Ireland ... Their duties will be defensive and protective, and they will not contemplate either aggression or domination ... Their ranks are open to all able-bodied Irishmen without distinction of creed, politics, or social grade. Means will be found whereby Irishmen unable to serve as ordinary Volunteers will be enabled to aid the Volunteer forces in various capacities. ... The Volunteers, once they have been enrolled, will form a prominent element in the National life under a National Government. ... In the name of National Unity, of National dignity, of National and individual Liberty ...

This first Provisional Committee of thirty included United Irish League/Irish Parliamentary Party (IPP), Ancient Order of Hibernians, twelve members of the Irish Republican Brotherhood (IRB) and among those not affiliated to any organisation were Patrick Pearse, Thomas MacDonagh and Joseph Plunkett, but all three of these later became members of the IRB. The biggest group, the IRB, being a secret organisation, did not declare themselves but, apparently acting as individuals, hoped that in time the Volunteers would become the means of separating Ireland from government by the British, and, prominent in the IRB but staying in the background, 'rubbing his hands with glee' according to Piaras Beaslaí, was Thomas J. Clarke (Tom) the Old

Fenian, watching, managing and waiting.

Six days after the Rotunda meeting, on Monday 1 December, the first assemblies of Irish Volunteers took place and the drilling started. It was taken for granted at the beginning that drilling on a British Army plan was the first essential and this had its uses, but the ex-British Army drill-sergeants nearly drilled the Volunteers into the ground. Joe was one of the few who did not agree with this policy, believing that voluntary discipline was the real foundation for the kind of fighting he expected to happen. The drill-sergeants were helped by some of those who had been in the officers' training corps in English schools and were teaching the Volunteers to march using English music-hall songs. To counteract this Thomas MacDonagh wrote the words for a marching song and O'Brien Butler offered to set it to music, but his tune didn't fit the words and they argued about it for an afternoon in 17 Marlborough Road. In the end they gave up on it, but Plunkett published the words in the *Review* – all eight verses, a potted Irish history, and six-line chorus with lines like these:

Our fathers who foresaw the noon

Unfurled this flag before the dawn:

Its fringes caught the light, but soon

Back to the darkness it was drawn.

The dawn is come, the night is o'er:

With joy we face the future years;

And now in Freedom's cause once more

Arise the Irish Volunteers

After Plunkett began to publish Volunteer matters in the *Review* its principal supporters, mostly civil servants, could no longer afford to be seen with it and the circulation, which had only been, at most, around a thousand, severely decreased.

The Irish Volunteers were allowed to organise, hold public meetings, drill men and have route marches because these things had all been allowed to the Ulster Volunteers, but on 4 December, nine days after the Rotunda meeting, a ban on the importation of arms and ammunition to Ireland was signed into law by the English King, George V. Plunkett, like others on the Committee, expected that there would be more bans, proclamations and arrests from this time on, but he was:

> ... exhilarated at finding that his philosophic speculation on the nature and necessity of spiritual and political freedom was leading to a practical conclusion.

Geraldine Plunkett Dillon

The printer, Mr Latchford, used to set up poems on the linotype for Plunkett and Plunkett printed them, using handmade paper, on the hand press he had bought from MacDonagh and used to print Christmas cards, some designed by his sister, Philomena, and to experiment with printing nonsense rhymes. He made about fifteen copies of his book of poems, *Sonnets to Columba*, this way, intending most of them to be published in his next collection. The eight sonnets, 'Invocation', 'Daybreak', '*Virga Florebit*', '*Flos Virgae*', '*Eleusis Nova*', '*La Pucelle*', '*Occulta*', 'The Vigil of Love' and 'Your Songs' all appeared (although titles in English were substituted for the Latin) with other poems in the volume of his poetry published after his death in 1916.

Three poems, finished within eight weeks of each other, in 1914 vividly illuminate Plunkett's sense of himself, unrequited love, illness, choices and his likely fate. They are full of the contradictions he loved – light and dark, heaven and hell, finite and infinite and are contradictions in themselves. He was very clear about what he was doing and what he hoped would be the end of it, even though the end would almost certainly be death but he had already looked at death many times. Geraldine's accounts of him from this time on are peppered with 'Joe was ill again...', but she also records that he went to every Volunteer meeting he could, even when he was ill. Politics and revolution were exciting the young man in him, love and death were making him old.

WHEN I AM DEAD

When I am dead let not your murderous tears

Deface with their slow dropping my sad tomb

Lest your grey head grow greyer for my doom

And fill its echoing corridors with fears:

Your heart that my stone monument appears

While yet I live—O give it not to gloom

When I am dead, but let some joy illume

The ultimate Victory that stings and sears.

Already I can hear the stealthy tread

Of sorrow breaking through the hush of day;

I have no hope you will avert my dread,

Too well I know, that soon am mixed with clay,

They mourn the body who the spirit slay

And those that stab the living weep the dead.

JMP   22ⁿᵈ December 1913

THE LIONS

Her hair's the canopy of heaven,

Her eyes the pools of healing are,

Her words wild prophecies whose seven

Thunders resound from star to star.

Her hands and feet are jewels fine

Wrought for the edifice of all grace,

Her breath inebriates like wine—

The blinding beauty of her face

Is lovelier than the primal light

And holds her lover's pride apart

To tame the lions of the night

That range the wilderness of his heart.

JMP 31ˢᵗ January 1914

THE DARK WAY

Rougher than Death the road I choose

Yet shall my feet not walk astray,

Though dark, my way I shall not lose

For this way is the darkest way.

Set but a limit to the loss

And something shall at last abide

The blood-stained beams that form the cross

The thorns that crown the crucified;

But who shall lose all things in one,

Shut out from heaven and the pit

Shall lose the darkness and the sun

The finite and the infinite;

And who shall see in one small flower

The chariots and the thrones of might

Shall be in peril from that hour

Of blindness and the endless night;

And who shall hear in one short name

Apocalyptic thunders seven

His heart shall flicker like a flame

'Twixt hell's gates and the gates of heaven.

For I have seen your body's grace,

The miracle of the flowering rod,

And in the beauty of your face

The glory of the face of God,

And I have heard the thunderous roll

Clamour from heights of prophecy

Your splendid name, and from my soul

Up rose the clouds of minstrelsy.

Now I have chosen in the dark

The desolate way to walk alone

Yet strive to keep alive one spark

Of your known grace and grace unknown.

And when I leave you lest my love

Should seal your spirit's ark with clay,

Spread your bright wings, O shining dove,—

But my way is the darkest way.

JMP 12th February 1914

Plunkett's ability to manage his mother for large projects, despite her reluctance to provide him with the necessities of life and health, was useful again when the Provisional Committee needed a venue for its second meeting, which was held in the Hardwicke Hall before they rented offices in No. 206 Brunswick Street and then more of her properties, Sandymount Castle and Larkfield in Kimmage were used for drilling and training. She was pleased to let the Volunteers have anything she could give them, but it seems she didn't really know what it was all about. She did think that Joe was responsible for starting the Volunteers. On 21 January the first afternoon drill was held on the Plunketts' ground at Larkfield in Kimmage where the 4th Battallion had their headquarters while the 1st Batallion headquarters was in St Enda's; the 2nd and 3rd still had to hire places to drill.

The following story is best left to Gerry Plunkett to tell:

> On a night at the beginning of February, Joe told me that a Mr Nolan would be coming to see him and that I (not Mary) was to answer the door and bring him straight in without asking his business. He would be carrying a bag and I was to tell him to come right in with it. The man in question arrived on an outside car at our house in Marlborough Road. He had two old-fashioned Gladstone bags with him and he told the jarvey that he preferred to carry them himself as they contained valuable glass. He said his name was Nolan and asked for Joe. He came in, shut the door and put the bags down very carefully. 'Mr Nolan' was Liam [Mellows] (this was the first time I had met him) and there was a half-a-hundredweight of gelignite in one bag and 4,000 rounds of .303 ammunition in the other. Someone had stolen the gelignite from the Arklow explosives factory and the ammunition had been bought from English soldiers in the Curragh. It was presumed by everyone that the arms from the Curragh store had been given to the Ulster Volunteers by the English officers, but Liam had managed to get some of it. From this time on it was always possible to buy arms and ammunition in small quantities from English soldiers. We kept the ammunition in the house until a few

weeks later when Eamon de Valera, who lived round the corner in Morehampton Terrace, brought a message that Liam thought his journey (from the Curragh) had been traced. Joe was ill so de Valera and my brother Jack moved the ammunition to a safer place on the backs of bicycles. I helped to put the gelignite in a shed at the back of the house where Joe kept his motorbike. The gelignite was not strong enough to be of any use and was easy to get so it stayed there ... [GPD]

Liam Mellows was a redoubtable worker for socialism, which he took up on meeting Connolly, and for republican-ism. He was a member of Fianna Éireann, the Irish Repub-lican Brotherhood and the Volunteers and was jailed and deported many times.

Jack Plunkett who was then at school in Clongowes, where he had joined the Volunteers, said 'something must be done' was a phrase you would hear all the time. When the first issue of the *Irish Volunteer* was published that February with articles by Roger Casement, Patrick Pearse, Tom Kettle and Liam Mellowes, Joseph Plunkett was also a contributor and in sub-sequent editions he wrote both signed and unsigned articles. He was also still producing the *Irish Review* and February, March and April were dominated by three articles under the general title of 'From "Coffin Ship" to "Atlantic Grey-hound"' by Roger Casement writing as 'An Irish American'. The 'Atlantic Greyhounds' were the great passenger liners of the Cunard Line whose contract to serve Queenstown (Cobh) was now being broken and British Government and industry were ensuring that a lucrative business would be removed from Ireland:

> It would be hard to find a public obligation of Great Britain with other peoples that has been scrupulously kept whenever it was found to hurt British interests to keep it ... When the Hamburg-America Line wanted to step into the gap it was prevented from doing so.

Casement sent a covering note with the article for the March issue:

> Malahide 18 February 1914
>
> Dear Mr Plunkett,
>
> The Coffins etc. were found lying at the station this morning. They said they knew 'I was away'!
>
> I send you part two of 'Coffin Ship' – not to my liking ...
>
> ... there is a possibility of the *Cunard* being forced back and also (I hope) the shadow of a possibility of the German line being forced in. In the latter event I would annul all abuse of the Anglo Saxons and send you a different article.
>
> Yours truly,
>
> R. Casement

Neither his hopes nor his fears were realised and all three articles duly appeared. Plunkett gave them pride of place in the *Review*. They were also the cementing of a friendship and mutual respect between the two men.

Plunkett was now pushing the *Review* more towards confronting political and economic issues: 'The Connemara Islands' by Alice Stopford Green, Harold Barbour, Douglas Hyde and Alec Wilson concerned a report on the appalling problems of disease, poverty and overcrowding in Connemara, which had been handed in to the Congested Districts Board and not even acknowledged, still less acted upon; 'Ensilage and the Production of Milk and Beef During the Winter Months' was by Digby Hussey De Burgh, 'A Word for the Police', a poetic satire on police actions in the Lockout by Harry Reginald King and in every issue, under 'Economics' Justin Phillips on 'Taxation of Land Values – the Irish standpoint', 'Afforestation', 'The Policy of The Department (of Agriculture)' and 'The Post Office Savings Bank'. In Arts and Literature, 'Within the Temple' by Thomas MacDonagh, 'Obscurity and Poetry' by Joseph Plunkett, and 'A New Poet' by Lily Fogarty, a celebration of Francis Ledwidge Poems by James Stephens, Thomas MacDonagh and Joseph Plunkett; 'The Tree of the Field Is Man's Life' by M.A. Rathkyle (Marianne Young), 'George Henry Moore' by Maurice Moore, 'The Poetry of Susan L. Mitchell' by Winifred M. Letts. Other contributors were Patrick Pearse, Liam De Róiste, Peter McBrien; Hannah Berman, Maurice Moore, and Jean Malye, a French journalist and editor and diplomat in Washington connected to Irish affairs. Paintings were by Estella Solomons, Jack Morrow and Sarah Purser. Two articles were to have interesting consequences later: 'The Recent Performance of Ibsen's Rosmersholm' by Edward Martyn and 'Plea for the Revival of the Irish Literary Theatre' by Edward Martyn.

Below is one of three poems which Plunkett sent in February to *The Women's Magazine*, New York, at the request of its Assistant Editor, Leonarda Coss.

ARAB SONG

The dates are heavy on the palms,

The fountain bubbles up in song,

The nights are blue and gold and long,

Cool winds flood out their burning calms.

Come out, and swaying gently, sing

Beneath the far green waving boughs,

Come out and make the heavens your house,

Your heart my heaven, your soul my Spring.

17 Bothar Marl

An Domhnach Broc

4th IV 1914

My Dear Aidan

This is to hope that you are alive and well and to tell you that I am alive. Today is the thirteenth day that I have been in bed but I am going to be let up for a little while this afternoon. It has been (physiologically) bronchitis etc. I suppose you have not heard from any of them. My line of conduct has been rigidly pursued for eight weeks and will therefore probably continue. I am sorry for the *Irish Review* which only just wriggled out in March and was a fortnight late and of which the April appearance is quite problematic. I must get rid of it or let it die. I have even to stick in those verses of mine because they were four pages short and I had to write reviews for the other two in the small hours of the morning. Charley came over to see me while I was in bed. The rest I have not heard of. How are you and what have you been doing? Golf I suppose and such. I've been reading of course, magazines and weeklies, cheap novels and philosophers Plato and Plotinus, Henry James and Owen Wister, St Teresa and Hilaire Belloc and Louis Tracy Philip Openheim and Wordsworth and Francis Thompson and *London Opinion*.

Let us have a line if you're not too busy.

Yours what's left, if any,

Ó Pluingcéad

Geraldine, as well as looking after Joe was now also his messenger on Volunteer business; he could not use letters or telephone as it would not be safe and he was usually too ill to deliver the messages himself. She was his confidante – he used to talk through what had happened at each meeting when he got home and having someone to talk to helped him to think and, according to Gerry, 'thought was the principal and sometimes the only weapon we had'. There was also a need for secrecy, or at least discretion, so when Gerry put her name down to join Cumann na mBan when it was started in April 1914, Joe told her, because of her position as his *aide-de-camp*, not to go ahead with it. She already knew many of the women in the Cumann, but it was hard on her to be deprived of their camaraderie and also of her hard-earned visible place in history, but this could be said of very many people of the time and she was very proud of the position she did have.

In May, Redmond claimed that he and the Irish Parliamentary Party (IPP) had a right to representation on the Volunteer Committee and proposed to send twenty-five of his own nominees to the committee. This, along with the IPP members already on the committee, would give Redmond control. It was presumed that he had decided that the Volunteer Organisation was a force to be reckoned with as he threatened to dismember the Organisation if his claim was not accepted. Plunkett felt that Redmond was as afraid of an Irish army as if he had been an Englishman in the English Government 'The only explanation,' Plunkett said, 'of Mr Redmond is that he means what he says.'

At the Volunteers' Committee meeting on 16 June Plunkett voted with the majority in favour of the nominees, because he thought that if there were resistance to Redmond at this stage, nothing would survive, but he was very worried about it. A minority group from the Committee disagreed with the decision but after a meeting in Wynn's Hotel on the following day they issued a statement giving their viewpoint but saying that they would continue on the Committee. New schemes were held up until the nominees joined them and Plunkett was determined to keep an open mind and to give them every chance. Many nationalists thought the Irish Party's intention was to control the Volunteers in order to use them for Ireland since war was imminent and Ireland was particularly vulnerable. It was possible that the Irish Party would arrange to have the ban on arms importation lifted and the Volunteers could procure guns to defend Ireland's liberty when the army was out of the country.

Plunkett didn't tell his sister, Geraldine, that he had joined the IRB but, being his messenger and agent she began to work it out. Different kinds of people came to the house and meetings would be described as 'Volunteer business', but by degrees he began to refer to 'the organisation', which she realised was a controlling force in the Volunteers. From here on he used to say 'we have agreed' and of course in time it was quite obvious.

MacDonagh and Plunkett had continued with their quest to find a way to start a theatre company which would perform modern international plays, in particular those of Chekhov, Ibsen and Strindberg in the style of Stanislavsky and the Moscow Arts Theatre. MacDonagh's suggestion was that they would find a patron with money and, after Edward Martyn had written the two pieces for the *Irish Review* with ideas very similar to theirs, MacDonagh approached him. MacDonagh told Plunkett he had found a patron who was passionate about Ibsen and the Russian dramatists and when the three of them met things moved along quickly. In due course, a partnership was arranged between them to form a company and the agreement, signed on 30 June 1914 was for the production of plays in English, Irish or by Irish authors and for plays translated from foreign languages. The company was called The Irish Theatre and was to begin on 1 July 1914. Plunkett provided his mother's hall, the Hardwicke Street Theatre at a peppercorn rent with its furniture and fittings, and paid the caretaker; Edward Martyn paid for lighting, management expenses, stationary, stamps, advertisements, theatre programmes, printing and production expenses; MacDonagh, as managing partner, was responsible for the rehearsal and production of plays and supplying a company of actors and actresses. All monies received from any source whatever were to go straight into Edward Martyn's bank within a week. Fifty performances, five per month for ten months from September 1914 to June 1915, were agreed on and at least one half of the plays were to be written by Edward Martyn.

That month's *Irish Review* included a painting by Dermod O'Brien; 'Manifesto of the Irish Volunteers' by Eoin Mac-Neill; 'An Ideal in Education' by Patrick Pearse; 'Language and Literature in Ireland' by Thomas MacDonagh; 'The Walls of Athens, A Comedy in Allegory' by Eimar O'Duffy and Criticism included Padraic Colum on Lord Dunsany's Plays.

One of the poems was by Plunkett's sister, Geraldine:

JUNE

I fill my heart with store of memories

Lest I should ever leave these loved shores,

Of lime trees humming with slow drone of bees

And honey dripping sweet from sycamores

Of how a fir tree set upon a hill

Lifts up its seven branches to the stars,

Of the grey summer heats when all is still

And even grasshoppers cease their little wars.

Of how a chestnut drops its great green sleeve

Down to the grass that nestles in the sod,

Of how a blackbird in a bush at eve

Sings to me suddenly the praise of God.

Geraldine Plunkett, June 1914

When John Redmond's nominees turned up at the July
meeting of the Volunteer Provisional Committee there was
disappointment all round. Only twenty-one of the twenty-
five arrived; some who were known as bitter opponents of
the Volunteers had accepted the nomination, one priest had
not even known he was nominated until then and said that
he was not going to come again, most of them thought they
were only there to protect the interests of the Irish Party.
Joe told Gerry that from the beginning it was quite plain
that the nominees, except for John Redmond's brother,
Major William Redmond, were only obstructionist and not
interested in the Volunteers. Plunkett was convinced they
intended to destroy the Volunteers. The sub-committees had
to be reorganised and Plunkett was now on the Arms sub-
committee which was chaired by Major Redmond. Unlike
other committees there was no 'dirty work' on that committee and Major Redmond was one of the very few nominees
who treated the original committee members as honest men

according to Plunkett, and Bulmer Hobson concurred:

> William Redmond was a sincere congenial man who was
> not rigidly bound to his brother's policy...

Another co-opted member who did not behave like a
mere partisan was James Creed Meredith. Despite the great
benefit Plunkett was getting from all this he found it terribly
debilitating and depressing and was often ill, coming back
from meetings after midnight, saying he wouldn't go again
but he always did. He was disgusted at the conduct and ethics
of Irish Party men who were supposed to be leaders, but the
long discussions and arguments during this period were very
useful to him, as he began to see his own possibilities and the
ways he could be useful to Ireland:

> He told me after one meeting that John D. Nugent, a Red-
> mond nominee, tried to provoke a row by accusing Pearse
> of embezzling the funds, a well-known way to annoy men
> into resigning from an organisation, and Pearse slapped the
> man's face. As he said afterwards to Joe, it was the only argu-
> ment Nugent understood. Joe was delighted and said that
> he had wanted all the time to do it himself. The one priest
> who continued to attend the meetings drew a gun and
> threatened Pearse with it. Joe began to feel he knew more
> about political strategy, tactics, international politics and the
> conduct of business than the Party people and he had a
> better idea of how to treat the ordinary Irishman and the
> growing number of educated and intellectual young people

whom the Irish Party either ignored or tried to suppress.

Geraldine Plunkett Dillon

Joe Plunkett to Aidan McCabe:

17 Marl Monday July 20 1914

Moses, you old scoundrel,

Are you blooming? Blown away? I can't very easily wring your neck at this distance so consider it done. Now down to business. I would like various particulars from you. I leave the choice to your discretion (the better part of valour) so here's a chance for you to create a record. I saw your old exam in the paper. Greek to me so I suppose condolences is what you require. Please take one. Crofton is trying Tuberculin on me again but his own this time. It never succeeded before – quite the reverse – but now it looks as if it might. It hurts like the very deuce. Something to measure things by. (the hurt – not the deuce)

As to her and me, I have pleasure in life. It is to embrace the postman. And between the lucky days to let my pen wriggle over reams and post a slab now and then. Let me know then is she well? Is she well? And is she? Does she hate the place? Do I bother her? Damn – I can't send her my love but she has it all.

Good luck to you –

Joe

CHAPTER 11

• • • • • •

July to December 1914
Words, Actions And War

Plunkett was feeling the need for fresh country air, but didn't want to leave Dublin because he thought he should attend all the Volunteers' Committee meetings, so he and Gerry applied to their mother for permission to stay in one of the cottages in Larkfield in Kimmage, which was still very much countryside at the time, for a month or two and she agreed. With Mary, the housekeeper, they moved into the vacant cottage, which, Gerry says, was not comfortable and had no garden, but her mother had put bathrooms in each cottage, a very unusual luxury in houses meant for lower-paid workers. At first Gerry was going in to the university at Earlsfort Terrace every day on research work, but, apart from attending meetings Joe was in the cottage most of the time. When they had been there a while he had a haemorrhage and was very ill. This meant that he also needed a night nurse and that they had to stay on in the cottage until he was fit to move. He was still confined to the cottage when the guns were run into Howth.

Although the membership of the Irish Volunteers was estimated at between 100,000 and 150,000, there was very little money and even fewer arms. Since what they were supposed to be organising was a National Army, Gerry asked Joe what was going to be done about arms for the Volunteers but he just chuckled and said it had been taken care of. They were both in Larkfield on Sunday 26 July, the day of the Howth gunrunning. Joe was in a fever of excitement, waiting all day for news until finally Theo McWeeney arrived having run all the way from the city centre to Kimmage. In O'Connell Street he had heard shots fired on Bachelors' Walk, he heard women wailing on O'Connell Bridge and he had seen dead men. He heard people saying that the Volunteers had been fired on and the rifles captured by the military. Joe was bitterly disappointed and upset, but too ill to leave the house to check the story. Some hours later MacDonagh arrived with the true account.

The *Asgard* had sailed into Howth with nine hundred rifles and 29,000 rounds of ammunition, thanks to subscriptions by Alice Stopford Green, Roger Casement, Erskine Childers, Mary Spring Rice and Captain Berkeley. Darrell Figgis had bought the guns in Antwerp and Erskine and Molly Childers sailed them into Howth where IRB, Volunteers and Fianna members took the guns and ammunition off in less than half an hour, most being taken away in taxis immediately. The remaining rifles, without ammunition, were carried by the Volunteers marching into Dublin. It would have been embarrassing for the British Government if they had arrested the Irish Volunteers or taken the guns when they had turned a blind eye to the Ulster Volunteers' Larne gun-running in April, or Carson's 'lunch' with the Kaiser. However the Assistant Police Commissioner Harrell, acting without orders, called out police and military to stop them. The police refused to do anything and, after some hassle and some attacks on the Volunteers by the soldiers, MacDonagh negotiated with Harrell, while Volunteers with rifles quietly slid away in the background. The soldiers of the King's Own Scottish Borderers marched back into town, angry and frustrated at the whole thing. Word had spread fast; from the time they left Howth the Volunteers had been cheered all along the route and the crowds now followed the military into town. Rumour had spread that the soldiers had attacked and killed Volunteers and the crowd jeered and threw stones and banana peels at them. At Bachelors' Walk the Scottish Borderers turned on the crowd without warning, charged with fixed bayonets and fired, killing two men and a woman, James Brennan, Patrick Quinn and Mrs Duffy, and wounding more than thirty people. There were no Volunteers present for any of this.

Next day MacDonagh and Plunkett set out in a taxi driven by a Volunteer to collect the rifles from places where the Volunteers had hidden them all over the city. They were frequently followed by G-men (detectives from G Division of the Dublin Metropolitan Police (DMP)) and spies and at one point when they brought a carload of rifles to Larkfield, they had to take it away again and leave it in the Plunketts' house in Fitzwilliam Street overnight because they could not shake off one of these watchers. The next day the guns were removed, but it must have a strange, sharp awakening for members of the Fitzwilliam Street household.

MacDonagh to Joseph Plunkett:

> 28 VII 1914
>
> 29 Oakley Rd
>
> Sorry I missed you this morning, I simply slept and slept and slept. Hope to see you tomorrow. I find that nearly all the men of my company all but one as far as I have yet heard, have lost their rifles through standing fast and putting them in the motors that came. If you can keep some of those you have for my men they will be the right sort and will satisfy Holmes and the others...
>
> ...Good luck. Will you be at funeral at 5 tomorrow?
>
> Beresford Place at 5pm Company C, 2nd Battallion.
>
> MacD

There was a public funeral for the victims of shootings on Bachelors' Walk, a huge, political funeral with crowds lining the route, Volunteers in formation behind the coffins, and a volley of shots over the graves. Soldiers were confined to barracks. Songs and slogans appeared overnight. The Irish all over the world telegraphed their sympathy and indignation to John Redmond and the Irish Party, who passed a resolution calling for the ban on the importation of arms to be revoked. On 1 August, one week after the Howth gunrunning, six hundred rifles and 20,000 rounds of ammunition were landed, at Kilcoole, County Wicklow, from the *Chotah*, Sir Thomas Myles' yacht with James Creed Meredith on board after they had been transferred from Conor O'Brien's yacht off the Welsh coast. Plunkett asked MacDonagh to write his account of the gunrunning for publication in the *Irish Review* and it appeared as a supplement to the July/August edition.

From Geraldine Plunkett Dillon:

> After the gunrunning very few of the nominees took the trouble to attend meetings and Joe said it made him sick. Many long hours in our house that summer were taken up in going over the rights and wrongs and internal difficulties of the Volunteer Committee. The conclusion reached in all discussions was that Ireland's honour had to be redeemed. Ireland's spiritual and material needs required strong action and 'England's difficulty was Ireland's opportunity'. There had been no armed protest against British rule since the Fenians and the approaching war with Germany could be the opportunity.

By now the *Review* was drowning financially, spies, pretending to be poets, were calling to 17 Marlborough Road and to Larkfield. Joe, putting what energy he had into Volunteers' business, was more frequently ill and exhausted. He knew, since he was making the magazine more and more political, that it was only a matter of time before it was censored, banned or seized since that was becoming normal British Government practice. MacDonagh was always equally involved and enthusiastic – in fact he had been creating the magazine longer than Joe had, but he also had his own pressing considerations, his much-loved wife, Muriel and baby, Donagh, his university teaching and the Volunteers. This double issue was to be the second-last *Review*.

The Irish Review July/August 1914:

> Picture: From a Painting by Casimir Dunin Markievicz; Supplement: 'Clontarf 1914' (an account of the Howth gunrunning) by Thomas MacDonagh; 'Manifesto of the Irish Volunteers'; 'Some Thoughts on the Industrial Question' by Harry Reginald King; 'The Doctor', a poem by Winifred M. Letts; 'The Post Office Savings Bank: A Bonus Scheme' by Justin Phillips; 'Storm-Struck' by Daniel Corkery; '*An Coill* / The Wood' by P. H. Pearse; 'The Ideal of the State in Irish Education' by Proinnsias Airmeas; Stories: 'Youth at the Cross-Roads' by R. B. Anderson and 'The Devout Murderer' by Jane G. Mitchell; '*Le* Home Rule *et la France*' by Jean Malye; critiques by Peter McBrien and Thomas MacDonagh of *Boxing Literature* and *The New Anthology* respectively.

On 4 August England declared war on Germany.

In the House of Commons on the same day Redmond offered the Volunteers for the defence of Ireland from any invader except England. Many thought he was cleverly using the situation to further the cause of Home Rule. Plunkett, Pearse and MacDiarmada thought that it was really a plan to hand over the Volunteers to the British War Office to be drafted into the army and Plunkett thought this was treason. They had to wait until this became plain to break with Redmond. Droves of Irishmen joined up and over the months lists of casualties full of Irish names began to appear. Pressure to join up was put on separatist nationalists with the suggestion that those who had not signed up were not supporting those who had. They all had friends and relations who had gone to the war and there were divisions within families and communities, but all experienced the war's heartbreak of death and destruction. Plunkett read every speech made at home and abroad, creating an ongoing analysis of the situation and one of his many conclusions was that the war would last at least three years, instead of the three months prophesied by the Irish Party. At least 300,000 joined up and Joe used to get Gerry to read the same national and international papers that he read and give him a summary of events from them; it all mattered to him. Those for whom Irish freedom was the cause, not a war between colonial powers, became a tighter-knit group and closed ranks.

In September thousands of rifles organised by Redmond arrived in Dublin to arm, equip and drill large numbers of Irish Volunteers for the defence of Ireland, but when Plunkett saw them he said they were completely useless, 1849 Garibaldi rifles with crooked barrels and no ammunition.

Geraldine Plunkett Dillon:

> I was wakened at five a.m. one fine September morning in Larkfield by the curious sound of 6,000 men talking quietly in the open air. They had gathered in the mill yard for the start of a route march and manoeuvres in the Dublin Mountains. Tomás led one section and Pearse the other. They were a very mixed crowd, some in morning coats and striped trousers, some in uniform and some in rags. Training was carried out as best as could be done but it was not easy, as a great unwieldy mass of men with little or no time for training had enrolled. The field in Larkfield where Andy Clerkin grazed his horses was also used for drilling and the horses were used to train cavalry ... The recruiters for the British Army had to be watched – Joe told me he was very surprised to learn that recruiters tried to join the Volunteers in the expectation of their being taken over by the War Office. The usual fee for every recruit handed over was 2s 6d, but one man I knew got a fee of £1 for each one.

In this letter from George Plunkett to his brother he describes cycling from Dublin via Kilcock, Kinnegad, Athlone, Athenry, Oranmore, to Galway city, Spiddal and Pearse's cottage in Rosmuc. They (he doesn't say who else is there) cycled from Rosmuc around Lough Corrib, through Cong and crossed to Aran.

Connemara 17 August 1914

A Ioseph a chara

I got your letter and enclosure .... we were on the rocks. We've had great time since we left ...We got an old boat there on the lake (we had the tent a few feet from the water) belonging to Pearse and we gave it a coat of tar and corked it a bit and went out in it....We've been using it ever since. PS We want some money. Tamid ar na gcarraigeachaí [We are on the rocks!]

We are coming home as soon as possible. The Pearses left on Wednesday. My gear <u>gave</u> when I was pushing up a small hill on low. I don't want a Pedersens gear I think .... will you call at the shop and get him to send it soon.

Best love to all Seoirse Give Eimar my love

[Eimar O'Duffy, playwright and novelist, was then living in Larkfield with Joe and Gerry Plunkett after his father threw him out of home because he wouldn't join the British Army. He then joined the IRB and the Volunteers.]

When, in early September, John Redmond said he would stand beside the British Prime Minister, Herbert Asquith, at a recruiting meeting in the Dublin Mansion House the IRB and the Citizen Army decided to stop the meeting by taking over the Mansion House. After a planning meeting Plunkett, for the first time, had a long conversation with James Connolly and arrived home very excited, telling Gerry that Connolly was the greatest and most intellectual man he knew. The military somehow were informed of the plan to stop the meeting and occupied the whole of Dawson Street before the IRB and Citizen Army arrived, so that they couldn't get near the Mansion House. Plunkett was terribly annoyed, but decided to relieve his fury with a strange joke: he wrote on an envelope *'Herbert Henry Asquith'* and gave it to his brother, George, who took it down the street shouting, 'Letter for Mr Asquith! Letter for Mr Asquith!' through all the soldiers and sentries, up to the door of the Mansion House where they opened the door and he handed it in. On it was a quotation from G. K. Chesterton, 'Your beauty has not left me untouched' and it was signed 'Little Snowdrop'! From here on Plunkett, like the rest of the Provisional Committee, was waiting for Redmond to 'cross the line', to commit himself to Britain and the War.

The Volunteers' Uniform Sub-Committee had reported, in August, that Messrs Morrogh Bros, of Douglas Mills, Cork, got special looms working and matched the sample the committee brought to them so the first order went to Morrogh Bros and they continued making the Army uniforms for decades after. No distinction was made between officers and others as all officers were purely temporary. Every item was made in Ireland. The report was signed by Eoin MacNeill and Laurence J. Kettle. Plunkett was a member of this committee which may be why he received a letter from Laurence Kettle:

> … informing you that you have been deputed to draft a scheme for the formation and government of a Motor Cycle Company in connection with the Irish Volunteers and that you were authorised to take into consultation any person you thought fit and to place a report before us.

On 20 September Redmond did cross the line. At a Volunteer review in Woodenbridge, he said that the Volunteers should be prepared to fight as members of the British forces. Plunkett was told by one of the Volunteers who was there that Redmond shouted at the men to 'go at once' that they were a disgrace, but this was not the way it was reported in the newspapers. Plunkett thought this was the final step and that they could not work with Redmond anymore.

He had been ill again so those on the IRB Committee came to him in Larkfield to discuss what should happen next and what should be in the *Manifesto*. A few days later the pre-Redmond Volunteer Committee passed the Manifesto wording which re-stated their position. As the newspapers were heavily censored Plunkett put it in the September/November number of the *Irish Review*.

The *Manifesto* stated: 'Mr Redmond is no longer entitled, to any place in the … Irish Volunteer Organisation' and announced its intention 'to call a Convention of the Irish Volunteers for Wednesday, 25th November, 1914.' It protested 'against the attitude of the present Government, who, under the pretence that "Ulster cannot be coerced" avow themselves prepared to coerce the nationalists of Ulster' and declared 'that Ireland cannot, with honour or safety, take part in foreign quarrels otherwise than through the free action of a National Government of her own;' and demanded 'that the present system of governing Ireland through Dublin Castle and the British military power ... be abolished ... and that a National Government be forthwith established in its place.'

Signed Eoin MacNeill, Ua Rathghaille, (The O'Rahilly) Thomas MacDonagh, Joseph Plunkett, Piaras Beaslaí, Michael J. Judge, Peter Paul Macken, Sean Mac Giobuin, P.H. Pearse, Padraic Ó Riain, Bulmer Hobson, Éamonn Martin, Conchubhair Ó Colbaird, (Con Colbert) Éamonn Ceannt, Sean MacDiarmada, Seamus Ó Conchubhair, Liam Mellows, L. Colm Ó Lochlainn, Liam Ua Gogan, Peter White.

Casement could not be there as he was in America.

They had no idea how many Volunteers would agree and remain with them and they could only wait and see and certainly the vast majority left to join Redmond's 'National Volunteers', but, after the first dip down to a few thousand, it started going steadily up again and continued to rise over the next year-and-a-half. Both Redmond's National Volunteers and the Irish Volunteers were drilling and forming companies but it was assumed the Irish Volunteers were too small a group to be considered so they were able to train fairly openly. Recruiting Volunteers was now done on the IRB lines, similar to Secret Service methods using 'Centres', a person who identified someone they trusted and brought them in. The numbers started to increase within a surprisingly short time, training methods became more effective and, behind the scenes, plans for an armed rising were taking shape. Arms became very important and guns began to come in more freely. On the other hand the National Volunteers, controlled by the Irish Party, was regarded by the British Government as an excellent recruiting resource for the British Army. Plunkett obviously thought that the whole thing was now more dangerous because he persuaded his sister, Gerry, to carry an automatic. He told her that 'if she carried it all the time she would not need it but if she didn't, she wouldn't have it when it was wanted'. She carried it nearly all the time in a holster under her jacket and then gave up on it altogether. Plunkett himself, an excellent shot, got a Mauser automatic, accurate up to 1,000 yards, and loved to take it apart and put all the little interlocking parts together again. Charlie Lawlor, who had a shop on Fownes Street where he sold sporting materials and sporting guns, used the business to bring in a lot of guns for the Volunteers.

The Irish Review finally came to an end with Plunkett committing a kind of editorial suicide by publishing his 'Twenty Plain Facts for Irishmen'. This was Volume 4 No. 42, September to November 1914. For the believer (and even the unbeliever) in signs and portents it has a strange prophetic feeling to its content beginning with the 'Manifesto To The Irish Volunteers'; which other newspapers would not publish, followed by 'Twenty Plain Facts for Irishmen':

Twenty Plain Facts For Irishmen

1. It is one thing to see the enemy's point of view: it is another thing to fight the enemy.

2. The Irishman who says he would prefer to be under German rule than under English rule is a slave.

3. The Irishman who says he would prefer to be under English rule than under German rule is a slave.

4. The Irish man who knows he should be under Irish rule and no other is capable of attaining freedom.

5. The Belgian owes no allegiance to Germany.

6. The Pole owes no allegiance to Russia, to Germany or to Austria.

7. The Irishman owes no allegiance to England.

8. The organisation of the Irish Volunteers was begun on 25th Nov 1913.

9. The British Government, on 4th Dec 1913 issued a proclamation prohibiting the import of arms into Ireland.

10. Under the Arms proclamation the British Government did what it could to hinder the Irish Volunteers from

obtaining arms necessary to equip them for the defence of Ireland.

11. The arms proclamation was withdrawn in August 1914 after the outbreak of an international European war.

12. Every foreign country from which the Irish Volunteers could have procured arms is in a state of war or neutrality.

13. Ireland, having no arms factory of her own, is thus still hindered from obtaining arms for her defence.

14. The Irish Volunteers have been organised first, to secure the rights and liberties of all the people of Ireland and then to maintain those rights and liberties.

15. The Irish Volunteers have not yet secured the rights and liberties of the Irish people.

16. The Irish Volunteers have no rights and liberties to defend.

17. The Irish Volunteers have not been enrolled to defend England and her empire, for the defence of which, according to the proclamation 'Your King and country needs you' the present war is being waged.

18. No body, committee or person has any right or liberty to use or to promise to use the efforts of the Irish Volunteers for any purpose other than the securing and the maintenance of the rights and liberties of the people of Ireland.

19. The Union Jack is the symbol of the Act of Union of

1800 by which the Irish nation was deprived of her last rights and liberties.

20. The Irish Nation lives.

In 'The Best Living Irish Poet', Thomas MacDonagh writes about Alice Milligan, claiming her as 'the most Irish of Irish living poets and therefore the best':

The only stand-alone poem in this issue is by Gerry Plunkett:

TO SAINT FRANCIS

O Francis, I have listened at your feet

And tried to catch your quick humility,

I caught the manning of your counsels sweet

And found the peace that is within your words.

I've loved with you the fishes of the sea,

I've been the little sister of the birds;

I am in fellowship with all the world

The rivers singing to me as they run,

The flowers spoke to me as they unfurled,

The dumb earth sobs to me in earthquake jars-

As you were little brother to the sun

I am the little sister of the stars.

Geraldine Plunkett 1914

M. Holmes, writes unenthusiastically on 'Futurist Poetry', but cites, with slight approval, Walt Whitman, Nietzsche and Verlaine. There is a diatribe on the state of Irish education by E. Creagh Kittson and the continuation of a story in English and Irish, '*An Choill* – The Wood' by P.H. [Patrick] Pearse, at the end of which it says 'to be continued'! 'A Story Of Land and Sea' is by Lord Dunsany, the unsigned and very favourable review of O'Neill and Ormond. 'A Chapter in Irish History' by Diarmid Coffey is probably by Joseph Plunkett and the rest certainly is. 'Notes' has two items: a promotional piece for the opening production of the Irish Theatre – 'The Dream Physician' by Edward Martyn, and an explanation of the theatre and its philosophy and second, an explanation to the readers of the dire circumstances in which the *Review* finds itself:

> Our entire staff has for some time past been working full-time and overtime (if such a thing is possible) in the Irish Volunteer organisation. Owing to international complications, copies of the *Review* sent to foreign subscribers have been returned to us ... readers should know our real position. For four years we have been giving them for sixpence a copy a magazine that has cost considerably more than that

to produce. The difference in normal times could be made up by advertisements. During national and international disturbances, when advertisements cease, the loss falls somewhat heavily on us. Was not most of the work of producing the *Review* entirely voluntary, it could not be produced at all. We have never issued an appeal for funds – what is more, while we in the beginning promised a forty-eight page magazine, we have constantly given fifty-six pages. We are content to do this for the advancement of Irish letters and the consequent credit of our country...

He goes on to ask readers to give their opinions on what should happen now but he was forced to give Manico, the publisher, the bill of sale to get MacDonagh's *Lyrical Poems* published the previous October so now the *Review* was really bankrupt He knew that, with the content in this issue, it would be suppressed or censored in some way and if so, it wouldn't survive but there is one more thing to mention about the content of this issue: the picture, a cartoon entitled 'Cupid and Psyche' by Grace Gifford. He certainly knew her by then, he probably met her in MacDonagh's flat in Baggot Street, but he was still in love with Columba O'Carroll, maybe more than ever and Grace is never mentioned, but, by another prophetic tweak, the word 'grace' is draped all over his poetry. The *Review* was not suppressed, but all the copies of it were seized and that was, indeed, the end.

During that September Joe and Gerry moved back to

Marlborough Road and Joe's health got worse again; whenever he had a temperature, perhaps a third of the time, he had to stay in bed. Their sister, Moya, decided to go into a convent, Philomena (Mimi) came back from working in London and wanted to try living in Larkfield, George was doing Engineering in UCD and supervising the laying of a sewer pipe under Larkfield avenue, Jack had finished in Clongowes and was also starting Engineering in UCD and Fiona (Josephine) was at home in Fitzwilliam Street. Many of those they knew from their schools and parties and dances in Fitzwilliam Street, Merrion Square and University College were joining up, going to war, becoming nurses and officers and they were torn between sympathy for them and feeling the need to turn inwards, to the group where their arguments and aspirations were understood.

The first Volunteer Convention in the Abbey Theatre on 25 October was attended by about 160 delegates (including Plunkett), a large number of whom were in uniform. Eoin MacNeill gave a vigorous and angry speech, tracing the year and the behaviour of John Redmond, the Irish Party and, most of all, the British Government who he accused of pressurising and deceiving Redmond. He mentioned Redmond's agreement to the exclusion of the four Ulster counties from Home Rule, the killings by the soldiers after the Howth guns were brought in and the offering up of Irishmen for the Army and all without consulting the Irish people.

This is one the many fragments of writing which appear in Plunkett's papers. It seems that when they are dated, as this one is, that he may be considering them for publication.

THE FIRST VISION WITNESS

[a fragment]

The poppies flamed out against the grey wall. Many coloured asters shone from the dark clay. The green that was everywhere among the flowers was as living as the sea. It ran into waves and sparkled and fell in cascades and showers of fine spray. Every particle of it seemed in separate motion. The flowers set in it were whirlpools of quiet. The flowers were amazing, their colour and shape seemed for each one a single indissoluble thing. Solomon in all his glory was not arrayed as one of these. Some, like the asters had each petal curved and smooth and set in the awful stillness of a carven gem. Others like the poppies surged and drooped in lambent fire. In this oneness of colour, light and form, this impossible or incredible harmony and symmetry of dissimilar qualities, they seemed to have reached the limit...

JMP 7th November 1914

The Hardwicke Hall, now becoming the home of 'The Irish Theatre' (often referred to afterwards as 'Edward Martyn's Theatre') was an eighteenth-century building which had been a convent, a Methodist teacher-training college and a Jesuit house. The hall itself held about ninety people and there was a balcony, which had been the entrance to a hiding place in Penal days. There were many small rooms upstairs, used as dressing-rooms and, downstairs, a green room and a good-sized stage. The entrance went straight into the hall from a noisy street without a porch or foyer, it was all very shabby, the lighting and curtains often failed and there was a musty smell but it constituted a fulfilled dream for this group and was bringing ideas of more international theatre, techniques from Stanislavsky and design from Gordon Craig. The producer was Thomas MacDonagh's brother, John, who, like his brother, was an excellent actor and producer; and just back after years working with European and American theatre companies.

Edward Martyn had been a founder member, with Yeats and Lady Gregory, of the Irish Literary Theatre in 1899 and of the Abbey Theatre in 1904. When MacDonagh approached him to be involved in an international, modern theatre company, Martyn was delighted and prepared to put his money behind it. *The Dream Physician* was Martyn's revenge on George Moore's portrayal of him in *Hail and Farewell* and this was the first play produced by the Irish Theatre, opening on 2 November 1914, to an audience of about a hundred people, in Madame Rock's little theatre on Upper O'Connell Street, because the Hardwicke Hall was being re-wired and was not quite ready. The play was 'not a success', but Edward Martyn was delighted with it.

The quality was usually much higher than this and over

the next year there were about ten Irish Theatre programmes, including Chekhov's *The Bear, The Proposal, Song, Uncle Vanya* and *The Cherry Orchard* and Ibsen's *Pillars of Society* and *An Enemy of the People*. Regular members of the company were Kitty and Gracie McCormack, George and Philomena Plunkett, Willie Pearse, Andrew Dillon, Joseph MacDonagh, Helena Moloney, the three eldest Reddin brothers, Columba O'Carroll, Thomas MacDonagh, John MacDonagh and Joseph Plunkett, who was a very good character actor. As time went on, Edward Martyn got meaner and made more difficulties, but he did pay for a dress for Una O'Connor (Agnes McGlade) when she played the lead in The *Cherry Orchard* and *Uncle Vanya* and although she was a really good, professional actress, that was the only payment she accepted. Critics from the newspapers came to the theatre, some finding it too *avant-garde* or too foreign or too amateur, but the indefatigable Joseph Holloway went to all the productions, kept a record of them in his notebooks and was very encouraging.

On 21 November 1914, Joseph Plunkett was twenty-seven and two days later he wrote:

O Bright! thy stateliness and grace,

Thy bearing and thy dignity

Bring intuition of the place

That still is native unto thee.

Solely thy native airs delight,

Can still thy silences embalm,

Solely thy native levin smite

Through thunders of unbroken calm.

A twyfold presence is and seems

To emanate from thine atmosphere,

Clothed in reality and dreams

It is in heaven, and it is here.

The forms of love enfolding thee

To flowers of earth and heaven belong,

Whose roots take hold in mystery

Too deep for song, too deep for song.

JMP 23rd November 1914

As a result of the split in the Volunteers the Irish

Volunteers Committee had had to be re-organised. It was now a large committee, meeting once a month with the Central Executive meeting once a week. The new headquarter's staff were: Chief of Staff, Eoin MacNeill; Director of Organisation, Patrick Pearse; Director of Military Operations, Joseph Plunkett; Director of Training, Thomas MacDonagh; Director of Arms, The O'Rahilly; Quartermaster General, Bulmer Hobson. The Volunteers bought many guns from British soldiers (the first prosecution of a soldier for stealing rifles to sell was that December), but it was a dangerous game so when Plunkett himself was approached by an officer from Beggar's Bush barracks he decided not to follow it up.

The Irish Volunteer Committee still had the offices in Kildare Street and members of the Committee who had had experience of John D. Nugent of the IPP and his violent tactics for dealing with political opposition, thought it necessary to protect the office with barbed wire and Joe agreed with them. There was no physical attack on them, but there were plenty of spies who turned up in and around the office. They had not been quite sure who to spy on before, but the Irish Volunteers were now easily identified and watched:

> A husband and wife team had been hanging round young nationalists for several years; they had even founded some organisations like 'The Irish Self-Government Alliance' as a front and they belonged to every real and phoney organisa-

tion there was … We had been watching these two people for some time; they had been asking curious questions and would not be put off. The wife was the first sympathiser into Kildare Street where Joe came in and found her telling Tomás how right he was. He did not know whether Tomás knew she was a spy so he kicked his ankle a couple of times until Tomás said, 'What are you kicking me for?' Joe was mad and when she had gone away asked him what she had said. 'To tell you the truth,' said Tomás, 'I wasn't listening to what she was saying, I was watching the flea that was crawling up her blouse!'

Geraldine Plunkett Dillon

The following description of Plunkett is by G.N. Reddin, who was at Belvedere with him and was one of the actors in the Irish Theatre:

Ardent and enthusiastic by nature, he delighted in controversy of any kind. How often have I seen him rush away from people with whom he was in conversation in one part of the room in order to settle a point in dispute with a noisy group in the other corner, then rush back to the people he had forsaken, and, taking up the thread of conversation where he had left it, settle their difficulty to his perfect satisfaction too. Not over-robust physically, all his activity and virility seemed to have been concentrated in his mind. His mind could never be at rest; if he was not reading or writing, he was evolving plans for the accomplishment of the most extraordinary things; not childish plans, mark you; no, but plans brilliantly formed and rendered practicable by the concrete logic and reason which gave them birth. This mental activity was a disease with him. Many a time I have heard him, in some heated argument, first prove conclusively that he was right, and then turn round and prove that he was absolutely wrong! Yes, and his listeners, both those who agreed with him in his first standpoint and those who disagreed, assent to his reasoning in both cases.

From Plunkett to Aidan McCabe

17 Marl

Christmas 1914

Dear Old Aidan,

You're quite right, I'm a devil not to have written to you- the fact is that there are so many things that I don't do, it is twice as hard to do any of them, I have written to nobody and they are very pleased.

Well its near midnight Christmas Eve so I can only wish you all the luck in the world and promise to write soon – yourself and me. Thanks very much for letter - the damned old white elephant *Review* has been seized in London – I wish them luck with it!

Olive oil

Goo'nigh' mise

PS A Happy Christmas and a bright New Year to you – Joe

CHAPTER 12

January To April 1915
To Germany Through The War

MY HOUR IS NOT YET COME

My hour is not yet come

And shall I do this thing

For them that need a sign?

Not you nor I, but some

That thirst shall hear me sing,

That praise the best of wine.

Fill then up to the brim

This heart of heavy stone

With suffering divine,

Then draw, and bear to him,

The steward Love alone

Who serves the gods with wine.

He'll know not whence it came

When my life-blood runs bright

To grace the gods' repast

But praise the Bridegroom's fame

Who kept for their delight

The best wine to the last.

JMP 17th Feb. 1915

It was after Christmas of 1914 that Joe told Gerry that he might be going away on IRB business to Germany. The Military Council now had a date for the Rising and had decided to send Plunkett to Germany to negotiate for arms and, if possible, some officers. This may have been Plunkett's own idea as he already had a military plan, one he had now been working on for some months and being Director of Military Operations for the Volunteers gave him extra opportunities to refine it.

Roger Casement was already in Germany trying to set up an Irish Brigade with Irish prisoners of war, supported by the German Government; he was also trying to negotiate an enormous invasion force with officers to lead it. This was not part of the IRB plan. Joe taught Gerry the cipher he would use in any letters he wrote, a variation of the 'Diplomatic' cipher, which depended on a key word order. Letters would be sent to Aidan McCabe and signed 'James Malcolm'. Aidan would pass them to Gerry who would bring them to Seán MacDiarmada or Patrick Pearse. Plunkett grew a little beard, destroyed all the photographs of himself that he could find and spread the idea that he was going to Jersey at Easter for his health. He and Geraldine heard afterwards that Dublin Castle opinion was that he had grown tired of the Volunteers and was making an excuse of his health to leave them.

There was danger of all kinds on the journey; due to the war there were spies all over Europe and in Ireland watching for anyone acting suspiciously. Because of this, Plunkett took a more circuitous route to Germany.

He kept a diary in a small notebook for most of his time away, which became more limited as the journey went on. Discretion was clearly crucial. He used code names and Irish to disguise people and places, and described it all to Gerry on his return.

MARCH

WED. 17TH St Patrick's Day 1915 left Dublin 8 o'c boat North Wall. City of Dublin Co's SS Carlow 1200 tons. Captain Williams. All lights out. G man [Spy from G-Division, Dublin Castle]. Arrived Liverpool before 8 o'c

THU. 18TH To PSq Co. and others. Found all sailings to Spain cancelled. To Cooks. Decided to go overland through Paris to San Sebastian. To French Consul and got passport viséd. Caught 11.25 train Central Station for London. Arrived London St Pancras about 5 o'c. Saw Gerald Gurrin at his office and went to Victoria Sta. where luggage and person was searched and letters read. Left London 8 p.m. for Folkestone where boarded SS Arundel for Dieppe. Arrived Dieppe in the small hours. Passports examined everywhere.

FRI. 19TH Left Dieppe 6 a.m. and arrived Paris St Lazare 9.50 a.m. Brought luggage to Quai D'Orsai and found I had 12 hours to stay in Paris. After an enormous dejeuner in the Gare Quai D'Orsay (more like a cathedral than a station – as my friend Chesterton says, 'What poetrace/Shot such cyclopean arches at the stars.') bought Edmond About **'Le nez d'un notaire'** (which is good fooling) and a map of Paris. Studied both of these for a short while and then with my sole piece of luggage (a black portmanteau) in the cloakroom, set out on my feet and my adventures.

I turned to my right coming out of the station and walked down the quays till I came to St Michel. Then up the whole length of the Boul' Miche' and again to the right into the Bould Montparnasse. On the left side of this, a little way up is a narrow street called Rue Campagne Premiere and up this I walked till I came to No.11 on the left side, where I rang and asked the concierge if M. James Stephens lived there. To my great surprise she pointed out a door and said, 'au premiere.' I went up the winding stairs and knocked at the first door. It was answered by Mrs Stephens and two small children, a boy and a girl. Mrs Stephens told me that she was to meet Seumas at 3.15 in front of L'Opera so I went there and met them and we had talk and coffee in the Café de la Paix.

Stephens is writing things about the war as he sees them. He seems to have become orthodox (in the right sense) in his opinions about Irish affairs, but otherwise is lamentably concerned with ideas (pur et simple) instead of realities, the things that may (or may not) be or become instead of things that are.

Left Paris 9.50 p.m Friday 19th and travelled most uncomfortably all night as I could not get a 'wagon-lit'.

Sat. 20TH Also all next morning and arrived at San Sebastian about 1 p.m. I had extracted the name and fame of the Hotel de France in a very subtle manner from a man in the train who was 'agent provocateur' for another 'fonda', so I went there in a motorbus and ordered a room a wash and something to eat. These being had I walked about the town and disliked it profoundly, mostly bad temper on my part. The town is not too bad but small. Architecture departs a trifle from usual cosmopolitan French/Italian by being more coloured and more fantastic while less 'Scirocco' (as someone ought to have called it). But this is only in spots. There are many churches which you don't find till you are inside them, I went to half eleven Mass on Sunday in a small church of the Capuchins beside the hotel. It reminded me of Mass at the same hour at Westland Row on account of the crowd and the style – mostly good-looking people (but comment is needless).

I arrived on Saturday,

SUN. 21ST On Sunday my bronchitis was very bad and I had fever.

MON. 22ND On Monday worse,

TUES. 23RD On Tuesday I contrived to find a doctor with a few words of French.

WED 24, THU 25, FRI 26, I was well enough to leave on Friday morning, through a strict regimen of quinine and creosote. When passing through London I had called on Gerald Gurrin to get Laurie to give me some introduction to San Sebastian. Gerald said he would get him to write to me but of course he never did. ... The result was that I was altogether alone and knew nobody.

On Friday 26th I was glad to take the train for Barce-

Iona. I was to change trains at Zaragoza but owing to their peculiar timing the train left the station before I did, (one way of losing a train). Well, it was lucky it did because in the Stacion Fonda I made a friend, one Candido Tomey Delado who was in an elevated state of happiness as he was engaged to be married. He had also once known a tremendous big great Irishman and was in consequence a Home Ruler (he took Home Rule to mean autonomy). He congratulated me on attaining our national aspirations. Poor fellow – I did not undeceive him. As I spoke to him in a becoming spirit and with due sympathy and modesty (he spoke French by the way) he did everything for me – interviewed the station master, ordered my meals, and brought me round the city and showed me everything. Saragossa is extraordinary beyond prose. I shall have to write verse about it or be inarticulate. The Cathedral is astonishing, immense, beautiful and antique – crammed with precious things of all kinds. (There are two Cathedrals but this one is the Basilica. It was once a mosque). Of the city it is impossible to speak – everything said would be wrong. It is all paradoxes. In it all contraries and contradictions are unified. It is big and small, clean and filthy, ugly and beautiful, new and old. I rushed it and escaped in a kind of dream for Barcelona. This town is perhaps no less wonderful but it is possible to take it in sections. It has 800,000 inhabitants, or 300,000 more than Dublin and they consist of the nations of the earth (for the most part). Spanish predominate, Mediterranean come next. I can speak their language but cannot understand it.

SAT. 27ᵀᴴ The lodgement I have secured (at 8 pesetas compris is in the Fonda de Espana and it sure is. It is situated in the Calle de San Pablo, very far from the Plaza Catalina and there you have it. Of course it is new to me and I have some fever still but the rest must be real.

FEVER RIMES

Through Saragossa should you rush

You'll find the place a mass of mush

To Saragossa should you go

And you'll be deluged with the rain

All Saragossa is the floor

Of just one single stream of mud

Follow the Saragossa trail

And you'll be hammered with the hail

When I am Dead

When I am dead let not your murderous tears
Deface by their slow dripping my ... tomb
Lest your grey heart grow greyer for my doom
And fill its ... corridors with fears
Your heart that my stone monument appear
While yet I live — O give it not to gloom
When I am dead but let some joy illume
The ultimate victory *that stings and sears*

Already I can hear the ~~dear~~ *stealthy* tread
Of Sorrow breaking through the hush of day.
I have no hope you will avert my dread
Too well I know that soon am mixed with clay
They mourn the body who the spirit slay
And those that stab the living, weep the dead

1914 [3]

And those that stab the living, weep the dead
~~They~~ mourn the body who the spirit slay
~~And those~~ that stab the living, weep the d[ead]
... the room of colours and light
...

Above: 1914 Poem: 'When I am Dead' by Joseph Plunkett.

Left: 1915. Plunkett from the photograph for his German passport.
Below: Passes given to Plunkett for entry into the Limburg Prisoner-of-War Camp.

Brotkarte.
Gültig für die Zeit vom 17. Mai bis einschließlich 28. Mai 1915.
4. Woche.

Brotkarte.
Gültig für die Zeit vom 17. Mai bis einschließlich 23. Mai 1915.
4. Woche.

Right: 1915. Plunkett in Germany wearing his cloak.

Above: Dr Joseph O'Carroll (second row, fourth from left) and Columba (third row, fifth from left).

Above: 1915. Plunkett working at wireless.

Opposite top: Letter from Joseph Plunkett to Grace Gifford, January 1916.

Opposite bottom: 1916. The exploded tram on O'Connell Street.

Of a Thursday on the twenty seventh day of
the month of January in this year of grace
(1) 1916. In the Gaelic tongue called διαρδαοιη
27 Εαηαιρ 1916. Written and indited in the house
upon the Field of the Larks at Kimmage in
the County of Dublin by (Joseph Mary Plunkett)
Ιοσεφ Ο πλυηγζέηδ to his betrothed Ζραγηε ηις
Ζιοφραιδ (Grace of the family of Gifford) at the
house of her father Frederick Gifford number
8 of Temple Villas in the road called Palmerston
in Rathmines also in the County of Dublin.

   Now I'll drop this old nonsense for
business.

   My hearts delight my lovely dear I will
not pretend I am not disappointed at
not seeing you but I know you must
be very busy and I know too that
you are sorry as well as me so I dont
want to make it worse for you by

Above: 1916. Marriage certificate of Joseph Plunkett and Grace Gifford.

Right: 1916. Grace Gifford Plunkett.

Left: 1916. Newspaper photo of George and Jack (Seoirse and Sean) Plunkett after their arrest with Jack O'Brien and an insert photo of Grace Gifford Plunkett.

Right: 1916. Memory Drawing of Joseph Plunkett in his Kilmainham cell by Grace Gifford Plunkett.

Above: The ruins of the Metropole Hotel, O'Connell Street, where Plunkett stayed before the Rising. The GPO side wall is on the right.

For Saragossa make a bust

And you'll-be choked to death with dust

In Saragossa make your beat

And you'll be smothered with the heat,

To Saragossa should you run

You'll sure be stricken with the sun

SUN. 28TH Everyone in the town had bought palms on Sunday for the next day, and that was all I saw of Palm Sunday because next day I was not well enough to go out, thus missing Mass and my last chance of seeing a bull-fight. I saw what is built of the Temple of la Sagrada Familia – but whether it is real or not is hard to say – certainly I never saw anything in the least like it in stone before, nor don't expect to again.

MON. 29TH On Monday 29th felt better and walked round a bit also booked a passage in the Italian SS Siena for Genoa. Saw very little of Barcelona except from tram and café. Had to go to Italian Consul to get passport viséd before getting boat tickets.

TUES. 30TH On Tuesday 30th unexpectedly heard that the Siena would arrive at 7p.m. and leave at 9. She did the first, but not the second. It is now 11 p.m. and she is still loading – so I'll have a drink and go to bed. 'God bless everybody' as le Bon Ton used to say.

['Le Bon Ton' is Theobald Wolfe Tone who made a similar expedition, on his own, to France, looking for help for Ireland, nearly a hundred and twenty years before.]

WED. 31ST We left sometime in the small hours and the voyage was uneventful until on Wednesday evening, a shot was fired across our bows and we were hailed by a couple of French torpedo boats to heave-to or they'd sink us. We hove to. (We had to). After some inquiries and replies had passed we were graciously allowed to proceed which we did until at about 2 a.m. all the passengers were hauled out of their bunks and ordered to proceed to the saloon, passport in hand. This time it was a French warship which had boarded us and her officers were holding a proces-verbal in the saloon. The examination of papers – (and, when doubtful, of luggage) was most strict and stringent, four passengers being held up, two only temporarily and two, who, it seemed were German, being taken off as prisoners to Toulon. There was also a question of 80,000 cases of (shall we say?) cocoa consigned to Switzerland, being part of a very miscellaneous cargo, and about which telegrams had to be exchanged with Toulon for instructions before we were allowed to proceed. One of the (2nd class) passengers who was held up temporarily had a very narrow shave. His passport had been raccommodé and touched up by hand. He had declared himself a Mexican being in reality a native of (shall we say?) Honolulu, but fortunately another Mexican (?) on board spoke up for him saying that he recognised the Mexican accent in the voluble Spanish of the doubtful one, (who was certainly a very good linguist) just in time to save him from much unpleasantness.

I made several acquaintances on board, among them a Chilean from Buenos Aires whose wife came from county Cork and who had been trying to sell horses to the British. Also a Secretary of Legation from Venezuela who had been Venezuelan Consul General in London and Secretary in New York – a very pleasant caballero indeed.

THU. 1ST APRIL We arrived at Genoa about 1 p.m. on Holy Thursday and I went to the Hotel Meuble Splendide right in the centre of the town. Dined in the evening at the most modest restaurant I've ever been in and afterwards to a cafe with a friend whom I had to see off by train for the North.

FRI. 2ND Next morning took the train to Pisa and from there to Florence where I arrived at about 5.30 p.m. Went to the Hotel Metropole recommended by Cooks as reasonable and good. It is both. Before dinner to the Poste Restante but got nothing. Dined with very good Chianti. Le Bon Ton again !

SAT. 3ᴿᴰ Holy Saturday. Still a bit tired and of course rather weak after my bout of fever – besides everything is closed for Easter, so just strolled round the old familiar places and find I love them more than ever – even the David statue that I was so angry with for being out of proportion. I have almost forgotten my way about and have to re-discover localities. This hotel is just behind the Piazza Vittorio-Emanuele and beside everything. Went to No. 9 Via Torrebuoni where they told me Dr Dunn could be seen on Tuesday next. Wrote to Mrs Dunn in case my other letter had gone astray, as I can get nothing at the Poste Restante.

[These were the same Dunns that Plunkett and his mother had visited in 1911.]

SUN. 4ᵀᴴ Easter Sunday. To the Duomo where I got one or two Masses and heard very good singing. Then advised to go to the Boboli Gardens and went but found them shut. About 5 o.c. Charlie Dunn called, very sunburnt from being in the country he has just returned. It seemed that my letter from Barcelona never reached them but Mrs Dunn will call for me tomorrow between 5 and 5.30 p.m. It is astonishing but I never heard anyone speak English with a worse accent than Charlie.

MON. 5TH Easter Monday. I must have caught a very bad chill last evening and have had to take enough chlorodyne to kill a regiment of artillery, also quantities of mixed Malaga and cognac. I could eat no dejuener and both ears are roaring. Yesterday I went out to have a look at David and then came back and read 66 of his songs. He was some writer as well as some fighter. I wonder which chilled me? The Dunns came (Mrs, Miss and Charlie) and we had a talk then Mrs Dunn, asked me to dine with them tomorrow (Tuesday) of course I said I would and afterwards Charlie took me for a drive in the Cascine where we saw everybody coming back from races. Then to café at Mucke's. I am to meet him at Mucke's tomorrow at 5.

TUE. 6TH My heroic regimen (and a bottle of Lacrima Christi) has succeeded. In the morning to the Uffizi. Hunted up all the Lorenzo di Credis and had a look at all the Tuscans. Then bought some necessary books also C. G. Leland's **Legends of Florence** – also a box of fine sweets for Eileen. Met Charlie at Mucke's also Beucci ... I am learning to spot Italian G-men – a useful accomplishment. Charlie described to me several fights that took place between the aristocratic nobles and other students. At 7 we went to fetch Dr Dunn and drove to the Villa Alimari Pian dei Giallari – where I gave them politics as a bad return for a good dinner. Tremendous bombardment of statements and arguments on both sides.

They took it very well.

WED. 7TH Got renseignments, did a quick change stunt and bought a ticket to Lausanne an imaginary difficulty having vanished into thin air. More necessary books, finished the wine and took the 2.20 p.m. for Milan. Read the first series of **Legends of Florence**, spilt a fiaschettino of red Chianti into my pocket and arrived at Milan at 10 p.m. Went to Hotel Terminus, another quick change. This is a good and comfortable hotel.

THU. 8TH Did nothing, but eat in Milani then left it by the 2.20 (or so) p.m. for Lausanne. Arrived Lausanne by P.L.M. with no trouble from customs or passports. At 10 p.m. – this seems to be becoming a habit – I must break it off – went by taxi as it was raining to Hotel National small and moderate, but quite comfortable. Why should I say anything about the scenery? It's been done before and I've seen such and other though this was my first sight of Como.

FRI. 9TH I seem destined to see nothing of Lausanne – or very little – and to leave again by the 2 something, this time for Berne. Lausanne would be a pleasant place to rest awhile but I'm hot on the trail now and spurred. Well, 'tis but in vain [for the soldier to complain]' vide le Bon Ton. Here also I cut my acquaintance and am growing a beard this last fortnight.

[He has now changed his identity to 'James Malcolm']

Same day, later. I arrive at Berne before 5pm and go to the Hotel Bristol. It is too late to do anything so I take a rest. Here endeth the first stage of my journey.

SAT. 10ᵀᴴ This hotel is full of devices including one for waking me which I duly set but it didn't … So in the afternoon I go to see the 'Hill of Rome' [the German Embassy] but find only a hermit to whom I confide my cause and who, promising that he will seek the aid of Higher Powers, bids me wait with patience. The which I do promise and intend in faith. This same hermit being much frequented by all nations for advice, whom do I meet at his lowly cell but my Chilean horse dealer, come doubtless to do penance for his evil ways. With him do I repair to my hostelry and, I fear me, prolong his days of necessary repentance by indulging in the flowing bowl. Therefore I pray God bless everybody. PS it snowed heavily and I spent Fr14 on taxis.

SUN. 11ᵀᴴ To 11.30 Mass at Dreifaltigkeitskirche, Seems new. Imposing exterior, interior very poor. Gaudy decorations in worst style. My Chilean has departed. More heavy snow. Read Bernard Shaw's **The Perfect Wagnerite**.

MON. 12ᵀᴴ The flower Patience flourishes on barren rock. I went in search of the Fine Arts Museum, but of course it was shut. The accompanying sonnet came easier than most (but that does not mean without the sweat of the pen) and I hope none the worse for it. The

Shakespear form is unusual with me.

If I were told the chair of Peter waits:

Nolo episcopari! I would cry,

Nor have the courage to take Heaven's gates

Were they set open — first I'd surely die;

How then, O sum of all that Heaven hoards,

Could I support the splendour of your love

If for one moment you might sheath your swords

Spreading for me the white wings of a dove?

For in the front of battle I may wield

My words as weapons while I fight for you

Against your beauty, yet if you should yield

I'm stricken by a bolt from out the blue:

But death I seek that cannot Heaven quell

Until I've proved my power over hell.

TUE. 13TH This morning I went and saw the Spiritual Father, other aforementioned Hermit the German

Ambassador, Herr von Romberg, who received me kindly and gave me good advice ... He also counselled Patience. I am acquiring a deep respect for this lady. I long for my Chilean or the doubtful egg from Mexico wherewith to carouse and make merry, I cannot drink by myself. Besides the egg was flippant whereas the bears are farouche. In afternoon to the Kunst museum where I saw some excellent and original pictures. The gallery is very small but the modern pictures are quite exciting. Plinio Colombi is by far the best modern in fact in the first rank. There is a great picture by Giron 'Schwingfest'.

WED. 14TH To nowhere and did nothing – just waiting. Tomorrow I shall have to buy a book or something to keep me quiet.

THURS. 15TH Still waiting for news. Went on a bust in a book shop and bought H.G.Wells: **An Englishman Looks at the World**, George Moore: **Vale**. George Borrow: **The Romany Rye** and Arnold Bennet: **Hilda Lessways.**

FRI. 16TH Read **the Romany Rye** – an utter fraud ignorant and badly written and yet with certain bright spots in it. On the whole it disgusted me and is not worth reading. Wells in this book (**supra**) is not as good as he was. His optimism is crazily unreal but very interesting. It improves as it goes on. **Hilda Lessways** is a dreadful delight to read – especially when I have read **Clayhanger** but I must read it — both again. I can't say enough for them.

SAT. 17TH Just a month away today. Summoned. My waiting is over. I leave on Monday. Went and got photographed. Began an essay on Hiberno-English poetry I mean literature. Now I am (temporarily) almost happy for the first time on my journey. I project things again.

SUN. 18TH To 10.30 Mass. Sermon in some tongue I do not know. Either German or Bernese. Got my photographs – very faithful and horrible – I finished Wells, his book. Wrote to Moses. [Aidan McCabe] I motored to the German embassy at Berne and got my German passport (made out in my own name) to take me to Berlin. The German Ambassador, Herr von Romberg, who was very friendly and wished me every success, had told me that he had telegraphed to the German frontier and that if I went to Leopoldshóhe they would be prepared for me. I thanked him 'and, waving my hands in a most graceful manner, took my departure'.

MON. 19TH The next morning I took the 10.45 train (as instructed at the embassy) having bought a 2nd class single ticket to Berlin via Basle and arrived at Basle about 1.30 where (also according to directions) I took a motor to the German frontier there (Basle by the way is a very pretty town and a place I would like to revisit). The Swiss authorities of the customs made the usual perfunctory enquiries and to my surprise asked to see my passport. I produced it and replied to his question as to whether I was English by a most vigorous denial and an asseveration that I was Irish. Next he stated that I aught to have had it viséd by the Swiss something or other (which I had of course omitted to do) but I jumped suddenly upon him and deprived him of the use of his weapon stating that I had not been told that that was necessary nor asked at any previous time in Switzerland for a passport. He then hemmed and hawed and ended by asking whether I was coming back into Switzerland. I answered him as I thought good that I hoped not, where-upon he graciously permitted me to depart. I had not gone far upon my journey to be precise about two feet or two thirds of a yard, when my progress was again brought to a halt this time by the German customs offi-cial who ran his hands rapidly through my effects, thus giving me the greatest difficulty in re-locking my poor plethoric portmanteau, in which of course I had noth-ing dutiable − all I wished to smuggle I had taken the precaution to conceal about my person. The next ordeal that I had to face was the scrutiny of myself and papers by the Kaiserlich military authorities. My papers gave them not the same satisfaction as my person, though I had anticipated a different state of affairs, and they could not release me from my quandary until they had made an extensive use of the marvel of modern science, the telephone. Two hours wait but great courtesy and, at the end, all the illustrated papers and a quantity of bar chocolate eaten out of the hand, the drawbridge was lowered the portcullis raised and, preceded by a flourish of trumpets, I resumed my journey. Id est what really happened was that there were three officers, they asked me for my passport and perceiving that I was a 'British subject' (mar dheadh!) wanted to know if I had any other papers e.g. a special permit. I, of course, referred them to von Romberg and they asked if I had a letter from him. I said not, so then one of the officers, a very decent young chap, brought me into another room where I told him something of myself and said that the German Ambassador at Berne had told me that he would wire to the frontier and make it all right for me. He enquired then whether the other two officers knew anything of a communication about me but they had not heard of such a thing. He (my beautiful officer) spent the next two hours trying to get hold of the persons in command – providing me meanwhile with **The Sketch** and other papers – and at length succeeded, coming in very happily to tell me: 'you can go to Berlin, it is all right'. He then marked my passport, called a porter for my bag and bade me goodbye and good luck on my journey. I replied as well as I could and picked up myself and set out.

The porter was a hunchback with a drooping straggling

moustache and thin arms and legs. He picked up my bag
and putting it on a handcart set off pushing it down the
white and dusty road. The day was hot and still, I wore
a fleece overcoat that accentuated the weather without
giving me too much discomfort. In a very short time my
black American shoes were thick and white with dust.
I walked pretty fast to keep up with the long stride of
the hunchback. On one side of the road the high railway embankment rose steeply covered with grass. The
ground at the other side of the road fell away sharply but
there was a little edge of grass on which I walked whenever I was not crossing the road which curved a great
deal. There were leafy trees standing straight up in companies in the fields to the left, and every now and then
a house looking fairly new. As we walked quickly and
silently we easily passed a countrywoman pulling what
looked like a toy wagon on four very tiny wheels, in which
sat or lay a small fat boy of about four or five years. Soon
we came in sight of Leopoldshóhe station where I was to
wait a few hours for the through to Berlin. Got a through
carriage but no wagon-lit. Twenty-three hours train and
train all day and night. Big towns and soldiers and soldiers and soldiers. Such was my entrance into Germany.
[He said later that he nearly died on that train.]

TUE. 20TH. Arrived at 8.30 a.m. The Ambassador at
Berne, Herr von Romberg, had told me that I ought to

ask for Herr von Langwerth at the Foreign Office at Berlin. So while on my twenty-three hour rail journey from Switzerland I tried to learn a few German words and phrases that would be necessary before I could reach the Foreign Office. Unfortunately the very term Foreign Office was omitted from the dictionary and phrase book that I had bought in Florence, and when I arrived at the Anhalter Banhof Berlin I had the greatest difficulty in conveying the name of my destination to the motor driver. At last an intelligent porter had an inspiration and asked me whether I meant Answartges Amt to which I also had the 'intuition born of desperation to reply in the affirmative'.

Fortunately the foreign office was close by in Wilhelmstrasse and when we stopped the motor at a door I entered and demanded Herr von Langwerth. They directed me to No. 76 in the same street and when I had rung the bell I thought I had come to the house of some relative of the late Robert Houdini for the great doors unlocked and opened of themselves showing no-one in the hall. It was of course an electrical device worked from the porters rooms. This little detail as I was afterwards to find out, is quite typical of Germany – or at least of Berlin. I went upstairs and demanded Herr von Langwerth. The porter asked for my card. I wrote out my real name in full and handed it to him. Almost immediately Herr von Langwerth came out and very courteously informed me that he was very pleased to meet me but that Herr von Romberg had made a slight mistake and that the person I should see was Georg Graf (Count) von Wedel who would know what business I had come about. He recommended me to return to that house 3 hours later at 2 o'clock when von Wedel would be there to see me. Excelsior Hotel to breakfast. Then a 10 franc hair-cut. Worth the length. My only enemy in the world is Johann M. Peters of San Francisco. [Himself! This is Plunkett's current alias].

To 76 at 2. Count von Wedel received me and rang up Roger Casement who said to come round. Went. While there Capt. Hans Boehm came and we had a few words. Casement said he would dine with me at Excelsior Hotel. He did and I met Virendnarath Chattopadhyaya [Chatto – the Indian nationalist] Casement has some flu. Very tired and ankles all swollen as I have not been able to lie down for forty hours.

[Sir Roger Casement, a British civil servant knighted for his outstanding humanitarian work, had now been in Berlin for over six months and had published his reasons for being in 'enemy' territory. This made him a severe embarrassment to the British Government and a willing and useful enabler for Plunkett and his mission.]

From Roger Casement to Herr Peters [Plunkett]:

Dear Herr Peters!

Here is your bread ticket. I did not want to wake you up before I left. You are going to FO to get your pass today aren't you? Then tomorrow morning we go to the Police Station and get you registered.

Well I hope you have slept well and feel good

With my best regards

I remain as ever

Sincerely yours

Roger Casement

WED. 21ST Casement came in morning. Brought Quin, Kehoe and Dowling [three members of the Irish Brigade] and we had a talk. At one p.m. I went to Casement's to lunch and met Princess Evelyn Blucher. In afternoon he had to lie down and Capt. Boehm came, later Dr Richard Meyer, [brother of Kuno Meyer]. Then as he was not well he gave me a letter for George Wedel and I went to 76, the Foreign Office, by myself. Had a long talk. Quite satisfactory. Before I went I had seen to marriage settlement [the Agreement] and had also met Adler Christiansen, [Casement's servant]

[Plunkett said that Christiansen had a curiously immobile face, not easy to decipher, so he did not allow Christiansen to be told his real name in spite of Casement's conviction that he was reliable. Berlin was swarming with spies, so Plunkett did not allow anyone under the rank of ambassador to know his real name.]

In evening found official telephone.

THURS. 22ND Official called with paper for me. Left Excelsior Hotel. Moved to Casement's, The Eden Hotel. Telephone from George Wedel to go to No.8 to see Nadolny [German General Staff]. Motored there but he was too busy. Am to go tomorrow. Stayed with Casement.

FRI. 23RD In morning Prof. Schiemann came. Casement was up. Said he would see Kehoe about the Irish Brigade at Limburg.

[Kehoe, Quinlisk and Dowling were Limburg prisoners delegated to establish the Irish Brigade; Roger Casement had persuaded the German Government that an Irish Brigade could be created from the Irish prisoners–of–war captured from the British Army if these were kept in a separate camp, in this case, Limburg. Casement was convinced that many would sign up and make an effective invasion force for the Irish cause, but by the time Plunkett arrived it was clear to the Germans – and subsequently to Plunkett – that this was not going to work as too few were interested.]

At 3.30 to Nadolny at No. 8. Casement came later. Sketch later.

['Sketch is probably the Ireland Report by Casement and Plunkett, a summary of Ireland's military status, location of troops, geography of the coast and so on. An information file, rather than a proposal.]

SAT. 24TH. Rain all day. In the evening George Chatterton Hill to tea. Talk all day. News still good. Bad tooth-ache.

SUN. 25TH. To 11.30 Mass by train. Sermon, good weather. Proposal begun. Not satisfactory. Crab for lunch. Talk of Sicily in evening.

['Proposal' was probably the Agreement between the German Government and the Military Council in Ireland.]

MON. 26TH. Sketch improving. News better. After lunch to choose rooms, good and cheap. Capt. Boehm to dinner, very cheerful. Off tomorrow at last so all looks bright.

TUES 27TH. Quin and Dowling. Left Casement. Estab-lished in apartment 42 Hardenbergstrasse. Bought bag. German lesson. Unpacked.

WED. 28TH Proposal. Purchases.

THU. 29TH Casement to 42. Great talk.

FRI. 30TH Mum's birthday. To Casement in the morn-ing. Long talk. Stayed to supper.

CHAPTER 13

May To October 1915
Decision And Command

F rom this point on Plunkett wrote the diary in Irish to conceal information as much as possible. He assigned new Irish code names to the protagonists – Limburg prisoner-of-war camp is 'Luimnuigh', Quinlisk, Kehoe and Dowling are 'Triúr', the Irish Brigade is 'Fianna Fáil' and 'Iolair Bán MacGiolla Chriost' is Adler Christiansen, but the form is so contracted as to make it largely unreadable, even with the interpretation by Geraldine Plunkett Dillon and Jane Kissane, so an account is given here instead.

As May began he was ill again and couldn't go out, but he was under pressure now from Capt. Boehm to finish the draft agreement with Germany for the purchase of arms which he had been writing for nearly two weeks so he worked on that all day for three days to get it finished. Capt. Boehm had told him that the Ireland Report, already submitted to the Foreign Office, was good and that he should get this other document finished quickly. In the evenings he was dining with Casement, Adler Christiansen and sometimes Capt. Boehm. Plunkett was finding the work very tiring but, with Boehm's approval of it, he finished on Wednesday ('Thank God!' he says) and he sent it to Nadolny at his office. He notes that he will be going to Limburg next day (Friday 7 May) and that he finished this poem:

THE LADY ELECT

This breast has nourished Christ, these hands

Have played with him in infancy,

These eyes, when at the cross she stands,

Shall weep for him, shall weep for me.

This soul, this body, this white Dove

Whose bride-song is the Canticle

Shall yet delight his heart in love

When he has won her heaven through hell.

Her fate, her future cross and crown

Those praises do but prophesy;

In grief the weeping stars bow down

That by his sword his heart must die.

JMP Berlin 28ᵗʰ April-6ᵗʰ May 1915

On Friday 7 May Plunkett left Berlin for Limburg on the Lahn near Frankfurt, a twelve-hour train journey, to visit the camp with Casement, Capt. Boehm, Quinlisk, Kehoe and Dowling. Next day Fr Nicholson and Fr Crotty, two Irish priests working with the prisoners, came to his hotel. Fr Crotty was the Chaplain to the Limburg Camp but Fr Nicholson had been sent from New York specifically to recruit prisoners into the Brigade and was having very little success with it. Plunkett stayed at the Hotel zur Alten Post and over the next week he and this group of about eight discussed what would happen next, talked, had 'lunch in the open air', 'dined under the stars', had 'plenty of beer', talked, discussed the Irish Brigade, the Agreement, Ireland, politics, tactics, talked.

Nightingales are singing

The whole night long

Crickets are chirping

Their cheerful song

Branches are rustling

On every tree

My heart my heart is silent

I cannot sing of thee.

JMP 10th May 1915

Plunkett, who temporarily took over the recruitment process from Fr Nicholson, wrote a speech, 'The Betrayal of Ireland by England since the passing of the Home Rule Act', which he delivered at the camp on his first visit there. Boehm had told him that a real Irish Brigade would be worth an army division to Germany and a rebellion would have the same value but Plunkett, once he went to Limburg with no dependence on the creation of a brigade, could see there was little chance of success. Casement had not been in Ireland when the war started so he had a false idea of why men had joined up. Plunkett knew that many of the recruits to the British Army were Loyalists of some kind, and for a large number it was a well-paid job they could not afford to turn down. Some joined because they thought Redmond had made a bargain for Home Rule and some because they believed Germany wrong to invade Belgium. Most would not be interested in joining a brigade to fight even for Home Rule for Ireland. The American Ambassador,

James W. Gerard, had also noted that the Irish Limburg prisoners were riddled with tuberculosis and particularly subject to neurotic and mental problems. As a result of all this only eight had signed up for the Brigade by the time Plunkett arrived in Limburg.

Plunkett did not interview men himself but he swore them in having written a Declaration for the purpose:

> … severing all connection with the British Army and state, volunteering for service in this brigade to fight for Irish independence … the Imperial German Government has generously undertaken to arm and equip the Brigade, and we may therefore hope with the assistance of Divine Providence to achieve our independence victoriously or to die fighting for the glory of God and the honour of Ireland.

> Sat 15th Big battle – the 2nd between me and Casement. The deck [Declaration] was the cause of it.
>
> JMP

The men were interviewed by Kehoe and Dowling outside the camp. Those who joined had their kit brought out of the camp to the barracks where they stayed. Later they were moved to another camp where they were given special status. Plunkett swore in over fifty men over a two-week period, but it stopped there and Casement's hopes for a significant Irish contingent were effectively dashed. Plunkett only hoped that the Germans would honour the Agreement, which was now being scrutinised. Newspapers in Ireland reported that 'a tall man with a black beard was with Casement' and had made a speech to the Irish prisoners urging them to join Casement's Brigade, but they did not identify him as Plunkett. Between 10 and 20 May Plunkett was having almost daily meetings with Boehm and his diary gives these figures – 174,000; 10,000; 194,000, 25,000 plus big ships; 12,000 plus ship; 4,800 plus ship; 12,000.

These are probably war statistics as Plunkett followed the war closely. In a letter to Casement the following month he gives his view of each country's position and quotes 42,000 as the number of prisoners taken.

A lot of Plunkett's time now was spent hanging around, waiting for things to happen, but the meetings with Boehm while Casement was away were developing the IRB and Military Council's position and Plunkett had the chance to restore German confidence, seeped away by the failure of the Irish Brigade recruitment.

THE MASK

…Now is my claim from thence

That you should hear your heart's

Pleading in my defence

Before your praise departs

And all your grace goes hence.

JMP 22nd May 1915

Two days later he wrote this 'talk–song'

If there is one thing about you more beautiful than another

It is the back of your neck

I am almost afraid to write of it

It is so beautiful;

Years ago – before you were grown up

It was hidden by your hair.

But I used to catch glimpses of it

And go crazy;

I used to walk behind you on purpose

And feel like a criminal

And I would think:

'Some day she will put her hair up

And everybody will be able to see'

And I was horribly jealous

And I swore.

Weather very hot. Nothing but talk with the three – Dowling, Kehoe and Quinlisk and with Fr Nicholson. I am smoking and drinking. I am doing nothing else at all. I visited the nuns. We had a long talk and they gave me books – stories and poems, George Moore, Browning and Christina Rosetti

Letters and papers and books from Casement. (Rhoda Fleming by Meredith)

At night I read Maguire's book on King William and Irish freedom. I had a cramp in my leg.

JMP

[He read all these and they helped, along with being invited out here and there and taking a day trip to Frankfurt, anxiety taking its toll while he waited for the verdict on the Agreement and for a date to be fixed when he could go home.]

JUNE Tue 1ST With Casement to Frankfurt in train. Town very nice. Saw Charlemagne's house. There from 2.15 to 11.25 at night. Casement went back at 4. I was the whole night in the train. JMP

[This all-night journey was his return to Berlin, reaching his apartment at 42 Hardenbergstrasse at 8.30 a.m. where he slept, even through Adler Christiansen's call.]

Thursday 3 June Wrote letters to Casement, Virendnarath Chattopadhyaya, and Fr Nicholson. Taxi in a hurry to 76 [Wilhelmstrasse – the Foreign Office] and saw Count George von Wedel, gave him a letter from Casement and my book, **The Circle and the Sword**. He says that I will be working wings (flying) ... Photographed again. Great hope now. I wrote a song 'Dolores La Paloma', cigar etc.' JMP

From Roger Casement to Richard Meyer:

Thursday 3rd June

Dear Mr Meyer,

... It is about Mr P's passport. I came with him, I am very anxious to get him away quickly – and after the failure of the first idea it may be necessary to send him out of Germany as a released prisoner or something of that kind.

I am very anxious to have him got away quickly as he is ill and may break down and be unable to travel which would be a calamity. So I beg that everything possible may be done to expedite his departure ...Yours Sincerely

Roger Casement

Extract from document by Plunkett:

Germany's Future World Policy

JMP June 4th 1915

A World Power must have a World Policy. The recognition that a world-Power must have a world-Policy is due to England. The necessity arises from her choices. She parcelled out the world into places she would dominate, places she would permit her friends to dominate and places or states she would wait for the opportunity to strike.

Germany was one of the latter.

England left no political entity out of her count. When she ignored some part of the world she did it with both eyes on it and on the future. Nevertheless her policy was not prepared beforehand. It needed no working out as it was not based on a principle; it was based on the absence of principle; it was a rule: Rule Britannia, the rule of Piracy.

Germany's future World-Policy should be worked out beforehand as far as circumstances allow with all the completeness of the plans of the Great General Staff. It can be so worked out if it is based on a principle; the principle of justice.

On Saturday 5 June a letter came to Plunkett by hand from Richard Meyer asking him to come to the Foreign Office. He saw Meyer there, got his passport from 'Koch' and went to the Post Office with Adler Christiansen for 'breadcart' – possibly a ration book of some kind. The evening of the next day, Sunday, he met Meyer again at the Foreign Office and they talked about the 'school wings (flying school).' This might refer to the aeroplane idea which Plunkett offered the Germans; two narrow planes mounted parallel, a short distance apart. Joe and Jack Plunkett made a version of it with cardboard. The model they made behaved like a glider with very slow descent. The idea was to reverse the process and create lift. Jack heard later that the Germans tried it out, but it was not successful.

In Plunkett's diary he says:

> Capt. Nadolny says that that is all right but that my life is very precious now (great hope of me for the cause). Perhaps so but I await Casement's advice.

> Monday 7th June Very early morning 1-2oc. I wrote a poem 'The Spark'.

THE SPARK

Because I used to shun

Death and the mouth of hell

And count my battle won

When I should see the sun

The blood and smoke dispel,

Because I used to pray

That living I might see

The dawning light of day

Set me upon my way

And from my fetters free,

Because I used to seek

Your answer to my prayer

And that your soul should speak

For strengthening of the weak

To struggle with despair,

Now I have seen my shame

That I should thus deny

My soul's divinest flame,

Now shall I shout my name,

Now shall I seek to die

By any hands but these

In battle or in flood

Whether I burn or freeze

No more shall I share ease

No more shall I spare blood

When I have need to fight

For heaven or for your heart,

Against the powers of light

Or darkness I shall smite

Until their might depart

Because I know the spark

Of God has no eclipse

Now Death and I embark

And sail into the dark

With laughter on our lips.

On Tuesday 8 June Casement came home from Limburg and Fr Nicholson left for New York. Plunkett saw Meyer again at the Foreign Office and the following day he met the German Chancellor, Theobald von Bethmann Hollweg (Plunkett's code-name for him was 'the bald head') with Casement and Capt. Nadolny and they discussed the Agreement, a long talk which Plunkett felt was 'quite satisfactory' and, finally, they came to terms on it. Germany would send a cargo of arms, paid for by the IRB, to Ireland on a date to be confirmed later, but approximately Easter 1916. A German offensive in the war was planned for the beginning of May 1916 (this did not actually happen until October 1916) and, if possible, a skeleton force of officers and trained men would come to Ireland with the arms. They all met again on Thursday 10 with Casement, Count von Wedel and Capt. Boehm who came from Limburg for the meeting. Plunkett was very disappointed this time because the Agreement couldn't be finalised without 'hearing from James', but there is no indication of who James is.

Fri 11th Waiting. Dinner with Casement at C.

Sat 12th The same. Waiting.

Sun 13th Mass at Ludwigkirche 11.30. At 1.00 with Casement to 26. Lunch with Adela O N [a friend of Casement's, Ada O'Neill] and Gussai. Playing and writing a poem in the book. God is very good.

Mon 14th Casement at the Foreign Office. ..

Tues 15th Again to 26 and lunch with Adela O N and Gussai. She gave me a flower. Good things. With Casement to Foreign Office. Richard Meyer. Drop of blood on the paper.

Wed 16th At No. 8 in the morning. Got my passport. There is nothing at all to do. Lunch with Casement. Capt. Boehm came. At Foreign Office with Richard Meyer.

Thu 17th 3 months today. At Foreign Office in the morning. Waiting 1 hour. George Wedel, Richard Meyer and OR and attendant, secretary, with Casement. JMP

This is where the diary ends, just when the Agreement was concluded and he could think of leaving for home. First he had to send a message to the Military Council in Ireland to make sure that it was safe for him to go home as any wrong timing or indication that he had been in Germany could destroy the whole enterprise; while he waited for word from home he and Casement and others went to the Grünwald in Bavaria for a holiday. It was about three weeks before he got word to go home. Casement, whose ideas of how the insurrection should be carried out were completely different, wanted to come back to Ireland with him, but Plunkett considered that the combination of Casement's deep depression, his idea that he was going to lead the revolution and his very high profile with the British Government made him a liability and he took it on himself to impress on Casement that he must not come back yet and Casement appeared to accept this. Plunkett travelled back through Switzerland and France without incident until he reached the English border when he was stopped. He had bought a copy of *London Opinion* and when the official came to check his passport and search him he threw the *London Opinion* on the window ledge and handed over his keys. They found nothing on him – the documents were in the magazine. He also met John MacDonagh on a tram who said, at the top of his voice (as a joke) 'I don't believe you were in Jersey at all, Plunkett, I think you were in Germany'. Joe nearly jumped out of his skin.[1]

Plunkett arrived home to Larkfield; Gerry had moved the household there in the middle of July. Both Gerry and Jack Plunkett noticed how well he looked and how busy he was. As soon as he arrived he asked about the two reports he had sent and when he found that a letter that Christiansen had undertaken to send asking for confirmation of his order to Casement had not arrived he went straight to consult the members of the Military Council to find out if he had been right in insisting on Casement remaining in Germany and was greatly relieved to find that he had. The old Fenian, O'Donovan Rossa, had died on June 30 and his body was brought home from the United States by an arrangement between John Devoy and Tom Clarke. The Volunteers acted as stewards and marshals at the funeral on 1 August and huge crowds followed the coffin to Glasnevin. Those Plunketts who were in the country were all there, all in different places; Count Plunkett was at the graveside, Gerry was at the Parnell Monument, Jack was there with his motorbike as a messenger for Thomas MacDonagh, who was the organiser and Jack said of it 'perfect organisation with a completely successful scheme to prevent arrests.' Joe went in his uniform but keeping a low profile as he was preparing to travel to the USA on behalf of the Military Council.

That month, two people close to Plunkett were killed in

the war, which was coming to the end of its first year: twenty-year-old Frank O'Carroll, Columba's brother, with whom Plunkett had grown up, who had gone to Donegal with him in 1910 and was in and out of the Plunketts' house every other day, was killed in Gallipoli on 4 June, and Sub Lieutenant Gerald Plunkett of Joe's grandfather's second family was killed in Gallipoli on 10 August after only three weeks in the war. He was twenty-seven years old, born within a month of Joe so they shared much – Joe had used the same cradle as Gerald after Gerald had grown out of it and there was a regular exchange between the Fitzwilliam Street and Palmerston Road houses.

Columba needed to get away from her father who had thrashed her for bringing home an 'unsuitable' man. As a result of this and perhaps also of her brother's death, Columba went to see Joe in Larkfield and told him that he would have to give up all his ideas of her and love, real or unreal and he agreed, as he could not do otherwise. Sadly she then had two bad marriages, but an exemplary professional life after her qualification as a doctor, working with the famous Alexander Fleming in England.

With that separation from Columba on his mind Plunkett set about preparing to travel to the USA to inform Clann na nGael of the German Agreement.

From Joseph Plunkett to Aidan McCabe:

13th August 1915

Dear old Aidan

James is off at short notice and has not had time to answer your letter. He received the book all right. He will probably be away a month or so. I will let you know when I hear. Your classification was great.

If you get a chance of coming down, take it,

Love P

I was asked to forward this to you ten days ago. Gerry

This is a coded letter to Aidan McCabe. 'James' is Plunkett's alias 'James Malcolm'.

Jack Plunkett, now in the Volunteers, became involved in the preparations:

I spent hours copying documents in code ... for Clan na Gael there was so many of them and they wanted details of everything. The code was very simple; there was an agreed relation between certain letters and certain figures. Joe brought a walking stick which I had bored and put back in the ferrule.

Jack Plunkett

Plunkett left Ireland for New York in about the third week of August. John Devoy was informed that Plunkett had been refused entry at Ellis Island because of his tuberculosis and he went there to see him. He said he knew immediately when he saw the distinct marks of tuberculosis on Plunkett's face and neck that he would not be allowed in to the USA.

BIG TALK

I have found a thing to do in the world,

It is to break chains

Not only the chains of the spirit

But the chains of the body also

Without whose freedom the spirit cannot be free.

Everywhere I see chains

And slaves hugging them

For fear of freedom

The unsensed to them is full of fear

How much more so the super sensible Liberty

Therefore they cling to chains

Of the body and of the spirit

Holding the body back from bravery

The spirit from good

The soul from God

And the heart from seeking the beloved

Slaves construct their own chain

Out of themselves.

JMP New York USA August 28th 1915

Devoy tried to persuade those in charge that Plunkett was dying anyway and nothing would be lost by giving him temporary admittance and in his account he says he enlisted the help of Senator O'Gorman who arranged that Plunkett would be allowed to stay for two months for literary pursuits if he deposited $1,000, which Devoy supplied. This was a double difficulty for Plunkett. It gave him more public notice than he wanted and it put him in debt to Devoy. John Devoy was now in his early seventies and had an extraordinary record of activities for Ireland, but he had been away over forty years and could not know what it was really like. Despite this, he and the Clann na nGael wanted to be the decision makers in any rebellion. They didn't trust the younger people and they had a more conservative programme. Plunkett was uneasy about Devoy's judgement so he waited for Joseph McGarrity to return from Philadelphia to give him a copy of the Agreement. Plunkett was also worried by the casual way people spoke of things 'which could cause a man to be jailed in Ireland'. New York had its share of spies and the US Government was passing information to the British.

While he was waiting Plunkett used the time making contact with people he knew and new contacts in the literary world but also to purge himself of his Columba passion. He wrote three letters to Columba which were never sent and never intended to be sent. Each different in character, they are quite revealing about his self-image, or lack of it, while giving a sense that his heart is not as broken nor his despair as deep as he might have expected.

The first letter is intense – on creation in art, beauty, expression and its part in the divine:

New York

Tuesday Sept 7th 1915

... I can speak within the truth and say that man is God's expression; art, poetry, life, is man's expression and you are my expression...

.. Does this to you savour of blasphemy? Believe me I would not speak it profanely.

'You are what God has made you – and my heart'

For your real being, the real you outside of me can only be known to God and you.

... In the best version of *Pygmalion* the statue that the sculptor made was so beautiful that it lived, showing the necessary connection between beauty and the reality of vision. In the second the Beast became beautiful when it was loved showing that beauty is the expression of the will and the consequence of its action.

The second letter is much more frivolous:

... I would like to incur your approval – even if I can't earn it to my own satisfaction. Now to do this it seems to me that I've got to conform – wait a minute – to some idea of yours about me ... I'm willing to attempt any behaviour on earth if you'll only just indicate which. If you don't indicate it I can't do it. That mightn't matter, only I'm sure to do something else. There is one thing I can't do if you refuse to specify. I can't just 'be myself'. Nobody can be themselves. They don't. There is only one way to be oneself and that is to be nothing. To sit down and say nothing and do nothing and behave ... nohow but just perform the curious feat of eating one's head off. That's bad besides being uncomfortable. Unless you'll admit as I do that anyone can be anyone and may behave any way. The only 'myself' that I know is me and all other people. ...What kind of things would you prefer? ...You can easily imagine something more interesting than this individual ... Would you like a classified list to help? Not Soldier Sailor Tinker Tailor Cowboy Gentleman Apothecary Thief but more wide and specific at the same time – Badman, Adventurer, Softie, Greenhorn, Sleuth, Napoleon, Toots, George Washington, The Thin Woman's Husband, Micawber, Romeo, St Francis, Don Juan, Robert Emmet, Boss Croker, Cuchullin, Kaiser Bill, Don Quixote, The Virginian, Dante, Danton, Tomás, Sir Roger Casement, Fr Browne, Fool (various qualities all the one price...) Explorer, Navvy, Old Moore,

Walt Whitman, Sophocles, or Endymion − ... unless you'll describe me, because I have no knowledge of such a person. It's up to you now.

The third is the closest to real life:

Sept 13th New York USA

... I am not writing this letter for you to read, that would be impossible because I know we cannot go back to before the irrevocable happened, but just to ease my heart where this has so often been written, if a new kind of pain can be called ease (I think it can.)...

... I never said rightly what I meant even so far as it could have been said by ... (thank you, such as I.) I just made blind rushes at speaking and got all tangled. I am not doing much better now, but the hopelessness seems to make it easier to be clear and anyway my failure this time wont make tragedy.

... This time I know you will not treat my words as they deserve with the impatience of which they were the necessary cause.

... but what a fool I am, labour is only a sign of love and love itself has failed. Have I not given you signs already? Am I not exiled? Have I not been silent? ...

... Is it not six months since I left my country, home, friends and you for your sake? Have I not even abstained from writing to you? What greater works could love have done than these? To have found what I did seek, honourable death would have been far easier to endure than the 'ordeal by life'.

...If these signs lack, do you not know that now as ever your name spoken or written brings to my heart a shock of joy as if the Heavens were opened and the moment of happiness were come?

'My heart is breaking
I cannot sing this song'
[Coventry Patmore's *The Angel in the House*]
But if I could it would not apply because in the next two lines he says
'Your life is in the rose you gave
Its perfume suffocates my heart'
But I, I have no rose.

...You would not stand accused to yourself of having led me to my hurt – you would give me no encouragement. Did you then know so little of love as to think it needed encouragement? Did you not know that love devours famine like a flame? That it follows lack as air fills a vacuum? And if encouragement were needed was there not yourself sweeter and more dreadful than any rose....Your hands at least will be clear of my blood ... perhaps, I do not know – a little in fear lest escape might be difficult, but chiefly because you would be truthful and not the slightest expression of what you did not feel.

...You did not know that in order to love, you had but to

throw yourself to the wolves – and the enchantment would be broken, or would begin. The Beast would be made a man and lovable by the power of your love.

It was my misfortune, it is my despair that the only hope for me lay beyond your understanding, buried in what was to you a foreign tongue. Only in my poems is there anything worthy of your love, and even the celestial glories of which I have written I seem to have obscured with my own murky personality. But I can at least praise God that I have seen his glory in you and have not kept silence.

The following two fragments are just intriguing....

I loved your beauty while you slept

And wept that you should wake to pain

While brain and heart the vigil kept

Stept lightly that your dreams remain.

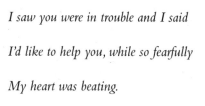

I saw you were in trouble and I said

I'd like to help you, while so fearfully

My heart was beating.

JMP 21st September 1915 New York

Plunkett wrote to Sydney Gifford (sister of Nellie, Muriel and Grace, a journalist who wrote under the name 'John Brennan') who had been in New York since 1914. They had a meal in a Turkish restaurant and Sydney was surprised that he seemed well and talked easily. She remembered him as 'taciturn, reserved and incapable of light conversation'. When she commented on the change in him he said, 'I am a different man since I joined the Volunteers.' He didn't tell her why he was in New York or that he had been to Germany. Plunkett also met up with Padraic Colum, one of the first editors of the *Irish Review* and Colum wrote of this meeting:

> Joseph Plunkett, for all his ill-health, had remarkable power
> of will … I was impressed by the decision and command
> he had attained to.

After his meetings with McGarrity in Philadelphia and with members of Clann na nGael in New York where he agreed to bring back with him their suggestions as to what should happen in Ireland, Plunkett met Joyce Kilmer. They were within a year of each other in age, both poets, both strongly identified with the Catholic religion and mysticism (Kilmer and his wife had converted to Catholicism) and both died young – Kilmer, aged thirty-one, died heroically in the war. Kilmer gave Plunkett his volume of poems, *Trees,* and, after the Rising, he wrote a poem, *Easter Week* dedicated to Plunkett.

Plunkett sailed back to Liverpool, arriving on 17 October on the *New York*.

Defence of the Realm (consolidation) regulations 1914

License to import Arms

Notwithstanding anything in regulation 31 of the Defence of the Realm (consolidation) regulations 1914

Mr J Plunkett of 26 Upper Fitzwilliam St Dublin

a British subject who has this day arrived at this port on board the New York from the port of New York is hereby authorised to bring into the United Kingdom the following arms ammunition etc namely: – 2 swords each marked US 1865

Signed T.J.G. Coady

Officer of Customs and Excise on behalf of the competent military authority port of Liverpool,

17-10-1915.

Late in 1915 I was in Aidan McCabe's flat. Joe came in. We were sitting by the fire. After a while, he took out a gold hunter watch which he wore. He opened it. He took out a small red wafer which was hidden in the back. He threw it into the fire. Saying, 'There goes the seal of the German Foreign Office.'

Arthur Cox

CHAPTER 14

• • • • • •

October 1915–February 1916
Passion And Plans

From the time Plunkett came back from the USA, the gland in his right cheek was troublesome and he had to stay in bed much of the time. He was still confined to bed on 31 October when the River Poddle overflowed at Larkfield where cows had trodden down the banks. Some of those who helped to make dams and trenches to direct the flood were the first of the refugees from conscription, christened 'the Liverpool Lambs' by George Plunkett. They were mostly Irish-born or of Irish descent, members of the Irish Republican Brotherhood (IRB) the Gaelic League or the Gaelic Athletic Association (GAA), men from Liverpool, Glasgow and London who had come to Ireland to join the Volunteers and fight for Irish independence. Before they arrived in Larkfield it was quiet enough; the bakers worked discreetly by night, the poplin weavers by day, sometimes Volunteers drilled in the barn and Tom Dillon and Rory

O'Connor were trying to get a tar still installed for their chemical factory. Suddenly one morning about forty young men arrived and accommodation had to be created for them. George Plunkett was put in charge and they set up living quarters in the barn. They had skills as plumbers, joiners, metal workers and so on and some of them found digs elsewhere, but most stayed in Larkfield where they acquired new skills in looking after themselves. They put all the mattresses together to make one enormous bed in the barn and George brought his own mattress out and slept there to stop the initial grumbling. They cooked huge pots of stew and bigger ones of potatoes. Some of them found work and Dillon's chemical company gave others a day's work now and then, but mainly they were training as Volunteers and becoming The Kimmage Garrison.

Countess Plunkett had left for an extended holiday in America at the beginning of September leaving financial chaos behind her and by now all the Plunketts, except Moya, who had become a nun, were living in Larkfield. Bills of all kinds started coming in from the grocer, the builder, the rates, mortgages, and repairs on the rental houses and a substantial annuity due to their aunt, Margaret Cranny. Gerry was told by a friend that Dublin Castle was out to bankrupt the Countess, believing, wrongly, that she was funding the Volunteers and businesses were pressing for accounts to be settled sooner and faster than usual. Gerry managed to let twenty of the houses that were vacant to begin the rescue of the family finances. Larkfield was by now effectively an armed camp with the growing Kimmage Garrison living in the mill and Gerry Plunkett was now minding the rental houses, looking after Joe, giving grinds and doing laboratory demonstration work, writing a paper for the Royal Irish Academy on dyes, seeing solicitors and business people and writing letters on family affairs. She told Joe she couldn't manage and would have to have a clerk for half the week and suggested he would get someone from the Volunteers as they could not bring an outsider into an armed camp.

A few days later Joe told her that two men would come that afternoon but only one arrived:

> This man was slim and of medium height and I thought not remarkable until I looked at his eyes. He was completely honest and direct and it was quite obvious that he was the right man ... This was Michael Collins (we knew him as Mick) and no one ever had a better clerk. He was shrewd, serious and downright, very quick and clear. I paid him £1 a week and he took pot luck with the family. For about three months he did a couple of hours' work every day making new rent books, answering letters and filing papers. ... I told Joe that Mick was much too good for the job and Joe, who had never met him before either, told me that he was very glad Mick lived up to the account which

had come with him from London.

Geraldine Plunkett Dillon

Plunkett put Collins on his staff after only a few days and they got on very well together, exchanging books and ideas, particularly on invisibility techniques: hiding in plain sight or, as Collins did, by walking up to the military at a barricade, pretending to be an ignorant countryman! Collins, who was very good to Plunkett, sometimes acted as his bodyguard. Occasionally, Collins also acted as bodyguard for Seán MacDiarmada, who had had polio from 1911, but was the most active and effective IRB organiser through the whole of Ireland, prime mover in the Volunteers and a very close friend of Thomas Clarke, the driver of the revolution. Collins came out to Larkfield nearly every day and collected letters from Plunkett to the other members of the Military Council. The rest of Plunkett's staff consisted of his brothers, Jack and George, Tom Dillon, his chemical expert and Rory O'Connor in charge of engineering, with Con Keating and Fergus Kelly working on radio. Plunkett was the only member of the Military Council who knew about radio and from early on he had realised its potential for sending the news of the Rising to the outside world, bypassing the British censor. Con Keating, trained in Atlantic College in O'Connell Street, had worked as radio officer on ships for several years and Fergus Kelly, an engineering student in UCD, was Con's assistant.

From Jack Plunkett:

> From 1915 I was full-time on Joe's staff. It was mainly work on wireless with an awful lot of work with no result. Joe was better than I was; he had sets working from 1907 but only at short range (up to 2 miles) in Morse and not portable. Con Keating had travelled around the world and used to describe Africa and other places he had been. He was a very fine fellow and everybody liked him.

[Plunkett recorded a radio signal on 11 March in his 1907 diary.]

In Larkfield there was constant practice at the targets in the big barn with the Howth .303 rifles and revolvers, sometimes resulting in injuries, there was an explosives factory in the outbuildings and the experiments on wireless in the house so, as an armed training camp, it had to become more organised. No strangers were allowed near the buildings; an English soldier in uniform who came in was chased down the avenue with knives, a platoon of British soldiers marched up to the gate one night but did nothing and the local spy and recruiting sergeants were often found hanging around. Guns of all kinds were quite common among the whole population as owning them was not illegal, but more small arms were smuggled in, revolvers and small automatics, and it was always possible to buy arms and ammunition from English soldiers. Tom Dillon showed Michael Collins how to make bombs out of big gun-barrel caps and the Liverpool men made bombs out of tin cans. Buckshot was cast in moulds and a few pikes were made by fixing twelve-inch knives on six-foot poles.

At some time during all this Joe Plunkett and Grace Gifford's relationship, very quietly and very discreetly, changed to love. They had known each other for a few years now, but Joe knew Grace's sister, Muriel, married to MacDonagh, much better. Plunkett was very ready to be in love, seven years of hopes from talks with Kathleen Cruise O'Brien, passion for Columba, moments with Ada O'Neill in Berlin and the un-named in New York.

Grace, one of twelve children, had been to Alexandra College, the Metropolitan School of Art in Dublin and the Slade School of Art in London. She was admired by many for her talent and painted for her beauty by William Orpen. She was now living independently, a member of the United Arts Club and drawing caricatures of well-known Dubliners, selling them when she could, but it was a difficult life. Her mother, Isabella, was Church of Ireland and her father, Frederick, Roman Catholic, both strongly unionist, and they adhered to the convention that the boys were brought up as Catholics and the girls Church of Ireland, but the girls were drawn to Catholicism mainly because their nursemaids when they were growing up were Catholic and nationalist. Grace was not really interested in politics, but in 1911 she was with Maude Gonne protesting against a 'loyal address' to the English King George V and from the time of the 1913 Lockout and Strike she was made aware of the overwhelming poverty of most of Dublin's people and had helped distribute James Connolly's school meals for the inner-city poor. Like her sisters, she was committed to the idea of votes for women and a supporter of the Irish Women's Franchise League. She had begun to go to the Pro-Cathedral to hear the Palestrina Choir where, because of its central location, there were many very poor people in its congregation. Grace felt they were more fervent and spiritual than those she met at her parish services in Holy Trinity Church, Rathmines. This was one of the incentives for her conversion to Roman Catholicism and that in its turn was what drew her into conversations with Joseph Plunkett.

From Grace Gifford Plunkett (Military Archive Statement 1949):

> I did not know anything about the military side of Joe's life. ... I was a committed Catholic as was Joe. We talked all the time about it. When I became interested in becoming a Catholic, Joe was the first person I met that I could talk to about it. It's what we talked about all the time. He was very athletic and could jump six chairs at a time. He was reckless about his health; he used to wander around the house in his pyjamas looking for books. He was all the time composing poetry. Joe was in bad health, I think he might have had bronchitis. The doctor told him three weeks before our

engagement that he didn't have TB.

It isn't clear from this whether Joe lied to Grace about his health or whether she misunderstood, but it seems very unlikely that Plunkett could have thought at this time that he did not have tuberculosis given that he had faced it so often already and that he had just finished one flare-up and was starting another.

NEW LOVE

The day I knew you loved me we had lain

Deep in Coill Doraca down by Gleann na Scath

Unknown to each till suddenly I saw

You in the shadow, knew oppressive pain

Stopping my heart, and there you did remain

In dreadful beauty fair without a flaw,

Blinding the eyes that yet could not withdraw

Till wild between us drove the wind and rain.

Breathless we reached the brugh before the west

Burst in full fury — then with lightning stroke

The tempest in my heart roared up and broke

Its barriers and I swore I would not rest

Till that mad heart was worthy of your breast

Or dead for you – and then this love awoke.

JMP

Plunkett was twenty-eight on that 21 November. In two-and-a-half years he had been editor of the *Irish Review* and made it a more political journal, he was joint secretary on the Industrial Peace Committee of the 1913 Lockout and Strike, he had joined the Irish Volunteers and gone straight onto committees and, after the 1914 split, he had become the Volunteers' Director of Military Operations, he joined the Irish Republican Brotherhood at their invitation and became a member of the Military Council, he had travelled through the war to Germany and negotiated with the Foreign Office, the General Staff and the Chancellor and assisted Casement in the Irish Brigade, he had travelled to the United States and informed John Devoy and Joseph McGarrity and now he was the deviser of the military plan for the Rising at Easter 1916. Through all this he continued to write poetry. He had endured illness and faced death several times, but kept his sense of humour. He was seen as flamboyant, eccentric, a bit continental, a slightly flashy dresser in a very conservative society, but those who knew him respected his brain, his passion, his learning, his love of technology and invention, his kindness and, above all, his inestimable courage. All through these things his friendship with MacDonagh was close and constant, 'always arguing, agreeing or disagreeing.' Plunkett was a strongly religious man, but it was mostly private. He read voraciously including books on religions of all kinds and his considerable religious reading led him to study Mysticism, in itself a part of many religions and traditions making it a catalyst as well as a deep, internal experience. Plunkett only spoke of it to the few he thought would understand, he didn't write about it in any depth and his few mystical poems were in a folder he had with him during the Rising which disappeared, probably in the GPO fires. He did not preach or try to convert anyone to Catholicism, he went to Mass on Sundays, but not weekdays, he did not live by the authority of bishops and priests but, like most people of his time, he knew plenty of them and he writes of dying 'for the glory of God and the honour of Ireland' not 'saving Ireland for God' as was said later. His relationship with his god (he rarely capitalises 'god' or anything else religious) comes through in his poetry as both close and all-embracing; all of good and evil here together, not fearful or puritanical but confident and delighted. More than anything, his reading, thinking and experience make him believe that, in a truly democratic and egalitarian system, every individual must have complete freedom to choose their own religion.

On 2 December Plunkett wrote to Grace:

> I do love you. I hope to become more worthy of loving you. Will you marry me?

And in a postscript:

> By the way, I am actually a beggar. I have no income and am earning nothing. Moreover there are other things more desperate, practically speaking, to prevent anyone marrying me.

There was no reason for Grace to believe that he was 'a beggar' as she had already seen the family lifestyle, but Joe had no income, no allowance, no property. His illness made it impossible to hold down a job so he was completely dependant on his mother's handouts and Gerry's contributions. The 'other things, more desperate' must be his illness and his expectations of the Rising.

Later that day he wrote:

> Darling Grace,
>
> You will marry me and nobody else. I have been a damned fool ... but thank God I see. I love you and only you and will never love anyone else ... I was never meant to be so happy. I can't believe what I know ... I love you a million million times ...
>
> We got engaged on the 2nd December 1915; I remember because it's in a book I have.
>
> Grace Gifford Plunkett

The other Plunketts were flabbergasted, they knew nothing

of any connection between Joe and Grace and Grace did not tell her parents then as she knew they would not approve.

From Joe to Grace, 4 December:

> It seems awfully silly that we should not be able to be together all the time and especially at the end of the day and all through the lovely hours of the quiet night. I want to hold you close and feel your happiness that is mine ... you have taken the harm out of all my troubles and made the whole world beautiful for me. You have made me happy – never forget that whatever happens because it's a kind of miracle.

By Christmas the engagement was well-known to many although not yet official.

Joe to Grace on St Stephen's Day:

> It's awful to be without you – you know if I was only coming home to you after my work it would be different ...

From Joe Plunkett to Aidan McCabe

> 5 Nollaig 1915

> Dear Old Moses,

> You may have noticed that I have not been writing to you very regularly. Well it is because of happenings. Listen I am going to astonish you. I don't know if you have ever met or seen Grace Gifford. Well she and I are engaged to be married. She is a sister of Tomás' wife – anyhow you have seen her drawings.

> I wrote a note to Columba to tell her about it and

when leaving your house I met her so I took the opportunity to tell her. She was looking very well. She congratulated me very kindly. Please write to me exactly what you like to say and don't be shy about it. Yours

PS Can you come here on or about the 23 Dec and stay over Christmas?

The Family and the Blood Royal

Just after Christmas 1915 the Military Council sent Philomena Plunkett to New York with despatches, the date of the Rising and word of the arms from Germany for John Devoy and Clann na nGael. For some time now James Connolly had made it known that he intended to bring out his Citizen Army in a Rising very shortly. It would have been no more than a very angry gesture by a few hundred virtually unarmed militant men and women, but people of great conviction and courage who might have given the authorities a bad fright before they were massacred, jailed or deported. Connolly had no faith in the Volunteers and knew nothing of the IRB plans for a Rising. The Military Council now had to prevent Connolly's Rising and persuade him to become part of theirs. They sent him repeated requests to meet them but he kept evading them so, on 19 January, some of them waited for him outside Liberty Hall …

From Joseph Plunkett:

A taxi waited not far from the steps of Liberty Hall. Two

men in it, one outside, and the driver. Padraig [Pearse] and another inside, Sean McDermott [Seán MacDiarmada] outside. When Connolly came level with the taxi the man outside stopped him to talk to him, persuaded him to enter and came in after him. Connolly was momentarily disturbed and thought of calling to those who were at the entrance to Liberty Hall, but was persuaded not to, and in any case he was a powerful man who had not to be afraid. An explanation of what was wanted rapidly followed his entry to the taxi. 'We want to talk to you for half an hour. If you don't think it worth while continuing the conversation after that you can do what you like.'

The taxi soon reached the house where the discussion was to continue, a two storey house with no carpet on the stairs. The three men Connolly, Pearse and McDermott went into the top front room facing the street. Someone pointed out to Connolly that he had only to put his head out the window to call for help if he wanted to. Four men were provided as a guard. These stayed in the house very quietly. The discussion with Connolly, at first very vehement, was quieting down after the first few hours, was first of all to convince Connolly that the Volunteers were sincere and about to start a Rising...

The house was in Dolphin's Barn and the guards were under strict instructions not to injure Connolly in any way. After a couple of angry hours in which Connolly said that he felt they had been less than honest initially, Pearse, MacDiarmada and Plunkett explained their plans and the German and American connections. They also emphasised that their aim was not just to have an Irish state, but one with social equality and justice, civil and religious liberty for all its citizens. As it went on, Connolly was completely converted. He spent the three days walking up and down, talking and asking questions. When Plunkett became exhausted he rested on a bed with a bare mattress for a few hours and when he returned Connolly was still walking and talking. He and Plunkett came to very close agreement on the style of campaign. They were both city-minded and understood the way that buildings could be taken over and used.

> Connolly had some unexplained (and to us inexplicable) poor opinion of Tomás MacDonagh, and when Tomás came in to the room he good-naturedly stated that if Tomás had been in the business earlier he would not have come into it. He also explained how glad he was not to have called out to the men at Liberty Hall to rescue him. One of the guards in the house was discovered by Tomás as he was going away not to have had sleep or food for a long time. He and the other guards were dismissed because the party was now on a friendly basis. We talked to him almost continuously for three days.
>
> Joseph Plunkett

Connolly later changed his mind and had great respect

for MacDonagh. Thomas MacDonagh is mentioned as being present on this occasion by Joe, Gerry and Jack Plunkett and in another note possibly by Count Plunkett. This begs the question about when he became a member of the Military Council, usually given as April 1916, but those in the room for discussions with Connolly were all members of the Military Council; the secrecy of the date and plans for the Rising being paramount. Kathleen Clarke also mentions a heated meeting about secrecy and publications at the beginning of that month with Clarke, Pearse, Plunkett and MacDonagh present suggesting that MacDonagh was already on the Military Council. They had to persuade Connolly to go home (it was now 21 January) and when he arrived first at Countess Markievicz's house on Leinster Road he discovered that his 'disappearance' had created great anxiety and foreboding in many quarters. After this Connolly and Plunkett worked together on the Rising plans, becoming very close in the process.

From Joe Plunkett to Grace Gifford:

Jan. 27th 1916

... My hearts delight my lovely dear I will not pretend I am not disappointed at not seeing you but I know you must be very busy and I know too that you are sorry as well as me so I don't want to make it worse for you ...

... Listen beloved – this is what I believe. I believe that God created you in his image and likeness that you might know and love him and his love for you through seeing his glory in the beauty of the things he created and especially through your love for me and mine for you. I believe that we were created for an eternal happiness. I believe that you are the temple of his holy spirit. I believe that Jesus Christ God and man suffered shameful torture and death on the cross that we might see and know what was right to choose and choose the right by our own free will when it would be most difficult. I am prepared to act on those beliefs and to follow him in the most difficult way for love. I believe that we are intended for great joy in this life – that happiness is to be hoped for while living in this world and not that we are to be only looking for something unknown till we reach heaven. We are meant to realise his glory in order to be able to love him. I do not ~~think~~ believe for a moment that it is meant that you should be unhappy in your life, but I know that there is great happiness in store for you if you love – the greater your love the greater the joy.

I am ready to go into darkness, danger and death trusting in his love that the issue will be joy. That is what I mean by the trust of love. I would not think it much for me to be willing to suffer all things for love, because I know the joy, but for one who does not know it is the sublimest virtue and the final and ultimate proof of perfect trust and love.

Joe [celtic cross symbol]

On the side of the page it says:

Darling I will see you at Oakley Road tonight.

Thomas MacDonagh and his wife, Grace's sister, Muriel, lived at 29 Oakley Road, Ranelagh and at this period Grace lived there a good deal of the time. That February, Grace also went out to Larkfield often to visit Joe. She was aware that he had a cold for weeks and that he had problems with the glands in his neck, but not how serious things were with him. She said later that she knew nothing of his 'military life', but she must have seen and heard some strange things going in and out of Larkfield! Their engagement was finally announced in *Irish Life* magazine on 11 February 1916:

> An engagement is announced between Mr Joseph Mary Plunkett, 26 Fitzwilliam Street Upper, eldest son of Count Plunkett Director of the National Museum, Kildare Street, and Miss Grace Gifford, daughter of Mr Frederick Gifford, 8 Temple Villas, Palmerston Park, Dublin.

This is one of the very few occasions when he uses his middle name, Mary. Five of the young Plunketts were christened with versions of their mother's name – Josephine Mary. Plunkett used 'Joseph Mary' when he published *Sonnets to Columba*, but not for *The Circle and the Sword* or any poems published in journals. He usually signed himself 'Joe' or 'Plunkett'.

Plunkett to Aidan McCabe:

> *Hic et Nunc* St Valentine's Day 1916

My dear Mose

Thanks for letter. I mislaid it. Also I've been worked to death and am now in bed with a cold. Sir Philip Sydney will hang on for a bit while you get through with Psyche. I have not got Jen his religious varieties tho' often wanted it – sure it is worth reading. But I know a lot of the matter in it from other sources – Dame Julian of Norwich and Catherine Emmerich – dialogue of St Catherine of Siena, Blessed Angela of Foligno – St Francis (of Assisi) – St John of the Cross – Ruysbrock – Suso – cf. Psychology of the Saints (Joly) and Underhill's Mysticism besides the Quietists, Sufi, Psychists, Gnostics, Quakers and in fact the religious history of all mankind (Catholic Mystics and Mysticism are being more fully treated of every day. Treatises in English include Scaramelli, S.J., Fr Poulain (I think translated but perhaps not) Algar Thorold. E Lambelle (*Mystical Contemplation* v. good) Sharpe's Catholic Mysticism (very simple and includes translation of Dionysius Areopagite) Abbé Le Jeune, *An Introduction to the Mystical Life* (just translated) Devine – *A Manual of Mystical Theology*. Baron von Hugel – *The Mystical Element of Religion*, Ven. Augustine Baker Holy Wisdom. The fullest treatise that I am acquainted with is Evelyn Underhill's *Mysticism*. It covers most of the ground and deals with most of the great mystics but the author is not a Catholic and the book suffers somewhat from modern psychologism. James of course examines all kinds of curious phenomena from the psychological standpoint and equally of course has no criteria of validity or proportional importance to go by – he just treats of phenomena as such.

There is no news – or very little. Philomena has gone out to her mother and we expect them home soon. Georgie has charge of a show to run. Fiona is complaining of boredom. Jack is as usual. Gerry and Tommy are well but overworked like myself. I have not met any of the O'Carrolls. Aunt Josie spoke to me on Grafton Street. Grace is working like a nigger as are all of us. We all wish you well and would like to see you as soon as the fates are willing.

PS Please write me disquisitions.

(unsigned)

In the final paragraph he is carefully concealing several truths: Philomena has gone to New York on Rising business, the 'show' George is running is the Kimmage Garrison, Jack is working on radio, Tommy· is making explosives among other things and Gerry is keeping revolutionary bodies and souls together!

Plunkett was now working constantly on the Rising plans. Over the last few years he had developed his own ideas about tactics and strategy. A lot of the work was done in his sick bed, which was always covered with maps procured from the Ordnance Survey by Robert Monteith and British military handbooks, which he studied to measure mentality rather than for Volunteers' plans. Plunkett took ideas from many sources and had been observing tactics, real and strange from at least 1911: the Siege of Sydney Street, one man in a house against hundreds of soldiers; the game of *Little Wars;* the violence of police and soldiers on the streets in 1913; working as Director of Military Operations in the Volunteers; creating the *Ireland Report* with Casement and discussions on tactics with the military in Germany. He believed that Dublin Castle's expectation of an Irish rebellion was 'Ten bloody fools in a field surrounded by rifles', that they would take to the hills in small numbers without proper plans. He wanted to do something completely different and unexpected, a defensive approach, which put the aggressor at a disadvantage, something that became a standard tactic later. This may explain why many have not understood the Rising plans or believed that they should have resembled conventional warfare.

He knew that there weren't enough troops in the city to deal with any Rising and believed that the route the British Army would take to the city when they brought in reinforcements, landing in Kingstown (Dun Laoghaire), would go through Ballsbridge, Northumberland Road, Lower Mount Street and Nassau Street to College Green. He thought he might be presuming too much but, as it turned out, the Army did follow its own textbooks.

'We need not keep their rules, but they have to,' Plunkett said. The choice of buildings occupied was based on strategic placing to enable control over the Army routes and using high buildings prevented them being overlooked or dominated. General Friend, in command in Dublin was known to have said at a meeting in the Castle that he was completely opposed to the shelling of the city and Connolly believed that the British would not shell 'their own' buildings. Unfortunately, General Friend was on leave in England that Easter. The taking of Dublin Castle was not part of the plan because it could be easily dominated, but Ship Street cavalry barracks beside it had badly needed arms and was a definite target. Connolly in particular, supported Plunkett in these ideas and worked with him on the plans. Because Plunkett's health was so bad the other leaders used to come to Larkfield for meetings; Tom Clarke rarely came as he said that his presence would endanger everything because he was always under surveillance so Seán MacDiarmada acted as Clarke's eyes and ears. Nothing of the plans or orders was written down; they were memorised and assigned to individuals to prevent access by informers and, uniquely in Irish history, this succeeded. Dublin Castle never did discover the actual plan. On 9 February Colonel Edgeworth Johnstone, Chief Commissioner of the Dublin Metropolitan Police, gave a plan to a conference, which included Chief Secretary Augustine Birrell, to arrest about twenty Volunteer leaders and 'Sinn Féiners', deport them and then search premises all over Dublin. The plan was delayed because there were not enough troops in Dublin to carry it out. It was estimated that it would take four field batallions to control the rebels. As February closed Plunkett and the Military Council were agreeing on a final plan for a Rising and the Chief Secretary and Dublin Castle were agreeing on a plan for arresting the leaders of the Irish Volunteers.

Plunkett was apparently becoming disenchanted with the Irish Theatre and a couple of incidents finished his involvement with it. An actress, not associated with the Irish Theatre, wanted to stage an Ibsen play there as a benefit for St Enda's school. Plunkett objected and a row ensued. When it was proposed that the Irish Theatre itself would stage Strindberg's *Easter,* Plunkett again objected. John MacDonagh, who directed many of their productions, said that Plunkett wrote to him saying that he did not blame him as he was an artist, but that Edward Martyn and Thomas MacDonagh had no right to produce this 'contemptible piece of profanity', but this 1901 play is one to which 'even Strindberg's severest critics have never been unkind'! The theme of the play concerns a family who are deep in debt because of their father's embezzling, but find reconciliation and restitution through a mentally-unbalanced sibling. None of this makes any sense in terms of Plunkett's taste, reading, admiration of Strindberg or love of the theatre so there is only one other explanation: it was a cover-up so that his leaving the theatre would not cause comment. It would simply be thought that he was being his eccentric self and MacDonagh may even have known what he was up to. He had no time for the theatre with the Rising fast approaching. Strindberg's *Easter* was performed in the Irish Theatre in March, 1916 but by then Joseph Plunkett had left.

CHAPTER 15

1916
Brinks Of Disintegration

Towards the end of March Philomena Plunkett arrived home from New York. She had given Easter Sunday as the date for the Rising to John Devoy and asked him to send that message to Germany and to stress that the arms should not arrive in Ireland before Easter Sunday. She also confirmed the requests Joe Plunkett had made to the German Government for a skeleton staff of German officers with the arms he had bought and a submarine in Dublin Bay. Philomena felt that Devoy did not take the messages seriously, as he sent her back to Ireland with a message saying that arms could be smuggled in beforehand, which the Military Council felt would endanger everything. Joe sent Philomena straight back to New York with a reply for Devoy to make it clear that the timing of the arrival of the guns was vital and saying that arms must not be landed before the night of Easter Sunday, 23 April. John Devoy did send this second message and it arrived in Berlin on 6 April before the arms ship left, but in the previous message he said 'between Holy Thursday and Easter Sunday' and the German Government took this as correct.

Plunkett told Gerry that Casement had written to the Military Council wanting to come to Dublin in a submarine, land in Howth or Bray and meet with them in order to change the Rising date and completely change the plans because he believed that the Germans 'were going to make a mess of the whole thing'. Casement still believed that the Rising would have to be officered and supported by a large invasion force from Germany and that he would have to be its leader. Casement was no leader, the Military Council were not depending on a German invasion force and if guns were landed early, all the initiative would be taken from the Volunteers. Plunkett believed there were enough arms to start the Rising and, with commandeered trains and trucks, the consignment could be distributed once it was landed. Unsuccessful attempts were made to dissuade Casement from his course of action and his heroism and dedication to Ireland were to cause some of the major problems in the Rising.

Throughout these months the Volunteers and the Citizen Army were regularly out drilling and on manoeuvres in full public view and, on St Patrick's Day, 17 March, they took over College Green in the centre of Dublin and held a review with Eoin MacNeill taking the salute. At the same time police and military, who had been watching Volunteer manoeuvres and the build-up of weaponry, including the activity at Larkfield, were practising their response to the Volunteers. At the end of March police and soldiers with rifles surrounded Larkfield house and mill. Jack Plunkett, Fergus Kelly, Con Keating, Rory O'Connor and Tom Dillon barricaded the house and prepared for a siege. George Plunkett was out in the mill with the Liverpool Lambs armed to the teeth. Joe was planning the defences as it could have been the expected move against the Volunteers. A few hours later the police and soldiers just went away as suddenly as they had come.

It had been reported in the papers that Asquith, the British Prime Minister, had visited Pope Benedict XV, confirming Casement's warning to MacNeill that England was influencing the Vatican against Ireland, the same warning Plunkett was given in Germany. This could lead to the Pope condemning the Rising so Plunkett swore his father, Count Plunkett, into the IRB and, at the beginning of April, sent him to Rome on behalf of the Military Council. His father had a right, as a Papal Count, to an audience with the Pope. Joe also got his father to memorise a letter to Casement, which he was to write and send from Switzerland on his way to Rome. In Berne he went to the agent at the Argentine Consulate, but he was uneasy about the agent's attitude and, in fact, this letter never arrived. He left a duplicate letter to be sent to Casement in the German Consulate and that was delivered through the Foreign Office. The letter was signed 'A friend of James Malcolm' and had Joe's authenticating word 'Aisling'. It got to Casement on 6 April before the German arms ship, the *Aud,* left for Ireland and it was essentially the same message that Philomena Plunkett had brought to New York giving the date for the landing of the arms as 'no earlier than Sunday' (23 April). Count Plunkett then went on to Rome and saw the Pope who told him that Asquith had informed him some months before that the Irish now had Home Rule and the Irish question was settled. Asquith did not tell him that Home Rule was suspended or that there had been no elections since 1910. Count Plunkett gave the Pope a more accurate view of Irish affairs and told him that the Volunteers intended insurrection and that 'the prospects were desperate'. Arriving back in Ireland on Holy Thursday Count Plunkett went down the country to visit various bishops and ask them to refrain from condemning what would happen. He thought afterwards that none of those bishops he interviewed did condemn the Rising.

The tubercular abscess on Plunkett's cheek was becoming so acute that he could do very little and it had to be opened. He was booked into Mrs Quinn's Nursing Home on Mountjoy Square where he was operated on by Charles McAuley. It was clear to the medical team after the operation that he only had weeks to live. Plunkett almost immediately started working again on the plans and, after the first week, going out to meetings in the city and in Larkfield. Michael Collins was with him constantly, guarding and looking after him. Grace visited him in the nursing home a number of times but, she said, they never discussed the Rising. She was baptised a Catholic in University Church, St Stephen's Green, on Saturday 7 April, 1916, by Fr Sherwin, a friend of Count Plunkett's.

TO GRACE

ON THE MORNING OF HER CHRISTENING,

APRIL 7th 1916

The powerful words that from my head

Alive and throbbing leap and sing,

Shall bind the dragon's jaws apart

Or bring you back a vanished Spring;

They shall unseal and seal again

The fount of wisdom's awful flow,

So this one guerdon they shall gain

That your wild beauty still they show.

The joy of Spring leaps from your eyes,

The strength of dragons in your hair,

In your young soul we still surprise

The secret wisdom flowing there;

But never word shall speak or sing

Inadequate music where above

Your burning heart now spreads its wing

In the wild beauty of your Love.

JMP

It was arranged that Joe Plunkett and Grace Gifford and Gerry Plunkett and Tom Dillon would have a double wedding on Easter Sunday in Rathmines Catholic Church and the banns were duly read.

From Grace Gifford Plunkett:

> He wanted us to get married in Lent, but I was a bit shocked by the idea; I said why not Easter? He said 'We may be running a revolution then'. He wanted me to be secure. I had been thrown out of the house when I became a Catholic. Joe wanted us married and going into the Rising together, but I knew nothing about it and wouldn't have been any good as a soldier.

The pieces were beginning to come together now and late in the evening of Tuesday, 17 April the wording of the Proclamation of the Irish Republic was finalised at 21 Henry Street, Jenny and John Wyse Power's restaurant. Meanwhile a Dublin Castle official was collecting information for the Volunteers: Eugene Smith had access to a document from General Friend to the Chief Secretary, Augustine Birrell, in London. Smith believed the document was a response to questions about action by the armed forces when conscription was introduced. The document was lengthy, but as he dealt with it himself he had enough time. He was 'deeply interested in the political situation in Ireland and in the threat of conscription to Ireland'. He decided to give the document to those it would affect and, having memorised it, he wrote it out and gave it, complete, to one of his contacts – he wasn't sure which, but probably one of Seán MacDiarmada's agents – he dealt with several. It is likely that Smith's contact passed the document to MacDiarmada who put it into a 'cipher', a simple mixture of shorthand and word contractions. The IRB could not risk a document like this being found if the carrier were arrested. The document was delivered to Plunkett in the nursing home where he 'de-coded' it with Grace sitting on his bed and writing it down. Plunkett then brought it to Larkfield, where there was a meeting of the Military Council, and George Plunkett, Rory O'Connor and Colm O'Lochlainn were told to print it on Plunkett's small handpress. Colm left after a while, but the other two carried on. They had no experience of printing and found it slow and difficult, passing the time by singing ballads and *God Save the King*. They ran out of capital letters and punctuation almost immediately, but continued anyway. They found that the wrong name '*Ara Coeli*' had been given to Archbishop House and sent Jack Plunkett across to Joe, who was now back in Mountjoy Square, to check it and Joe told them to change it to Archbishop House. As tiredness grew, a tray of ready type was knocked over and they had to start again, but at last it was done and, on the orders of Plunkett and the Military Council, copies were sent to all the papers on 15 and 16 April, and to many prominent people.

None of the papers would print it. Censorship was heavy and papers and journals were being seized and closed down. Patrick J. Little, now the editor of *New Ireland* had told Rory O'Connor that if at any time he wanted to use his paper especially for national purposes, he was willing to take any risk and O'Connor now approached him. Little sent the document out to the papers with a covering letter from himself, which said that attacking the Volunteers would only create an armed resistance by them. He also started to print his own paper, *New Ireland,* with the text of the document in it; Eoin MacNeill, also involved in *New Ireland*, was hesitant about this but P.J. Little persuaded him into it. After only seven copies had been printed, the manager of the Wood Printing Works, Mr David, 'not an Irishman' says Little, went across to the *Irish Times* office who telephoned Dublin Castle and the 'brass hats' came down to the printing works and suppressed all reference to the document from the paper. Little could not get the paper out again until June. Francis Sheehy-Skeffington brought a copy of the document and a letter signed by P.J. Little to Alderman Tom Kelly, and Kelly read the document into the minutes of Dublin Corporation on the Wednesday of Holy Week, 19 April. He said he took the responsibility of reading the document in discharge of his public duty. Now the document could no longer be ignored. Below is a section of the document as it came from Larkfield with no capitals or punctuation giving actions to be taken on receipt of an order from the Chief Secretary's Office:

> the following persons to be placed under arrest – all members of the sinn fein national council, the central executive, irish sinn fein volunteers executive committee county board irish sinn fein volunteers, executive committee national volunteers, coisde gnota gaelic league, dublin metropolitan police and royal irish constabulary in dublin city will be confined to barracks under the direction of the competent military authority an order will be issued to the inhabitants of the city to remain in their houses until such time as the competent military authority may otherwise direct or permit pickets chosen from units of territorial

forces will be placed on all points accompanying mounted patrols will continually visit all points and will report every hour the following premises will be occupied by adequate forces and all necessary measures used without need of reference to headquarters first premises known as liberty hall beresford place no 6 harcourt st sinn fein building no 2 dawson st headquarters volunteers no 12 d'olier st nationality office no 25 rutland square gaelic league offices no 41 rutland square forester's hall sinn fein volunteer premises in the city all national volunteer premises in the city trade council premises capel st surrey house in rathmines the following premises will be isolated and all communications to and from prevented premises known as archbishops house drumcondra mansion house dawson st no 40 herbert park larkfield kimmage woodtown park ballyboden st endas college hermitage rathfarnham

Surrey House was Madame Markievicz's house, 40 Herbert Park, The O'Rahilly's, Woodtown Park was Eoin MacNeill's and St Enda's College was Patrick Pearse's school.

There were also references to lists and maps, but Smith says they were not in the original so Plunkett must have added them. Plunkett hoped that publication would do two things: make the Castle hesitate to do the things they were planning and make the public realise what the Castle planned to do. Others hoped it would prevent bloodshed to publish it. Nationalists were certainly angered, but Dublin Castle simply put it out that the document was 'bogus' and, despite the confirming evidence by Castle officials at the Royal Commission of Inquiry into the Rising, this was believed for decades by a substantial number of people. It is worth saying that the lack of upper case letters and punctuation make it look very unprofessional and probably helped the Castle's prevarication.

On Good Friday, 21 April, MacDonagh and others came to the nursing home and talked with Plunkett and then brought him to a meeting in Larkfield. Con Keating was leaving Larkfield with the radio equipment on his way to Cahirciveen in Kerry to capture the radio transmitter. The hope was that they could transmit in Morse Code the message that the Rising had begun and a Provisional Government was declared. Con Keating looked in to say goodbye to the Plunketts, including Joe, and they, who had loved him and found him charming, never saw him again. Joe had slept every night in the nursing home until that Friday when his aide-de-camp, Michael Collins, brought him and his luggage to the Metropole Hotel on O'Connell Street.

Saturday and Sunday, 22 and 23 April, were two of the blackest days the leaders had encountered with a trio of disasters over twenty-four hours. Casement was arrested on Friday 21, and the 20,000 rifles and their ammunition consigned to the sea with the *Aud* by Captain Spindler when he was captured by the British Navy. Eoin MacNeill cancelled the Volunteers' parades on Easter Sunday that were meant to become the Rising by sending out countermanding orders and putting notices in the newspapers. One of the cars on its way to capture the radio transmitter at Cahirciveen missed its turn and went straight into the sea at Ballykissane and three men were drowned, Dan Sheehan, Alf Monaghan and Con Keating, who got caught under the car hood. Keating was the only one in the two cars who knew what the orders were. The Rising could not happen at all unless there was strict secrecy, but secrecy sometimes seemed to cost too much.

Plunkett, like the others, was at many meetings that day and met with many people, starting in the morning in Larkfield with MacDonagh and ending up close to midnight with several of the leaders. They had to guess what the effects of all this would be and they presumed that their arrests were likely to be next. This was correct, but not as imminent as they thought. Some of the Castle officials had decided that once Casement had been arrested (they thought he was the leader) the countermanding orders were issued as a result and whatever action had been planned would not happen. They identified the car in Ballykissane, but didn't know how it fitted in. For the Rising leaders the loss of the radio scheme was not crucial, but the loss of life was; they were not depending on the German arms and they had hoped

Casement would not come at all, but the cancellation of the Sunday parades would mean the loss of possibly thousands of men and women and of a countrywide movement.

From Grace Gifford Plunkett:

> I didn't go back to Larkfield in Holy Week, I was doing the churches, Collins came to Palmerston Park on Holy Saturday with twenty pounds and a revolver. He said that Joe sent the revolver to defend myself and the twenty pounds to bribe the military. Collins said, 'He wants you to come down and see him this evening'. 'This evening' meant after six to me, but it meant between four and six to Collins. I arrived at the Metropole just as Joe was coming down the stairs. His uniform looked like a new one, his hair was completely shaved and he was wearing a wide-awake hat. He looked awful and said 'I waited all afternoon for you'. We took a cab to Gardiner Street and stopped under the wide overhead bridge. We said goodbye there and he went in to a building that was not Liberty Hall … I went to Muriel's and had tea there.

Tom Dillon and Gerry Plunkett went to see Joe Plunkett in the Metropole Hotel at about 8.30 that night. They were to be married next day and they wanted to know what was going to happen. Joe gave Tom his orders, to take over any chemical factory captured and run the manufacture of munitions and he told them they should stay in the Imperial Hotel over Clery's on O'Connell Street, where Tom would be considered on duty. They asked him about the situation and he talked through everything he could.

He said that MacNeill's order had caused complete confusion. Hobson had told MacNeill that the parades on Sunday were to become a Rising and MacNeill accused Pearse of deceiving him, but Pearse reminded him that MacNeill, knowing Pearse's plans, told him a good while before to go ahead with them. MacNeill had agreed to join the Military Council after being told the plans for the Rising, which included the landing of arms. Hobson was arrested by the Military Council and kept in a private house until after the Rising started as they knew that he was opposed to the way it was devised. Then Plunkett told them that The O'Rahilly had come back from various places round the country where he had been sent by Hobson with documents, not knowing what they were. He had heard of Hobson's arrest and gone to St Enda's and threatened Pearse. Plunkett and MacDonagh had been trying to find O'Rahilly to tell him about the Rising and when they did he said he was absolutely in favour of it. Plunkett confirmed that Casement was the man arrested in Kerry and that the arms were gone and there was now no hope of MacNeill's co-operation.

Plunkett said there might be no Rising after all, but until they heard what the Castle was going to do, there would be no final decision so they were waiting for news of a meeting in Dublin Castle that evening. If the Castle decided to arrest the leaders at once the Rising would go on, no matter how few took part in it. The leaders had discussed escape, but decided against it. Plunkett said that if there was no Rising now that Ireland would get nothing, not even the Home Rule Bill, without fighting for it. He said the Rising could not be a success now but, in spite of this, he was satisfied that it was right to go on if forced to do so by a Castle decision. He thought that soldiers would have to be brought from England rather than from all over Ireland and that it would be victory if they held out against England even for a short time; it would be a first step on the road to freedom. He said that everything had been done to give the Volunteers military status and they would declare a Republic. (This was also a reference to their hope that the Republic would have a seat at the peace talks after the War). He said he did not want to die. He had postponed his wedding but, if he could, he would get married at once. He had told Grace that they might be able to get married in gaol.

When Tom Dillon and Gerry Plunkett were leaving at about 10 o'clock, Colm O'Lochlainn was arriving with the news of the Ballykissane drownings and Plunkett was certain now that his friend and colleague, Con Keating, was dead. He went on to the next meeting in Mrs Kissane's on Hardwicke Street where, for safety the only lights used were flashlights.

When Geraldine Plunkett left Larkfield for her wedding

to Thomas Dillon on Easter Sunday she was given a rousing send-off by the Kimmage Garrison – the 'Liverpool Lambs'. The marriage was in Rathmines Catholic Church and Gerry knew that her entire life was about to change. It was supposed to have been a double wedding with Joe Plunkett and Grace Gifford, but Joe was too busy with disasters.

James Connolly's daughter, Ina, and her sister travelled with other members of Cumann na mBan on the early train from Belfast to Dublin on Easter Sunday morning to inform Connolly that the Countermanding Order was published in Belfast and was having a disastrous effect, with Volunteers deciding not to turn out for the parades. Connolly took the news very seriously and sent each of them to one of the leaders to give them the news. In Ina's account she says:

> I went to the Hotel Metropole to Joseph Plunkett. The porter refused to admit me, but I insisted that I must see Plunkett at once. The Porter reluctantly gave in, 'Take a seat in the lounge; I'll go to his room.' He returned and informed me that Plunkett was coming down immediately. Wow, what sort of man was I going to meet? Could I talk to this man as I did to my father? All at once there appeared a tall, thin man in a dressing gown coming slowly down the stairs. He had his neck wrapped in bandages or a white scarf. Later I learned that he had just undergone an operation. As he came near me I stood up, he put his hand on my shoulder saying... 'We will sit over in this corner, we will

be by ourselves.' He made me feel at ease and talked to me just as my father did, asking questions, assuring me that he had plenty of time to listen to all my chatter. Bringing me to the door and in close proximity to the porter he said: 'I will dress and join you at breakfast' [in Liberty Hall.] I told my father of meeting Joseph Plunkett. After breakfast we went to Mass … Mass over we got back to Liberty Hall and there met all the signatories to the Irish Republican Proclamation.

The leaders, meeting in Liberty Hall, decided to go ahead one day later with the Rising. They believed that Dublin Castle was aware of their plans and ready for action; in fact the Castle was empty and asleep for the weekend. The same day Plunkett made a will leaving everything to Grace:

Will of Joseph Mary (Patrick) Plunkett made this day April 23rd 1916.

I give and bequeath everything of which I am possessed or may become possessed to Grace Evelyn (Mary Vandeleur) Gifford.

Signed Joseph Mary Plunkett

Witnessed George Oliver Plunkett.

He kept this with him for the rest of that week.

Geraldine and Tom had a wedding breakfast in their new home, No. 13, Belgrave Road, Rathmines and, putting their bicycles on top of a cab, proceeded to the Imperial Hotel, opposite the GPO on O'Connell St. Although it was just

across the street from the Metropole Hotel, they had no contact with Joe. Rory O'Connor came in that afternoon to tell
them that the Rising was off for that day but to look out
from noon the next day so they presumed that Dublin Castle
had decided, at least, to arrest the leaders. At nine o'clock
that Easter Sunday Joe wrote to Grace:

> My dearest heart,
>
> Keep up your spirits and trust in Providence. Everything
> is bully. I have only a minute. I am going into the nursing
> home to-night to sleep. I am keeping as well as anything but
> need a rest. Take care of your old cold, sweetheart. All my
> love for ever, Joe

CHAPTER 16

1916
Rising And Falling

On Easter Monday, 24 April 1916, Commandant Brennan–Whitmore was appointed to Joseph Plunkett's staff by Thomas MacDonagh who sent him to help Michael Collins bring Plunkett from the nursing home to Liberty Hall. Brennan–Whitmore was shocked when he saw Plunkett for the first time. 'If ever death had laid its mark openly on a man, it was here'. Plunkett sat on the bed while two nurses bandaged his throat.

> Both nurses sought to persuade Plunkett to go back to bed, but with a gentle smile and a wave of his hand he put their exhortations aside.... Tears were in the nurses' eyes as they followed us to the door.
>
> Brennan–Whitmore.

Collins helped Plunkett into his tunic and called a cab. Plunkett had to be helped down the stairs. They drove to the Metropole Hotel where Plunkett had kept his rooms and his arrival, in uniform and with a heavily-bandaged throat, caused a hush from the British Officers and their friends around the door. In his rooms he had to rest again and then he took maps, books and three revolvers from his trunk and, as they left said to Collins:

> You lead out and down the stairs. I and the Commandant will follow. We must not allow ourselves to be arrested under any circumstance. If necessary we must shoot our way out but not unless it's necessary. There is an intelligence officer in the vestibule, a stout dark man. If he attempts to interfere he is to be shot at once.

Arriving down, there was silence again and the stout dark man simply gave them good day. In the cab Plunkett said, 'So far so good' and on the way to Liberty Hall asked Brennan-Whitmore if Wexford would be a good county to fall back on, but Brennan-Whitmore said no, that Wexford was a *cul de sac* for insurgents.

Liberty Hall was alive with activity and as Plunkett got out of the cab there were many salutes, which he returned with smiles, as Collins helped him up the steps to the door. Inside he got a great welcome from Pearse and Connolly. Something was, at last, becoming real. When, after their meeting, they returned to the street to begin assembling the troops, Plunkett made it without help. The Citizen Army and the Cumann na mBan were there, already busy, and Volunteers were turning up from here and there. To the delight of all,

The O'Rahilly arrived, Frank Thornton arrived with his North Frederick Street men and Captain George Plunkett arrived with the Kimmage Garrison, 4th Batallion, the 'Liverpool Lambs', some of whom had come by bicycle, but most on the tram, which George had commandeered on Harold's Cross Bridge. Being the honest man he was, he had insisted on paying the forty-three fares to the mystification of the tram conductor. Jack Plunkett, now Lieutenant, came on his motorbike on Joe's instructions as he was to be on his staff. Joe Plunkett was twenty-eight, George was twenty-two and Jack was eighteen.

Just before noon the whole column left Liberty Hall, James Connolly at the head with Pearse on his right and Plunkett on his left, 'He looked dying,' said Eamon Dore, but Plunkett brandished his sabre as though very much alive. Behind them marched the Kimmage Garrison, armed with pikes, shotguns and an assortment of weapons and implements, and the Citizen Army men and women, the Cumann na mBan and the Volunteers. Two drays followed loaded with guns, pikes and explosives. Some left for different positions round the city, but the main body turned left up Abbey Street and right into O'Connell Street where they halted at the General Post Office. Plunkett stood with Collins, Pearse, Connolly, Clarke and MacDiarmada, George Plunkett lined up the Kimmage Garrison, Jack Plunkett had his motorbike near the front of the column between Prince's St and the door of the GPO

and, across the street, at a second-floor window of the Imperial Hotel, Geraldine Plunkett, now Dillon, watched with
her new husband. Unbeknownst to them, Grace Gifford was
also in the Imperial Hotel, also watching. She was there so
that, if the opportunity arose for them to get to the church,
she and Joe could be married. From their ringside seat they
waited for the Rising to begin and begin it did. Connolly
gave the order 'Left turn and Charge!' and when George
Plunkett gave this order to his men some couldn't believe
their ears; he had to say 'Take the GPO!' and in went the
Kimmage Garrison with whoops of delight. George said to a
friend, 'Did you know there was anything on today? I didn't,
though one must always be prepared.'

Plunkett established his own work area on the ground
floor alongside the other leaders and he started working on
recording the circle of positions around the city that had
already been captured if everything had gone according to
plan but, after the countermanding order, he had no way of
telling who or how many would turn out. He kept notes of
messages received during the week from Dublin and around
the country in his Field Message Book, which was composed of numbered perforated leaves, some of which he used
for sending messages. Geraldine Plunkett and Thomas Dillon
were still looking out their window and Grace was at hers
when the most important event of the Rising happened; Patrick Pearse came out of the General Post Office, accompa-

nied by the other leaders and, standing at the kerb step, or in one of many disputed positions, he read the Proclamation of the Irish Republic and then stood in the middle of the street, near Prince's St and read it again. It was a deeply-considered statement of aspiration to a fully egalitarian, democratic state by the seven leaders.

After a while Plunkett sent Grace a message that she should go on home, which she did; back in the GPO, Plunkett sent Fergus Kelly – who had worked on the whole radio project with Con Keating, now drowned at Ballykissane Pier – the Volunteer and Abbey actor, Arthur Shields, and four others including two wireless operatives to take over Atlantic College, the wireless telegraphy school. Here, all week, they sent out the message that the Rising had begun and Pearse had been declared first President of the Irish Republic. In the end, it was picked up by a small commercial steamer on its way to the USA. Plunkett's plan, to bypass the British censor had worked.

From Plunkett's Field Message Book:

> Easter Monday 1916. GPO occupied in the name of the Republic shortly after noon (about 12.15 p.m.) Republic proclaimed. About one hour later a detachment of enemy Lancers attempted to rush O'Connell Street. They were opposed at the Parnell Statue. A small number (described as 'about 20') succeeded in advancing as far as the GPO, but on our opening fire they retired in confusion leaving

a few casualties. Simultaneously with our operation positions were successfully taken up in the front and rear of Dublin Castle, and troops in that stronghold prevented from coming out.

Few enough people knew each other in the GPO apart from the members of the Kimmage Garrison who had trained together for months and Plunkett, for many reasons, was probably the leader least known by sight. James Connolly's secretary, Winifred Carney, had never seen him before and disapproved of Plunkett's appearance, which she thought 'unsoldierly' as he wore jewellery, but Connolly put her straight. He said Plunkett could please himself, as he could teach them all in military science, and that he was 'clear-minded and a man of his word'. James Connolly's son, Roddy, had a similar account:

> I had never seen Joe Plunkett and there he was gorgeously apparelled in his uniform with a long sword and a silk scarf around his neck ... someone procured a mattress and put it in front of the stamp counter and he lay down on it. I thought he was rather out of place, lying on a mattress in the middle of a revolution, I didn't think he was much of a leader. Of course as soon as I could I asked my father about him. My father said, and I remember his remark, I think it was very striking, 'That's Joe Plunkett and he has more courage in his little finger than all the other leaders combined'.

Liam Tannam took in two foreign seamen, a Swede and a Finn, who wanted to join the fight. He gave the Swede a rifle and the Finn, who had no English, a shotgun, but when he stepped off the barricade he hit the gun on the floor and it went off. Plunkett came running and shouted at the man not realising he had no English. Tannam explained that they wanted to fight the British as Russia oppressed their countries the same way. 'Amazing!' said Plunkett and, for safety, the two men were put filling tins with explosives. They stayed to the end and were captured with the rest.

Plunkett never intended barricades to form part of the rebel defences – they were 'simply to interrupt communication for the enemy, and enable us to cross the street' – but they became necessary on several occasions. Geraldine Plunkett Dillon who had seen the Lancers and the looters from their window now saw this:

> Joe and George and other Volunteers came out into the street. One of the Volunteers got into a tram which had been abandoned at Nelson's Pillar, and tried to get up enough speed to ram it into another one in the Earl Street opening to wreck it. This was to make a barricade, because Earl Street is just opposite the GPO, but he did not succeed. Then he threw a bomb at the Earl Street tram but it did not explode. Joe put another bomb in the tram and shot at it with his Mauser from about thirty yards – he was a beautiful shot. The shot exploded the bomb and smashed

the chassis. The tram settled down on the bogies and now could not be moved, which served the purpose intended. That was the last time I saw Joe.

At about six o'clock Plunkett sent Rory O'Connor across to the Imperial Hotel to tell Geraldine and Tom that they should go home. They were to try to make more guncotton and explosives in case the Rising lasted longer than expected. She had wanted to go into the GPO to work, but knew she had to obey.

From Geraldine Plunkett Dillon:

> It was getting dark and then suddenly the street lights flick-ered and lit up – great carbon arcs. We got our bicycles and with a small bag strapped on to one of them, we cycled without any opposition across O'Connell Bridge, along D'Olier Street, Brunswick Street, Westland Row, the Green, Harcourt Street, up through Belgrave Square to 13 Bel-grave Road. We met nothing on the way, very few people, no soldiers, no police. We saw that the Rising was a com-plete surprise to the English. The bulk of our luggage was left in the hotel and was, of course, burnt with the rest.

That night Dr Charlie McAuley was called in to the GPO to treat some wounded Volunteers. He had trained Volunteers and Cumann na mBan in First Aid before the Rising and he had operated on Plunkett only three weeks before and had had to tell him he had not long to live. In a small room in the GPO he saw Clarke and MacDiarmada and 'Stretched on a pallet on the floor ... Joseph Plunkett in riding breeches and wearing a green Volunteer uniform shirt.'

On Tuesday 25 April, Jack Plunkett went with a group to the National Volunteer Headquarters in Parnell Square where they found about a dozen rifles for which Jack had found ammunition in the GPO and they brought them back with them. Pearse and Plunkett went up to the roof to give the men up there encouragement and Count Plunkett, back from persuading the bishops to hold their fire, arrived at the GPO to report to his son, Joe. The Count wanted to stay there and be taken on as a Volunteer, but Joe told him that there were more than enough there and to go home.

Plunkett's changes between energy and illness were reflected in the comments made about him. Some only saw him active and others only when he was too ill to get up, lying on an improvised bed in the big hall on the ground floor where Desmond Fitzgerald, Quartermaster for the garrison, who admired his 'cheerful spirits' brought him food.

From Desmond Fitzgerald:

> Sometimes when there was only the two of us together we would talk about literature, writers and he would ask questions about writers who were friends of mine ... that Plunkett was a dying man inspired me with a great pity for him ... No matter what might be happening Plunkett could forget the facts that surrounded us.

This was a quiet day so they could guess that Dublin

Castle was not as ready for them as they thought and Plunkett's belief that they had to bring in troops from England was proving correct.

Wednesday 26th April 3rd Day.

Garristown Police Barracks taken. No guns or ammunition. P.O. wrecked. 40 I.R.A. under Commandant Ashe (5th Batt.) moving on railway N. of Gormanston. Finglas. News from Navan says 200 I.R.A. moving on Dublin.

It is almost certain that Plunkett, 'the IRB's most admired military thinker', did not know that his greatest military triumph happened that day. He had calculated when the British Army brought in reinforcements they would land at Kingstown (Dun Laoghaire) and march in to the centre of Dublin by the straight road. He posted men in houses around Mount Street Bridge, over the Grand Canal, to hold up the troops and the big guns they brought with them. The 5th and 6th Sherwood Foresters came in unchallenged by the inner road to the city centre and took up the battle for the South Dublin Union. Meanwhile the 7th and 8th came in the straight road and seventeen Volunteers with only one gun per man, sometimes too hot to re-fire, under gunfire from the hundreds of British troops with grenades, bombs and incendiaries, prevented the Foresters from getting any further, kept troops trapped in Beggar's Bush Barracks and prevented the big guns from getting to the city for over nine hours. Over two hundred and thirty British soldiers were killed and several compassionate truces were agreed to by both sides to remove the dead and wounded. It was a testament, not just to its deviser's plan, but also to the extraordinary courage of the men who carried it out.

By now there was Martial Law and curfew from six o'clock, making it impossible for the Volunteers' relatives to get any news. The big guns were being put in place and machine guns rattled all day and all night.

Thursday became a different kind of situation altogether; the reinforcements had arrived, the big guns began shelling and there were snipers on every high point ringing the city centre but there were more disasters.

From Plunkett's notebook:

> Thursday, 4th Day of the Republic.
>
> About one o'clock Commandant General Connolly was wounded in the left arm and ten minutes later in the left leg (by a sniper). The leg wound is serious as it caused a compound fracture of the shin bone.

From Jack Plunkett:

> It was George who found Connolly lying on the ground between Prince's St and Abbey St (William's Lane) unable to move as he was very badly hurt. He had fired his .45 Colt Automatic pistol a few times to try to attract the attention of those in the GPO. George heard the shots, went to investigate and carried him in. I saw him about a half-hour later and he told me about it.

Plunkett's notebook continues:

> The Linenhall Barracks, in the possession of the enemy, is on fire
>
> Signal to Imperial.
>
> Cut way to Liffey St.
>
> Food to Arnotts.
>
> Order to remain at posts unless summoned.
>
> Barricades in front.
>
> Henry St.
>
> Food.

The situation was becoming very serious and the GPO was surrounded by buildings burning so fiercely that its walls were heated by them. There was deafening noise from fires started by British incendiary bombs in the streets close by, the noise of breaking glass, oil drums exploding in Hoyte's across the road, sniper fire all day long and the first shell that hit the GPO, thunderously shaking it and the buildings round it. Morale was ebbing fast and Pearse, who had raised spirits several times already in what was patently impossible chaos, seemed unable to do it again but, according to Joe Good, one of the London Volunteers who had come over for the Rising and whose account is one of the most vivid and perceptive of all the accounts:

> Joe Plunkett moved amongst us all the time, his eloquent comforting words at odds with his bizarre, eccentric appearance, his sabre and his jewelled fingers. We all, some-

how, and in many differing ways, responded to his gentle urgings and praise. He was greatly loved. Most of us by now knew that he'd risen from his deathbed to lead us. … Joe's high uniform-collar didn't any longer quite hide that bandaged throat from his operation of only a few days before. He was already dying of a galloping consumption. Joe Plunkett realised, I felt, that the engulfing flames around us were far more frightening than machine-gun and shell fire. He said to one of our officers near by, with his typical surge of excitement: 'It's the first time this has happened since Moscow! The first time a capital city has burned since 1812!'

Plunkett could take a perverse delight in this as, against the odds, they had made the English burn what they considered to be 'their' city.

On Friday the British incendiary bombs were coming in to the GPO thick and fast, the hoses didn't work and the ammunition, which had been moved to the basement, was a threat to themselves and particularly their prisoners, who, for their safety, were also in the basement.

From Jack Plunkett:

I was very glad to have that rifle I took from Parnell Square when I was able to knock off a British sniper from the top of the burnt-out wall of the Imperial Hotel. He fell down so hard that his rifle broke in two. Gearóid O Sullivan saw what had happened and told me. That sniper was firing at the Volunteers who were trying to put out the fires in the GPO; one of them was my friend, Fergus O'Kelly.

The leaders could see that evacuation was imminently necessary and, as it began to get dark, all were gradually assembled in the courtyard of the GPO side-gate on Henry Street. Pearse explained to the gathering that they were heading to Williams and Woods factory, a large building off Parnell Street, but this was challenged by Seán McLoughlin who had been there and found it surrounded by snipers and artillery. They had to get away from the GPO, which meant crossing Henry Street under fire from Amiens Street Station at one end and Capel Street at the other. The O'Rahilly took about twenty volunteers to see if it would be possible to get up Moore Street, but they were cut down, several of them killed including The O'Rahilly himself in heroic action. The main group now made rushes across Henry Street to Henry Place while Connolly was carried on a stretcher and Pearse checked the GPO, making sure all were out, including the prisoners. Plunkett was at the front of the main group as it came to the corner of Henry Place and Moore Lane where they were held down by fire again. Plunkett ordered a van pulled across the end of the lane forming a very inadequate barricade and, as no-one wanted to cross under fire, he lined them up, held up his sabre and each time he lowered it sent a batch across shouting 'On! On! Don't be afraid, don't be cowards any of you!' In the glare of the GPO flames the rebels were an easy target; seventeen were injured, but they all got across.

Very thirsty from the fires, some of the men broke into O'Brien's mineral water factory while the rest of the group tried to find a safe place to stop. There were gunfire accidents resulting in injury or death, sometimes involving civilians; a Volunteer fired through a door to open it and killed the daughter of the house, but when Seán MacDiarmada wanted to have an inquiry about it the family said 'no', that it was an accident, and were generous in their support. After all kinds of difficulties, they managed to make their way to Cogan's, No. 10, on the corner of Moore Street. There the five leaders and many of the men spent that night. Mrs Cogan gave them the ham she had been cooking (other local families also cooked for them) before she and her family took refuge in the basement.

While George Plunkett, John Nunan and Frank Kelly were building a barricade at the junction of Moore Street and Henry Place, they heard moaning across the street. They could make out a soldier and hear 'water! water!'. George Plunkett took Kelly's water bottle, jumped the barricade and dashed across under heavy fire. When he carried the man back on his shoulder the firing down the street lessened and he realised that his rescuee was a British soldier. He dumped the man on the barricade 'Here take him' – to his comrades – and dashed back to get his rifle, this time under heavy fire both ways. That British soldier was with them and well-treated to the end. Julia Grenan and Elizabeth O'Farrell looked after the wounded that night. Patrick and Willie Pearse slept on a table upstairs while the others found wherever they could. After dark the sky was full of orange light, which changed to red and died away.

At 3a.m. there was a huge explosion as the ammunition blew in the GPO basement.

CHAPTER 17

1916
The Dark Way

Tunnelling began early in the morning to try to get into the protection of the middle of the terrace. From house to house they found themselves dropping different distances and Connolly, his foot now gangrenous and agonisingly painful, had to endure being carried in a sheet, sometimes held almost vertical to get him from one house to another. They took over the terrace of sixteen houses and established Headquarters in No. 16, coincidentally belonging to Plunkett's, the butchers.

> To Miss Grace Gifford,
>
> 8 Temple Villas, Palmerston Road
>
> 6th Day of the Irish Republic
>
> Saturday April 29th 1916. About noon.
>
> Somewhere in Moore St
>
> My Darling Grace,
>
> This is just a little note to say I love you and to tell you that

I did everything I could to arrange for us to meet and get married but that it was impossible. Except for that I have no regrets. We will meet soon. My other actions have been as right as I could see and make them, and I cannot wish them undone. You at any rate will not misjudge them. Give my love to my people and friends. Darling, darling child, I wish we were together. Love me always as I love you. For the rest all you do will please me. I told a few people that I wish you to have everything that belongs to me. This is my last wish so please do see to it.

Love x x x x

Joe

Plunkett asked Winifred Carney to deliver this note to Grace along with the bangle and ring he was wearing and she said she would. She was in jail until Christmas and delivered it on her release.

From Joe Good:

Joe Plunkett was sitting at the end of the bed. He had lost one of his spurs. I pointed this out to him, sensitive for his dignity when he would face the enemy. He must have known what was on my mind, and said, smiling, 'The doctors give me six months to live.' He took the other spur off and kicked it with a quiet tap under Connolly's bed.

Promoted by the leaders as someone of energy and ideas Seán McLoughlin was now looking for volunteers for a reconnaissance group to investigate escape. The British had been firing indiscriminately down Moore Street, killing civilians; Patrick Pearse, looking out the window of No. 16, saw the Dillon family cross the road carrying white flags and being killed by fire from the top of street. Pearse ordered a Volunteer ceasefire to discuss surrender with the other leaders at Connolly's bedside. The men waited in the houses, walked in the yards or walked up and down through the holes in the walls. Finally, the decision was made to surrender and Elizabeth O'Farrell was asked to take the note offering to treat with the Commander in Charge. Seán MacDiarmada gave her a small white flag and she had to walk alone into the guns at the top of the street. They would not accept any negotiation, it had to be unconditional surrender so she had to return and return again with Pearse who surrendered, proffering his sword, to General Lowe on Parnell Street and was taken away to Arbour Hill Barracks.

Instructions as to the form of the surrender were sent to the remaining leaders and, after Connolly had been carried down the stairs of No. 17 by four spruced-up Volunteers and taken away to Dublin Castle Hospital, the Kimmage Garrison had to be persuaded to surrender.

From Joe Good:

> Joseph Plunkett, with a talent for words, the maker of such luminous poems, leader of men into impossible battles, could not dissuade us from this certain last one.

These men, committed to the whole idea, trained, courageous and young, had most to lose with their English accents and conscription avoidance but, finally, it was MacDiarmada, telling them they were needed for the future, that they must survive who earned their agreement.

Plunkett now took up a position in the middle of Moore Street 'alone except for the dead, tall and elegant' opposite the door of No. 16, carrying a white flag and with his back to the guns, causing a curious silence from the British soldiers at the top of the street. The snipers were still firing so he called over Joe Good who was in the doorway and sent him up to the barricade to get them to stop the fire. On his return Good told him they needed to know what to do with the wounded and Plunkett sent him again to the top of the street, still standing with his back to the guns. The officer in charge was rude and dismissive to Joe Good until he mentioned that some of the wounded were theirs. The wounded were brought out onto the street to be collected, Willie Pearse joined Plunkett, the men lined up behind and the officers, including Clarke and MacDiarmada, took up the rear. Their ammunition discharged and guns at the slope, they marched in fours down Moore Street, Willie Pearse and Plunkett waving their white flags 'as if they were banners of victory', through Henry Place, Henry Street, to the opposite side of O'Connell Street, left up to Findlater's and the Gresham Hotel where they laid down their arms and stepped back as professionally as trained soldiers.

The British Army soldiers and officers were taken aback. They had expected much bigger numbers, far less discipline, attempts to escape and the shame or depression of defeat, but that was not at all what they saw. Their names were taken by British officers and Frank Henderson noticed that:

> Joseph Plunkett was singled out by one British officer for particular insult. Plunkett was ordered to step forward from the ranks and he was ignominiously searched. He had his Will in his pocket, and the British officer passed some very rude remarks about Plunkett's courage, asking him was he making his Will because he was afraid he would die. I remarked at the time that Joseph Plunkett paid not the slightest heed to what this British officer said to him. He had been talking to us in the ranks before the incident about the Rising generally, its effect, and about some steps he had taken in regard to publicity in foreign lands. When he had been maltreated by this officer, he stepped back into the ranks and resumed his conversation exactly where he had left off.

While they were there Ned Daly's men arrived, laughing and talking and smoking, but still in formation and all of them were marched off to the small garden in front of the Rotunda Hospital. Plunkett, hardly able to walk, almost fell and a soldier gave him a rough shove forward, threatening to bayonet him, but the sergeant pulled him by the arm and barked angrily, 'Do your duty and do no more; *that's* not your duty.' They were kept lying all night on the grass, made to lie on top of each other and hit with rifle butts if they moved. They were abused and screamed at by Captain Lea-Wilson, who stripped Tom Clarke naked and took Sean MacDiarmada's stick from him. Since MacDiarmada had contracted polio he couldn't walk without it. Jack and George Plunkett were also there on the grass that night, but nowhere near Joe who seemed to be dying; Winifred Carney covered him with her coat.

Plunkett's Field Message Book was found on Moore Street by a waiter from the Metropole Hotel who sent it to Grace Gifford Plunkett. Maybe Plunkett dropped it intentionally.

The following morning, Sunday 30 April, they were all marched the three miles to Richmond Barracks in Inchicore. As they arrived at the Barracks, Plunkett collapsed and had to be carried in. About one hundred men had been selected by the Dublin Castle Detectives (G-men) on their way in, including Joe, George and Jack Plunkett, and packed into the gymnasium.

From Liam O'Briain:

> My best friend Sean MacDermott was there – poor, lame Sean, affectionate, gay, handsome, warm-hearted. The first thing he said to me was 'What's that you have under your arm?' It was the old quilt I had brought with me from the College of Surgeons. 'Give it to Plunkett,' he said, 'he is very sick'. Joe Plunkett was lying on the floor near him, trying

and failing to rest. For a couple of days following he had the old quilt, sometimes under him as a bed, sometimes under his head as a pillow. Plunkett was wearing his Volunteer uniform and top boots, as were his two brothers, George and Sean ...

Jack Plunkett was talking to Joe that morning:

... we were sitting on the floor of that disgusting gymnasium in Richmond Barracks. 'Do you know,' Joe said, 'I don't feel half as bad as I ought to'. His enthusiasm for the coming events had made him forget his bodily sufferings. He said 'Here are some things you must remember' – I can't remember what they all were but he very definitely said that they were going to shoot him and shoot the signatories of the Proclamation but they would not shoot us. He was worrying a lot about Tomás McDonagh ... now there was no need for secrecy he dropped all reticence and spoke openly.

MacDonagh was brought in to Richmond Barracks on that Sunday, but Joe didn't know he was there. They had not seen each other since the previous Sunday and it is almost certain that they did not see or speak to each other again. On Sunday evening Plunkett wrote a brief message to his family.

Sunday, 30 April 6.25 p.m. Joe, George and Jack well and happy but detained at Richmond Barracks. Plunkett, Larkfield, Kimmage.

There were no Plunketts at Larkfield then. His parents

had been arrested within a day of each other, Tom Dillon, Gerry and Fiona Plunkett were in Belgrave Road, Rathmines, sitting on gun-cotton to hide it from the soldiers' searches, Philomena was still in New York having brought the Rising messages there and Moya, the Sacred Heart nun, was in Roehampton, England,

> Richmond Barracks Tuesday May 2nd 1916
>
> My Darling Child,
>
> This is my first chance of sending you a line since we were taken. I have no notion what they intend to do with me but I have heard that I am to be sent to England. The only thing I care about is that I am not with you – everything else is cheerful. I am told that Tomás was brought in yesterday. George and Jack are both here and well. We have not had one word of news from outside since Monday 24th April except wild rumours. Listen – if I live it might be possible to get the Church to marry us by proxy – there is such a thing but it is very difficult I am told. Father Sherwin might be able to do it. You know how I love you. That is all I have time to say. I know you love me and I am very happy.
>
> Your own
>
> Joe
>
> Miss Grace M.V. Gifford, 8 Temple Villas,
>
> Palmerston Rd., Rathmines

He wrote this note in copying-ink pencil on the back of the will, which he had written on Easter Sunday and kept with him through all those days. He gave the letter to a British soldier who duly delivered it to Grace.

On Tuesday, 2 May George and Jack Plunkett had one of several interrogations in Richmond Barracks.

From Jack Plunkett:

> I saw Joe before one of these and we spoke but the guard said not to (but he was nice about it). Frank Daly talked so much about how dreadful a disaster it all was and that there was no hope for Ireland for another two hundred years, that he made me very depressed, but Joe said if we hadn't come out, there really would be no hope for Ireland for another two hundred years.

Seoirse (George) and Sean (Jack) Plunkett were given life sentences, commuted to ten years penal servitude. They were taken from Richmond Barracks, to Kilmainham, to Mountjoy Jail and, in a cattle boat, to Holyhead and thence to Portland Prison.

Patrick Pearse, Thomas Clarke and Thomas MacDonagh, Plunkett's closest friend, were shot in the early dawn that Wednesday, 3 May while Plunkett was still at Richmond Barracks. In his last letter MacDonagh nominated Plunkett as his literary executor, 'if he survives me', along with his wife, Muriel. For the prisoners even rumour was hard to come by and there is no way of knowing which of these things Plunkett could have known.

Father Augustine, one of the four Capuchin priests who

helped the condemned through those last days, was at Richmond Barracks that Wednesday and

> ... recognised Joseph Plunkett who lay there in a sitting posture with his body thrown slightly back supported by his two hands which pressed against the ground. He was, I was told, awaiting his turn for Court Martial with his back turned towards us and his face towards the building he was soon to enter. My heart went out to him but I did not then know I was to see him so soon again.

Court Martial Wo 71/349 No.33 Joseph Plunkett

Colonel E.W.S.K. Maconchy, CB, CIE, DSO (President), Lieutenant-Colonel A.M. Bent, CMG, 2/Royal Munster Fusiliers and Major F.W. Woodward, DSO, Loyal North Lancs. Regiment.

The charge: That he did enact to wit did take part in an armed rebellion and in the waging of war against His Majesty the King, such an act being of such a nature as to be calculated to be prejudicial to the defence of the realm and being done with the intention and with the purpose of assisting the enemy

Plunkett pleaded not guilty.

Major Philip Holmes, Royal Irish Regiment identified him as one of the 'Sinn Féiners' who surrendered on 29 April who had retired when the Post Office was burnt:

> They had been firing on the troops for several days and had

killed or wounded several soldiers. He was dressed in the green uniform he is now wearing with a captain's badge of rank on his sleeves when he surrendered.

The second witness, Sgt. John Bruton, Dublin Metropolitan Police said:

> I know the prisoner, Joseph Plunkett. The Headquarters of the Irish Volunteer Movement are at No. 2 Dawson St. I have seen him on two occasions entering and leaving No. 2 Dawson St dressed as well as I could see in the uniform of the Irish Volunteers on at least one occasion. His name appears in the Proclamation issued by the Irish Volunteers and I believe him to be a member of the Executive Council of that body.

There was no defence of any kind, but Plunkett was allowed to cross-examine the witness and asked him, 'How do you know the Proclamation was issued by the Irish Volunteers?'

The witness answered:

> I know that the names of the men that appear at the foot of the Proclamation are connected with the Irish Volunteers. They include P. H. Pearse, Edmund Kent, Thomas MacDonagh, John Mc Dermot who are members of the Council of the Irish Volunteers and who constantly attended meetings at No. 2 Dawson St.

The third witness, Lt. Col. H. S. Hodgkin DSO, Sherwood Foresters also said that he had seen Plunkett when he surrendered:

> He was wearing a sword and pistol.

Plunkett then said:

> I have nothing to say in my defence but I desire to state that the Proclamation referred to in Sgt. Bruton's evidence is signed by persons who are not connected with the Irish Volunteers and the Proclamation was not issued by the Irish Volunteers.

General Sir John Maxwell sent this memorandum on Joseph Plunkett to the British Prime Minister, Herbert Asquith:

> This man was also a signatory to the Declaration of Irish Independence. He was a member of the Central Council of the Sinn Féin Volunteers and took part in their meetings and parades. His residence was a training ground and arsenal for the rebels. This man, being of good education, exercised great influence for evil over the other members. He took an active part in the fighting in and around the GPO where the British troops suffered severely. He held the rank of Captain.

Later that day the verdict, 'Guilty', and the sentence, 'Death', were given to Joseph Plunkett.

Count Plunkett had been arrested four days before and kept in Richmond Barracks, as was his wife, but in a separate section. He was in a first floor guardroom, standing at the window and, looking down into the barrack square, he saw his eldest son, Joe, standing there. Joe looked up and saw his father and they remained so for a long twenty minutes before Joe was moved on, transferred to Kilmainham Gaol and put in a cell in the East Wing.

From Grace Gifford:

> On May 3rd I was pulled out of bed by an extraordinary force; I got these things sometimes, a sort of telepathy

She 'saw the priest' probably Father Sherwin who may have talked to the Kilmainham Chaplain, Father Eugene McCarthy who would have needed the permission of Major Lennon, Governor of the Gaol. Grace went to Mr Stoker's jewellery shop on Grafton Street to buy a wedding ring and, although she was veiled he could see her tears and her distress and when he tried to comfort her, she told him she was to marry Joseph Plunkett that evening. She chose the most expensive ring, paid for it and left quickly. He rang the newspapers as soon as she had gone and the story appeared everywhere within days.

She got in to Kilmainham Gaol at six o'clock, but had to wait until after eleven o'clock before Plunkett was brought down the steps of the chapel to her. The gas lighting was gone and this should have pleased Plunkett because during Easter Week de Valera had dismantled the area gas supply to prevent an explosion so now the only light in the chapel was from a candle held by a soldier, but for Grace it must have enhanced the nasty atmosphere, being surrounded in the darkness by men with ready guns. Plunkett's handcuffs were taken off for the ceremony, which was the briefest it could be, and they were allowed no private conversation. Father Eugene McCarthy conducted the ceremony and two soldiers signed the marriage certificate, John Smith and John Carberry. Plunkett was handcuffed again and taken away and Father McCarthy took Grace out of the Gaol. She could not have made it home at that time, there was a curfew from six o'clock and the city was ringed with sentries so Fr McCarthy took her to James' Street which was part of his parish. He tried to get her a bed for the night in a convent, but they wouldn't let her in; he found her a place instead with Mr Byrne, the bell-founder where she was given a meal and a place to rest.

At 2 a.m. she was woken by a policeman with a message from Major Lennon, saying that she could go to the Gaol to visit her husband. Plunkett's cell, referred to by a soldier as a 'hospital cell', had a plank bed, a bench, a blanket and a bowl of gruel without a spoon. It filled up, wall to wall, with soldiers carrying bayonets and Grace found herself tongue-tied. Plunkett spoke to her of the bravery of his friends and comrades, of MacDonagh, Pearse, Connolly and The O'Rahilly. While he talked he was kneeling on the floor as she sat on the bench and she noticed how dirty his neck bandage was:

Joe's thoughts were so exactly the same; he was so unselfish, never thought of himself. He was not frightened, not the slightest bit, not at all.

They were given ten minutes, no more, and now the Sergeant who had his watch in his hand all the time said suddenly, 'Your ten minutes are up!' and Grace was taken out of the cell, out of the Gaol.

> We who had never had enough time to say what we wanted to each other found that in that last ten minutes we couldn't talk at all.

From George Noble, Count Plunkett:

> I was never let speak to Joseph my son during his imprison-ment in Richmond Barracks. I was not allowed to send him a message or receive a word from him. No official told me of my son's trial, his sentence, his execution, his burial – nor even of his marriage on the eve of his death.

Count and Countess Plunkett were brought separately to Kilmainham Gaol that day and put in separate cells. They were not told why they were there and next day they were returned to Richmond Barracks, but Count Plunkett was awake in the early morning and heard the shots.

Edward Daly, Michael O'Hanrahan and Willie Pearse were shot on that morning, 4 May.

Plunkett was the last to be executed that day. He was attended by Father Sebastian who said that while Plunkett waited to be called to the place of execution, he said:

> Father, I am very happy. I am dying for the glory of God

and the honour of Ireland.

Plunkett had used the same words earlier to Father Albert, words he had written just a year before in the Limburg Declaration. They were now his own declaration and he had beaten death for the privilege of owning them.

Plunkett took off his spectacles at the last minute and gave them to one of the priests, saying he would not need them.

> He was there, his hands tied behind his back, waiting to face the firing squad. I noted his courteous 'Thank you, Father'; his face reminded me of St Francis and 'Welcome, Sister Death'. He was absolutely calm, as cool and self-possessed as if he looked on what was passing and found it good. No fine talk. No heroics. A distinguished tranquillity—
>
> Fr Augustine F.M.Cap.

Joseph Plunkett's name was spoken and a signal given, a bandage placed over his eyes and, with Father Sebastian in front, two soldiers guided him out. The procession went along the yard and through the gate to the Stonebreakers' Yard where the firing squad of twelve soldiers, six kneeling and six standing, waited. It was said that the officer in charge of this firing squad, who was noticed saluting Plunkett, was Kenneth O'Morchoe, Plunkett's friend from Kilternan, who had been so sure that Plunkett would be given a reprieve because of his illness that he delayed the execution for as long as he could. No reprieve came and O'Morchoe retired from the scene, saying that he could not execute a friend. He was excused and replaced with another officer.

The youngest signatory of the Proclamation of the Irish Republic, Joseph Plunkett, was led in front of the firing squad and turned to face it. There was a silent signal from the officer then a deafening volley. Plunkett fell and the officer stepped forward to give him the certainty of death with his revolver.

> Up on Arbour Hill in the Barracks Yard, the priest, waiting beside the open mass grave, heard the shots and the sound of the Army ambulance bringing four bullet-ridden bodies, some of them warm, over the Liffey for his ministrations and burial, Edward Daly, Willie Pearse, Michael O'Hanrahan and Joseph Plunkett. The reality of all that life became part and parcel of a soul at once impressionable and as hard as nails, for he hated sentimentality, that which he had being of the Spartan type.

> No-one would dare to call in question the matter-of-fact, unsentimental sincerity of Plunkett's patriotism. It was a life of marvellous grit. In spite of ill-health, absorbing study, and hard poet-work, he was ever ready to meet the ventures that came his way.

> Frail as he was, it was not that impression the man himself left with you. Pain did not dismay him. There was nothing small in his personality. He had personality ... His conversation had wondrous charm, a rare combination of vivacity and reposefulness, of alertness and poise. With Plunkett it

was not so much his courtesy that struck one as his courtliness, not so much his politeness as his kindness and grace. He was what you call a decent fellow.

Peter McBrien on Joseph Plunkett, 1916

Appendix

[¬ means it is already in his collection]

TITLE PAGE
'*Homo Sum humane nihil a me alienum puto*'
Bibliography
Joseph Plunkett Ramise II Ciops XX Gotis idiots MemphesXX

Buddhism, History of Indian, by T.W. Rhys Davids (Hibbert Lecture 1881) Williams 10/6

Questions of King Milinda (Buddhic) by the same, (sacred books of the East vol XXXV) Clarendon Press 10/6

Buddhist Suttas – the same Clar. Press 10/6-

Dhammapada & Sutta Nipata, by Max Müller and Fausböll. (trans from original) Clar.Press 10/6-

Life of Buddha from Thibetan sources. Rockhill. Trubner. 10/6-

C. Hare Plunkett, *Letters of One*. [Essays, publ. New York 1907]

Socialism – A Critical Examination, Mallock, Murray 6/-

Wisdom of the East Various Subjects and authors, pub Murray 1/- and 2/- ea.

Explication Mechanique des Proprietes de la Matiere Cohesion Affinite Gravitation etc. by A Despaux, Paris, Febr. Alcan 1908 6fr. (Reviewed in Nature March 4 1909)

Experimental Zoology Dr Hans Spemann Cambridge University Press 1908 5 parts, part 1 Embryogency Eng trans 7/6-

Textbook of Experimental Psychology by C.S. Myer ed Arnold. 8/6-

Handbook of Wireless Telegraphy. Dr J Erskine Murray, 2nd Ed. 1909. pub Crosby Lockwood and Son

Methods and Aims in Archaeology by Petrie

Egypt by Ebers (V Good and readable)

Handbook for Travellers in Egypt, Wilkinson.

Egypt in 1898 by Steevens (Rotten, bad, no use)

Appendix

Popular Account of the Ancient Egyptians by Sir J. Gardner Wilkinson (V good)

Outlines of Ancient Egyptian History, Marrietta Pasha

Monuments of Upper Egypt, Alphouse Marietta

Dictionaire d'Archeologie Egyptienne, Pierret

Egyptian Archaeology, Gaston Maspero (valuable)

The Pyramids and Temples of Gizeh, Petrie, (too technical)

Ancient Koptic Churches of Egypt by Butler (Very valuable)

Leaves from an Egyptian Notebook by Taylor

History of Religions, transactions of the 3rd international congress Oxford,

Artificial and natural flight. H. Maxim 1908

Grammar of the Egyptian language, Tattain

Eucken, Philosophical works

Etruscan Roman Remains. C.G.Leland

Novels of J.B. Bergin, Elizabeth Robbins, Maurice Hewlitt, D. Christie Murray, Hilaire Belloc, G.K. Chesterton, G.B. Shaw, Maarten Martens, Georg Ebers, Fiona McLeod,

Works of Swinburne, Blake, Dante, Belloc, Chesterton, Herbert Spencer, Vaughan, Aristotle, Plato.

Elementary Histology, Scháfer

Notes for the Nile (containing metrical rendering of the hymns of ancient Egypt) H.D.Rawnsley 1892

Richard Crashaw nos. refer to Cambridge English Classics Ed

Henry Vaughan silurist. Temple Classics Ed Silence and Stealth p43 Some Electro-Chemical Centres by J.N. Pring, Manchester Univ Press 1908 1/6

Philosophy of Life and Phil. Of Language by Schlegel, Bell (Bohn) 3/6

Works, Schopenhauer 2 vols 5/- ea. Bell (Bohn)

Chief Works of Spinoza trans by Elwes 2 vols at 5/- ea . Bell (Bohn)

Malay Magic by Walter Skeat, pub Macmillan 1900

Light Visible and Invisible by SB Thompson, Macmillan 6/-

Discharge of Electricity Through Gauze, 4/6 JJ Thompson, Arch. Constable

Critique of Pure Reason, Kant 32/- Macmillan trans Max Müller

Táin Bó Cuailgne, Hutton 10/6 Maunsel & Co.

History of Human Marriage, Westermark, Macmillan 14/-

The Golden Bough J.G. Frazer Macmillan Part 4 10/-

The Origin and Development of the Moral Ideas by Westemarck

Religions Ancient and Modern Arch. Constable [1906] 1/- per vol.

Anti-Theistic Theories Prof. Flint. Pub Blackwood. 10/6-

Agnosticism the same   18/-

Henebry: Sounds of Munster Irish

The Talmud

A History of Hindu Chemistry, [Acharya Prafulla Chandra] Ray Vol. 1 10/6-W&N [1902]

Algonquin Legends

An Elementary Manual of Radio telegraphy and Telephony by Fleming. Pub Longman's 1908 7/6-

La Telegraphie sans files, Albert Turpain pub. Paris Guntier Villars 9fr

Flight

Studies on immunisationd and their applications to the diagnosis and treatment of bacterial infections. Sir A.E. Almroth Wright.

A Mystical Anthology- tentative selections

George Herbert (page nos. referr to Moxons popular editions)

The Agony p30

The Pearl p 87

The Collar p163

The Glimpse? p164

Richard Crashaw nos. refer to Cambridge English Classics Ed

A song p 344 and p 237 or 277

Henry Vaughan poisiliurst

Temple Classics Ed

Silence and Stealth p43

The Favour p136

The Queer p200

The Retreat ? p34

Quickness? P198

The Shower? P210

The Eclipse? P212

Page nos. refer to Oxford Ed

The Mental Traveller p162

Auguries of Innocence Quatrains First and last p171–175

The Book of Thel p241

I Seize the Sphery Harp from the 4 Zoas p351

The Divine Image p410

Modern Views of Electricity by Oliver Lodge Pub. By Macmillan 3rd Ed rev. 6/- ¬

Totemism J.G. Fraser A&C Black 3/6 net

World in the Making Sroub Armenius? Harper & Bros

Heredity by J.A. Thompson Pub. Murray 9/ ¬

The Radio Active Substances by W. Makower. International Science Series pub Keegan Paul 5/

Pysiological Psychology by W. Wundt pub. Sonischkeim trans Kitchener

The Outlines of Psychology by O. Kulp

Paid in His Own Coin, Comedy, by Thomas King Moylan, The Storm by Hugh Barden.

History of Egypt, 6 vols, 6/ each by Thinders? Petrie. Methuen

2/6 *Religion and Conscience in Ancient Egypt and Syria*

0

3/6 *Egytian Tales* ¬

3/6 *Egyptian Decorative Art* – Methuen ¬

Modern Spiritualism by Frank R. Podmore 2 vols @ 21/-

Dante, Studies and Researches 10/6

Dante Alighieri by Paget Toynbee

William Blake by Arthur Simmons 1907

Hilaire Belloc on Nothing

At the end Plunkett writes 'Are you coming? If you're coming then come along.'

[1910]

Endnotes

Ch 6

1: It was January 1912 before Thomas MacDonagh and Muriel Gifford were married and it was in Beechwood Avenue Church, Ranelagh, not University Church.

Ch 13

1: Plunkett left his German diary in the German Foreign Office when he was leaving. It was found by Gertrude Bannister when sorting Casement's belongings in 1918 and she brought it back to the Plunkett family. It was published in *University Review,* the journal of the UCD Graduates' Association, edited by Jane Kissane and Geraldine Plunkett Dillon.

Sources

The principal sources for all chapters are:

Joseph Plunkett Papers, National Library of Ireland, 10,999 including diaries, notebooks, letters, poetry and sundry prose.

Published poems by Plunkett: *The Circle and the Sword* (1911), *Sonnets to Columba,* (1913) and (posthumous) *Poems*, 1916★

Joseph Plunkett's diary of his 1915 German journey, NLI 10,999

Joseph Plunkett's GPO diary, 1916, National Library of Ireland, NLI 10,999

Joseph Plunkett's Court Martial proceedings, 1916. British Public Records Office.

'Joseph Plunkett' by Donagh MacDonagh, *An Cosantóir* No. 10, November 1945.

Geraldine Plunkett Dillon Papers, National Library of Ireland 33,731, assorted copybooks and pages of memoirs and family material, 1820-1930.

Geraldine Plunkett Dillon Papers Notebooks, articles on 1913-1916 for *University Review,* Bureau of Military History Witness Statements, Scripts for Radio Talks, 1959, manuscript and typescript for an unpublished book on 1913-1916, 1960s, ten articles for *University Review*, 1960s. Witness Statements for the Bureau of Military History.★

Letters between Geraldine Plunkett Dillon and Bulmer Hobson, William O'Brien, Cathal O'Shannon, Dan Nolan, Professor Desmond Williams, Professor William Feeney, Donagh MacDonagh, Professor Roger McHugh, Frank Robbins, Aidan McCabe, Professor F. X. Martin OSA, Arthur Cox and Padraic Colum, among others.★

RTE Radio interviews with Geraldine Plunkett Dillon by Donncha Ó Dulaing, courtesy of RTE Radio Archive.

Introduction by Geraldine Plunkett Dillon to *The Poems of Joseph Mary Plunkett*, The Talbot Press, 1916.

O Brolchain, Honor (Ed.) *All in the Blood, Memoirs of Geraldine Plunkett Dillon*, Dublin: A&A Farmar, 2006

Statements to the Bureau of Military History by Jack Plunkett, Grace Gifford-Plunkett, Paddy Little and Eugene Smith.

★Honor O Brolchain collection

CHAPTER 1

Plunkett Estate Deed of Family Settlement 1949★

Registry of Deeds: Plunkett and Cranny Estates.

Breathnach, Labhrás, *An Pluincéadach*, Dublin: Foilseachán Náisiúnta Teoranta 1972

Catholic University Schools (CUS) Archive: Archivist, Kevin Jennings

CHAPTER 2

Plunkett, George Noble Count: *Botticelli*, George Bell & Co., 1900.★

Ní Phluingcéid, Máire, Thesis: *George Noble Count Plunkett and his role in the Arts*

Belvedere College Archive: Tom Doyle

Reddin, Gerard Norman: 'Joseph Mary Plunkett: The Man', *The Belvederian* vol 4 no. 3, 1917

Plunkett Family: *The Morning Jumper*, 1903★

Plunkett Estate Deed of Family Settlement 1949★

CHAPTER 3

Joseph Plunkett, 1907 Diary entries, Art O Laoghaire Collection.

Stonyhurst College Archives: David Knight, Archivist

Sire, H.J.A., *Gentlemen Philosophers,* Great Britain: Churchman Publishing Ltd., 1988.

The Philosophers' Diary, Stonyhurst.

Knight, David: *Joseph Mary Plunkett*

Mercer, David: 'The Irish Enigma', *Stonyhurst Association Newsletter,* September 2010.

University College Dublin Archive

CHAPTER 4

Thomas MacDonagh Family Papers, National Library of Ireland 44,316-345

Internet Archive, Digital Library of Free Books, Anthony Cogan: The Diocese of Meath 1869.

Lydon, James, *The Making of Ireland,* London, Routledge, 1998

Plunkett, George Noble Count: Genealogical Research, National Library of Ireland, 33,933

Clery, Arthur, Ed. 'Poets of the Insurrection', reprinted from *Studies*, 1916, Dublin and London: Maunsel and Company Ltd., 1918.

Ó Ceallaigh, Seosamh, *Coláiste Uladh1906-2006*, Dun na nGall: Coiste Cuimhneacháin na Coláiste

Alice Nic Giolla Chearr, Grainne Nic Giolla Chearr

CHAPTER 5

Boylan, Patricia, *All Cultivated People – A History of the Arts Club*, Great Britain: Colin Smythe, 1988

Fairbrother, Henry, *Dr Joseph O'Carroll*, Old Dublin Society Paper, 2011

National Archive, 1911 Census Online.

CHAPTER 6

National Library of Ireland MacDonagh Papers

Clery, Arthur, Ed. 'Poets of the Insurrection', reprinted from *Studies*, 1916, Dublin and London: Maunsel and Company Ltd., 1918.★

CHAPTER 7

Thomas MacDonagh Family Papers, National Library of Ireland 44,316-345

CHAPTER 9

The Irish Review 1911-914★

Plunkett to McCabe letters.★

Plunkett Estate Deed of Family Settlement1949.★

CHAPTER 10

Martin, F.X., OSA, *The Irish Volunteers 1913-1915,* Dublin: James Duffy & Co. Ltd., 1963.

CHAPTER 11

Martin, F.X., OSA, *The Irish Volunteers 1913-1915*, Dublin: James Duffy & Co. Ltd., 1963.★

University College Dublin Archives.

Feeney, William J., *Drama in Hardwicke Street,* United States: Associated University

16 LIVES: JOSEPH PLUNKETT

Press, 1984.★

The Belvederian vol. 4 no. 3 (1917)

CHAPTER 13

Grant, David, 'Casement and the Irish Brigade' http://www.irishbrigade.eu/index.html

Joseph Plunkett's 'Plan of Campaign' Ireland Report, Roger Casement Papers NLI 13,085/5

Roger Casement letters, NLI 13,085

Fairbrother, Henry, *Dr Joseph O'Carroll*, Old Dublin Society, 2011

Plunkett to McCabe letters.★

John Devoy: Article in *The Gaelic American*, 15 Jan 1927

Sydney Gifford: *The Years Flew By* (Revised edition), Arlen House 2000

Colum, Padraic, Introduction to *Poems of the Irish Revolutionary Brotherhood,* Ed. Padraic Colum and Edward O'Brien. Small, Maynard and Company, Boston, 1916★

Grace Gifford Plunkett: Witness Statement in Bureau of Military History.

CHAPTER 14

Matthews, Ann, *The Kimmage Garrison*, Dublin: Four Courts Press, 2010.

Jack Plunkett: Witness Statement in the Bureau of Military History

Grace Gifford Plunkett: Witness Statement in Bureau of Military History.

O'Neill, Marie, *Grace Gifford Plunkett and Irish Freedom*, Dublin: Irish Academic Press, 2000.

Clare, Anne, *Unlikely Rebels*, Cork: Mercier Press, 2011.

Plunkett to McCabe letters.★

Ó Broin, Leon, *Dublin Castle and the 1916 Rising*, Great Britain: Sidgwick and Jackson Ltd., 1970.

CHAPTER 15

An Cosantóir, The Defence Forces Magazine, April 1991, April–May, 2006.

Grace Gifford Plunkett: Witness Statement, Bureau of Military History

Eugene Smith: Witness Statement, Bureau of Military History

Patrick J. Little, Memoir, courtesy of the late Donal O'Donovan

418

Carden, Sheila, *The Alderman,* Dublin: Dublin City Council, 2007

Jack Plunkett: Witness Statement, Bureau of Military History

Ó Broin, Leon, *Dublin Castle and the 1916 Rising.* Dublin: Helicon, 1966.

Litton, Helen, Ed. Kathleen Clarke, *Revolutionary Woman: My Fight for Ireland's Freedom*, Dublin: O'Brien Press, 1991.

Letters from Plunkett to Grace Gifford: National Library MS 21,590.

CHAPTER 16

Brennan-Whitmore, Commandant W.J., *Dublin Burning*, Dublin: Gill & Macmillan, 1996.

Jack Plunkett: Witness Statement, Bureau of Military History

RTE Television Series: *On behalf of the Provisional Government ...* 1966

Muriel McAuley of the MacDonagh Family.

FitzGerald, Desmond, *Desmond's Rising; Memoirs 1913 to Easter 1916.* Dublin: Liberties Press, 2006 courtesy of the late Garrett Fitzgerald.

Townsend, Charles, *Easter 1916*, London: Penguin, 2006.

Coffey, Thomas M., *Agony at Easter,* London: George G. Harrap & Co. Ltd., 1969.

Caulfield, Max, *The Easter Rebellion* (revised ed.) Dublin: Gill and Macmillan: 1995. (First pub. 1963)

Good, Joe, *Enchanted by Dreams,* Kerry: Brandon, 1996.

Ryan, Desmond, *The Rising,* Dublin: Golden Eagle Books Ltd., 1949.★

CHAPTER 17

Good, Joe, *Enchanted by Dreams,* Kerry: Brandon, 1996.

Townsend, Charles, *Easter 1916*, London: Penguin, 2006.

Coffey, Thomas M., *Agony at Easter*, London: George G. Harrap & Co. Ltd., 1969.

Caulfield, Max, *The Easter Rebellion* (revised ed.) Dublin: Gill and Macmillan: 1995. (First pub. 1963)

Hopkinson, Michael ed., *Frank Henderson's Easter Rising,* Cork: Cork University Press, 2006.

MacLochlainn, Piaras F., *Last Words*, Dublin: The Stationery Office, 1990.

Jack Plunkett: Witness Statement, Bureau of Military

British Public Records Office: Proceedings of the Court Martial of Joseph Plunkett,

Grace Gifford Plunkett: Witness Statement, Bureau of Military History

Count Plunkett: Letter of complaint to the British Government 1916★

Witness Statements by Frs Farrington and O Carroll to the Bureau of Military History.

RTE: *To the Stonebreakers' Yard*, Producer, Lorelei Harris.

Peter McBrien on Joseph Plunkett from 'Poets of the Insurrection', *Studies* 1916, reprint 1918.

Index

Fitzpatrick, Nora, 37

Fitzsimon, Nellie, 128

Fleming, Alexander, 323

Florence (Firenze), 118, 120, 291, 292

Fogarty, Georgie, 130

Fogarty, Lily, 245

Fogarty, Willie, 130

Foley, Justice Bride, 123

Founier d'Albe, Edmund E., 65

Frances, Blue-Sister, 116

Franco-German Club, The, 106-7, 111

Frankfurt, 309, 314 *see also* Germany

Freeman's Journal, 149, 150, 166

French Mullen, Mrs, 127

Friend, General, 355

Fry, Roger, 108

G-men, 258, 284, 293, 397

Gaelic Athletic Association, The (GAA), 334

Gaelic League, 84, 92, 192, 230, 334, 366-7

Galea, Mrs, 116

Genoa, 289, 291

Geoghegan, Joseph, 131

George V., King, 235, 340

Gerard, Ambassador James W., 311

Germany, 261, 268, 282-3, 298, 299, 300-7, 309-12, 314-17, 319-22, 332, 342, 346, 348, 354, 358-60 *see also* Bavaria, Berlin, Franfurt, Limburg

Gibb, Fr (Professor), 54-5, 57, 69

Gibson, Hon. William, 127

Gifford MacDonagh, Muriel, 164, 189, 172, 180, 189, 260, 332, 339-40, 351, 370, 400

Gifford Plunkett, Grace Evelyn, 272, 332, 339-41, 343-5, 349-51, 353, 362-4,

370, 372-5, 379-80, 392-3, 397, 399-400, 404-6

Gifford, Frederick, 339, 351

Gifford, Gabriel, 232

Gifford, Isabella, 339

Gifford, Nellie, 214, 332, 340

Gifford, Sydney (John Brennan), 214, 332, 340

Gleeson, Evelyn, 36-7, 122, 131

Gonne, Maude, 339

Good, Joe, 387, 393-5

Gran Canaria, 63

Greenan, Mr, 48, 52

Gregory, Lady, 275

Grenan, Julia, 391

Griffin, John, 131

Gudansky, Rabbi, 217

Gurrin, Gerald, 114, 284, 286

Gurrin, Tom, 51

Hackett, Dominic, 80

Hading, Jane, 139

Hardwicke Street Theatre (Hall), 200-1, 241, 250, 274-5, 372

Harrell, Assistant Police Commissioner, 257

Hayden, Mary, 206, 211

Healy, Tim, 146

Henderson, Frank, 396

Herzog, Rabbi, 217

Hobson, Bulmer, 231, 253, 266, 278, 371

Hodgkin, Lt. Col. H.S., 402

Hogan, Jim, 114

Holloway, Joseph, 276

Holmes, M, 271

Holmes, Major Philip, 401

Home Rule, 128, 187-8, 216, 229, 261, 273, 287, 310, 361, 372